IN THEIR SIBLINGS' VOICES

IN THEIR SIBLINGS' VOICES

White Non-Adopted Siblings Talk about
Their Experiences Being Raised with
Black and Biracial Brothers and Sisters

Rita J. Simon and Rhonda M. Roorda

COLUMBIA UNIVERSITY PRESS
NEW YORK

Columbia University Press
Publishers Since 1893
New York   Chichester, West Sussex
Copyright © 2009 Columbia University Press
All rights reserved

Library of Congress Cataloging-in-Publication Data
Simon, Rita James.
   In their siblings' voices : white non-adopted siblings talk about their
experiences being raised with black and biracial brothers and sisters /
Rita J. Simon and Rhonda M. Roorda
        p.   cm.
   Includes bibliographical references.
   ISBN 978-0-231-14850-4 (cloth : alk. paper) — ISBN 978-0-231-14851-1 (pbk. : alk.
paper) — ISBN 978-0-231-51994-6 (e-book)
   1. Interracial adoption—United States 2. Child development—Cross-cultural
studies. 3. Ethnicity in children—United States. 1. Roorda, Rhonda M., 1969–
II. Title.

HV875.64.S5578 2009
306.875089'00973—dc22

2008045103

Columbia University Press books are printed on permanent
   and durable acid-free paper.
This book is printed on paper with recycled content.
Printed in the United States of America

In Their Siblings' Voices is dedicated to all children, men, and women touched by transracial adoption and to those who are interested in learning more about this complex but powerful act. We hope that this book will present another way of understanding the wonderful discovery of adoption.

We also dedicate this work in loving memory to Mrs. Esther C. Solomon ("Ma Dear") and to others who have gone before us and who have helped pave the way toward racial reconciliation.

CONTENTS

PART 3: IMPLICATIONS OF SIBLINGS' VOICES ON
     TRANSRACIAL ADOPTION   211

PREFACE

This book, the third in the series on transracial adoption, follows the publication of *In Their Own Voices: Transracial Adoptees Tell Their Stories* (2000) and *In Their Parents' Voices: Reflections on Raising Transracial Adoptees* (2007). The first two books in the series continue to be extremely well received, especially among adoptees and adoptive parents; researchers; students; adoption agencies and support groups; the media; and those interested in social work, adoption, and race relations in the United States. One of the greatest joys I have gained from the publication of these volumes is that teenagers, adult adoptees of color, and adoptive parents living in the United States and in other countries have been able to identify with those interviewed in those first two books. Since the books were published, numerous students completing their master's theses or doctoral dissertations on transracial adoption have expressed that the two books, particularly *In Their Own Voices*, were useful resources in their research. It was also gratifying to learn that the students' own curiosity about transracial adoption was piqued by reading these books. *In Their Own Voices* and *In Their Parents' Voices* are included in social work, English, and ethnic studies curricula in higher education and in adoption and cultural competency training courses. Both volumes remain relevant to families, scholars, and practitioners in today's society.

This current volume, *In Their Siblings' Voices: White Non-Adopted Siblings Talk about Their Experiences Being Raised with Black and Biracial Brothers and Sisters*, examines the experiences of the white non-adopted siblings living in the original families that appeared in the first two volumes and elicits their views on transracial adoption. This third volume should add substantially to the adoption literature and further open the doors of understanding and dialogue about this vital subject.

For the first volume we interviewed black and biracial adopted men and women who were raised in white homes beginning in the late 1960s and early to mid-1970s, and who had long been the subject of controversy over whether transracial adoption was viable for children and families over the long term. In the first phase of our research, we focused on locating black and biracial transracial adoptees essentially through word of mouth, placing an ad in a magazine on multicultural issues, and soliciting well-known personalities. Some individuals who learned about our project through friends, teachers, and colleagues contacted us personally because of their interest in participating in the project.

Our objective in the first volume of the series was to explore how the transracial adoptees integrated themselves into their adoptive families, and how they developed their own self-identities and self-esteem in the process. We also wanted to know how they fit in with their peers throughout their child/adolescent and early adulthood years, and to understand the inner journey the participants took to reconcile who they were in relation to how their adoptive families and society perceived them. The questions posed to the participants in the first volume were therefore designed to address some of the most sensitive issues inherent in transracial adoption—race, identity, adoption, family, and society—issues that remain at the heart of the discussion on transracial adoption.

In the second volume we interviewed the adoptive parents of the men and women who participated in volume 1, *In Their Own Voices*. Our goal was to learn how these parents viewed transracial adoption thirty years later, after they had raised their children to adulthood and were establishing relationships with them as black men and women. Would their experiences be similar to those cited in the traditional body of research? Equally intriguing was to hear their responses in view of the fact that many of these parents had read the powerful and intimate accounts by their sons and daughters and other black and biracial transracial adoptees featured in *In Their Own Voices*.

As students of transracial adoption, my co-author, Rita Simon, and I felt compelled to include volume 2 in the series centering on the adoptive parents in order to provide a platform to hear their voices collectively and in continuum with *In Their Own Voices*. At the same time our goal was to offer readers insight into this complex issue from the perspective of parents who made the life-changing decision to adopt transracially. In most cases the parents who participated had limited resources to assist them in their parenting; they had to rely on their own skills, modeled for them by their parents, and they depended on the support of family members and friends, some of whom were taking similar paths. For these parents, transracial adoption was uncharted territory and did not come with a compass to guide them. In the course of interviewing the parents for volume 2, our hope was to elucidate the barriers these families broke through and to reveal the work that remains to ensure that transracial adoption can be successful for every family member.

Without question, the lessons learned by the transracial adoptive parents who participated (and others like them) are directly relevant for parents who are planning to adopt transracially or have already chosen this option as a way to build their families. Yet, on a broader scale, particularly as this nation continues to grapple with finding permanent and stable homes for many thousands of children in our foster care system, the parents of *In Their Parents' Voices*, with their journeys through transracial adoption and willingness to come forth, can educate families, practitioners, and policy makers on how to invest in our children (foster, adopted, birth) for the long term no matter how different or similar they are to us.

In the third volume of the series, *In Their Siblings' Voices*, we interviewed the white non-adopted siblings in the same families. This third volume argues that we must not overlook the urgency to study this important demographic group, especially in light of what we do know about transracial adoption. The white non-adopted siblings, though not the primary decision makers, are still significantly affected by transracial adoption, and there are unanswered questions concerning them: In what ways have their views of themselves and their families been influenced by having an adopted sibling of color? What do they believe are the underlying consequences of transracial adoption, and what must change to make this experience supportive for every family member, including the non-adopted sibling? *In Their Siblings' Voices* attempts to answer these critical questions.

The structure of this third volume on transracial adoption is similar to the previous two. We asked the siblings questions regarding their experiences growing up in a blended family and the choices they made in their adulthood years in creating their own families, careers, and relationships. We also wanted to know, of course, the siblings' relationships with their adopted siblings of color. These individuals' candid stories, it turned out, revealed more than first met the eye. The script was not one I had anticipated. As an African American transracial adoptee, I knew my own journey: the many blessings and challenges that came with discovering myself living in a family that did not look like me or often identify with the culture or rhythm of my ethnic community. Yet as I worked on this third volume, I was changed. I saw transracial adoption differently, this time not through my experiences but through the voices of those who had been silent for far too long, the white non-adopted siblings.

All three volumes in this series were created from a need to understand more about the long-term consequences of transracial adoption. All three phases of the study were qualitative by design, intended to bring together both the academic and human interest dimensions to this subject. Here it is appropriate to underscore that the first volume in the series looks primarily at the experiences of domestic black and biracial adoptees who grew up in white homes in the United States rather than transracial adoptees from other racial and ethnic groups (e.g., Native American, Hispanic) in this country or transnational adoptees (e.g., Korean, Chinese, Guatemalan, Ethiopian) born in different countries and raised in white American homes. Although the three volumes in the Simon-Roorda series cannot, of course, make universal claims about the experiences of all adoptees of color and nationalities raised in white homes in this country and abroad, we believe these volumes are relevant and meaningful to adoptees and families embarking on transracial adoption generally as well as those who want to learn more about this subject. That much more discussion and research is needed on transracial adoption cannot be stressed enough. Our volumes symbolize the value, commitment, and priority we and the participants in these volumes have to achieving that purpose.

A question often asked is this: "Why did you [Rhonda Roorda] decide to be interviewed for volume 1, *In Their Own Voices*?" That is a fair question. Early on in this process I made the hard decision, and Rita Simon agreed, to participate in that volume *because* of the sensitivity of the subject and our expectation that participants would talk openly and honestly about their personal experiences related to transracial adoption. In many cases, it was the first time participants had publicly shared intimate details of their experiences; indeed, some experiences that were described were not even known by family members until they read the volumes. I could not ask any of the participants to share their stories without also consenting to do the same, given the similar path I was on. I believe that my presence in the first volume helped to establish a sense of trust between the adoptees and their family members, which I believe added to the value of these volumes.

The Simon-Roorda study unites the only twenty-year longitudinal research, conducted by Rita Simon, on transracial adoption with the voices of veteran families at the forefront of the controversy over the subject. It unites empirical data with human anthology, and brings together a pioneer/renowned scholar of transracial adoption and an African American adult transracial adoptee living out this journey. It is our hope that these three volumes will change the way transracial adoption is viewed and discussed.

Rhonda M. Roorda

ACKNOWLEDGMENTS

In Their Siblings' Voices is a collaborative among special people across diverse racial and ethnic backgrounds, socioeconomic statuses, and interests, who share a common goal of promoting public awareness about transracial adoption. We warmly thank each of you—friends, family, colleagues, foster, adopted, and non-adopted youth and adults, parents and scholars—as well as our long-standing publisher and the media for your expertise, prayers, support, and exposure in making this important work come to fruition.

Although we are not acknowledging each individual or organization by name because the list would be quite extensive, you all know who you are. Your presence in our lives both personally and professionally has made us better people and has helped us stay the course in bringing our readers valuable information on transracial adoption.

Thank you.

IN THEIR SIBLINGS' VOICES

PART I

ARGUMENT, RHETORIC, AND DATA FOR
AND AGAINST TRANSRACIAL ADOPTION

LEGAL STATUS, HISTORY, AND REVIEW OF EMPIRICAL WORK

![decorative bar]

LET US begin with a section from *In Their Own Voices*, the first book in this series published in 2000, which describes the legal background and history of transracial adoption, and also provides empirical data, to give readers a contextual understanding of transracial adoption.

LEGAL STATUS OF TRANSRACIAL ADOPTION

Adoption is a legal process in which a child's legal rights and duties toward his natural parents are terminated and similar rights and duties are created toward the child's adoptive parents. Unknown in common law, adoption was first created in the United States through an 1851 Massachusetts statute. By 1931 every state in the union had passed adoption statutes.

Adoption, like other family law issues, is the province of the states; therefore the law of the state in which the adoption takes place controls the arrangements. The legal structure for adoption consists of the adoption statutes, case law interpreting those statutes, and—perhaps most important—the placement practices of the public and private adoption agencies whose role it is, first, to provide services to parents who wish to place children for adoption and, second, to choose adoptive homes in which those children will be placed. This legal structure shares the common objective of seeking adoptions that are in the child's best interest.

Federal Legislation

Before the United States Congress passed the Multi Ethnic Placement Act (MEPA) in 1994 and the Adoption and Safe Families Act in 1996, transracial adoptions were also governed by the same laws as other adoptions. The purpose of both these acts was to prohibit the use of race "to delay or deny the placement of a child for adoption or foster care on the basis of race, color, or national origin in the adoptive or foster parent or child involved."

While the major supporters of the 1994 act had the above objectives as their goals, the act also contained the following language: "An agency may consider the cultural, ethnic, or racial background of the child and the capacity of the prospective foster or adoptive parents to meet the needs of the child of this background as one of a number of factors used to determine the best interests of the child." That statement thwarted the act's original intention to remove race as a consideration and in fact freed agencies and states to continue to consider a child's racial background in determining placement. It took three more years for the passage of the 1996 act that clearly prohibited the use of race to delay or deny placements.

States found to be in violation would have their quarterly federal funds reduced by 2 percent for the first violation, by 5 percent for the second, and by 10 percent for the third or subsequent violations. Private entities found to be in violation for one quarter would be required to return to the secretary all federal funds received from the state during the quarter. In addition, any individual who is harmed by a violation of this proviso may seek redress in any United States District Court.

Before the intervention of the federal government in 1994 and 1996, twenty states included race as a consideration in the adoption process. Ten of those states simply stated that the race of one or more of the parties directly affected by the adoption was to be included in the petition for adoption. But their statutes were silent as to how the information should be used by those in a position to make final decisions concerning adoption. Arkansas and Minnesota had laws specifically requiring that preference be given to adoption within the same racial group. New Jersey and California statutes provided that an agency may not discriminate with regard to the selection of adoptive parents on the basis of race, but then provided that race might be considered in determining the child's best interest. Kentucky statutes claimed that agencies may not deny placement based on race unless the biological parents express a clear desire to so discriminate, in which case their wishes must be respected.

At the time this book went to press there were no data indicating the effectiveness of the 1996 Adoption and Safe Families Act in moving minority children out of institutions and foster care into adoptive homes. Were the states finding ways of ignoring the intent of the act and doing business as usual? The answer to this question is a very important one. Unfortunately it must await greater efforts at determining what is actually happening.

Adoption Statistics

Transracial adoption (TRA) began with the activities of the Children's Service Center and a group of parents in Montreal, Canada, who in 1960 founded the Open Door Society. The Children's Service Center sought placement for black children among Canada's black community. It worked with black community leaders and the mass media in its efforts to find black homes for these children. It was unsuccessful. The center then turned to its list of white adoptive parents, and the first transracial adoptions were made. Between 1951 and 1963 five black and sixty-six biracial Canadian children were transracially adopted by white families.

In the United States 1961 marked the founding in Minnesota of Parents to Adopt Minority Youngsters (PAMY). PAMY was one of the first groups to be formed in this country along the lines of Canada's Open Door Society. It provided similar referral, recruitment, and public relations functions. PAMY's involvement with transracial adoption, like that of the Open Door Society, came as an unexpected by-product of its original unsuccessful attempt to secure black adoptive homes for black children. From 1962 through 1965 approximately twenty black children in Minnesota were adopted by white families through the efforts of PAMY. By 1969 forty-seven organizations similar to the Open Door Society were operating in the United States.

The federal government began collecting national adoption figures in 1944 and stopped doing so in 1975. In that year the Children's Bureau reported that there were 129,000 adoptions, of which 831 were transracial.

In 1982 a statistician at the Administration for Children, Youth, and Families wrote, "There are no reliable national statistics available on virtually all ... aspects of adoption. To remedy the situation, Congress mandated the government to resume collecting national figures on adoption by October 1991. In December 1995 the U.S. Department of Health and Human Services published final rules implementing the Adoption and Foster Care Analysis and Reporting System. The rules require states to collect data on all adopted children who were placed by the state child welfare agency or private agencies under contract with the public child welfare agency. But as of the time this book went to press, national adoption data are still not available.

The following are approximate 1996 figures relevant to TRA:

1. There are anywhere from 450,000 to 500,000 children in America's foster care system, about 40 percent of whom are black.[1]
2. There are about 50,000 legally free-for-adoption children, many of whom have special needs (physically/emotionally disabled, sibling groups, older,

Table 1 Number of Adoptions by Year and Percentage of Change

Year	1987	1990	1992	CHANGE (%) 1987–90	CHANGE (%) 1990–92
Number of Adoptions	117,585	118,779	128,000*	+1.0	+7.7

* Interview with staffer, U.S. House of Representatives, Ways and Means Committee.

SOURCE: Victor Eugene Flango and Carol R. Flango, "Adoption Statistics by State," *Child Welfare*, CWLA 52, no. 3 (May–June l993): 311–19.

nonwhite). This figure rises to about 85,000 children if the formula used by many states is taken into account, namely, that about 20 percent of all foster care children eventually have adoption as a casework goal.[2]

3. Table 1 represents all adoptions in 1987, 1990, and 1992 and indicates the changes in percentage. Adoptions are not classified as related (those involving stepparents and relatives) or unrelated (those involving nonrelatives). In most years these are approximately equally divided. For example, in 1986 related adoptions accounted for 50.9 percent of all adoptions; unrelated adoptions equaled the remainder, 49.1 percent.[3]

4. TRA figures are extremely hard to come by. Most would agree that actual numbers are very small. For example, in analyzing 1987 data it was found that "92 percent of all adoptions involve an adoptive mother and child of the same race.... In only 8 percent of all adoptions are the parents and children of different races."[4]

But this does not mean that 8 percent of all adoptions in the United States were TRAs. Included in this figure are thousands of intercountry adoptions. In fact the 1987 TRA figure, where a black child was adopted by a white family, may be as low as 1.2 percent. There is no reason to believe that this figure is any different in 1999.

Opposition to Transracial Adoption

Organized opposition to transracial adoption began in the early part of the 1970s and was formidable enough by 1975 to bring about a reversal in policy on the part of major adoption agencies in most states throughout the country. The opposition was led and organized primarily by the National Association of Black Social Workers (NABSW) and by leaders of black political organizations, who saw in the practice an insidious scheme for depriving the black community of its most valuable future resource: its children.

Opposition also came from some of the leaders of Native American groups, who labeled transracial adoption "genocide" and also accused white society of perpetuating its most malevolent scheme, that of seeking to deny the Native Americans their future by taking away their children.

Both the black and Native American groups who were opposed to transracial adoption agreed that it would be impossible for white parents to rear black or Indian children in an environment that would permit the children to retain or develop a black or Indian identity. Even if some white parents might want their adopted children to grow up Indian or black, they would lack the skills, insight, and experience necessary to accomplish such a task.

At its national conference in 1972 the president of the NABSW, William T. Merritt, announced, "Black children should be placed only with black families, whether in foster care or for adoption."[5] The following excerpt establishes the flavor of the speech:

Black children should be placed only with Black families, whether in foster care or adoption. Black children belong physically, psychologically and culturally in Black families in order that they receive the total sense of themselves and develop a sound projection of their future.... Black children in white homes are cut off from the healthy development of themselves as Black people. The socialization process for every child begins at birth. Included in the socialization process is that child's cultural heritage which is an important segment of the total process. This must begin at the earliest moment; otherwise our children will not have the background and knowledge which is necessary to survive in a racist society. This is impossible if the child is placed with white parents in a white environment....

We [the members of the NABSW] have committed ourselves to go back to our communities and work to end this particular form of genocide [transracial adoption].[6]

In his testimony before a Senate committee on 25 June 1985 Merritt reiterated the NABSW position:

We are opposed to transracial adoption as a solution to permanent placement for Black children. We have an ethnic, moral and professional obligation to oppose transracial adoption. We are therefore *legally* justified in our efforts to protect the right of Black children, Black families and the Black community.

We view the placement of Black children in White homes as a hostile act against our community. It is a blatant form of race and cultural genocide.[7]

In addition, Merritt made the following claims:

- Black children who grow up in white families suffer severe identity problems. On the one hand, the white community has not fully accepted them; and on the other hand, they have no significant contact with Black people.
- Black children adopted transracially often do not develop the coping mechanisms necessary to function in a society that is inherently racist against African Americans.
- Transracial adoptions, in the long term, often end in disruption; and the Black children are returned to foster care.

In 1974, the Black Caucus of the North American Conference on Adoptable Children recommended "support [for] the consciousness development movement of all groups" and "that every possible attempt should be made to place black and other minority children in a cultural and racial setting similar to their original group."[8] In May 1975 the dean of the Howard University School of Social Work and president of the NABSW stated that "black children who grow up in white homes end up with white psyches."[9]

In 1972 Leon Chestang posed a series of critical questions for white parents who had adopted or were considering adopting a black child:

The central focus of concern in biracial adoption should be the prospective adoptive parents. Are they aware of what they are getting into? Do they view their act as purely humanitarian, divorced from its social consequences? Such a response leaves the adoptive parents open to an overwhelming shock when friends and family reject and condemn them. Are they interested in building world brotherhood without recognizing the personal consequences for the child placed in such circumstances? Such people are likely to be well meaning but unable to relate to the child's individual needs. Are the applicants attempting to solve a personal or social problem through biracial adoption? Such individuals are likely to place an undue burden on the child in resolving their problems.[10]

And, Chestang also wondered, what of the implications for the adoptive family itself of living with a child of another race? Are negative societal traits attributed to blacks likely to be passed on to the adoptive family, thereby subjecting the family to insults, racial slurs, and ostracism?

The white family that adopts a black child is no longer a "white family." In the eyes of the community, its members become traitors, nigger-lovers, do-gooders, rebels, oddballs, and, most significantly, ruiners of the community. Unusual psychological armaments are required to shield oneself from the behavioral and emotional onslaught of these epithets.[11]

But Chestang concluded his piece on a more optimistic note than most critics of transracial adoption: "Who knows what problems will confront the black child reared by a white family and what the outcome will be?" he asked. "But these children, if they survive, have the potential for becoming catalysts for society in general."[12]

Most writers who are opposed to transracial adoption have challenged two main hypotheses: first, that there are insufficient black adoptive parents willing to adopt black children; and, second, that the benefits a black child would receive in a white family surpass those the child would receive in an institution. They have observed that many potential nonwhite adoptive parents are disqualified because of adoption agencies' widespread use of white middle-class criteria selection. They also noted that blacks historically have adopted informally, preferring not to rely on agencies and courts for sanction. And they claimed that no longitudinal outcome data were available to show that transracial adoption of black children outweighed the known disadvantages of an institution or foster care. They predicted family and personal problems as the children grew into preadolescence and adolescence. A leading black organization pointed to transracially adopted black children who were being returned to foster care because the adoption was not "working out" or were being placed in residential treatment by their white adoptive parents who could not manage them.

One of the most prevalent arguments against transracial adoption is that white families—no matter how liberal or well-intended—cannot teach a black child how to survive in an essentially racist society. Many of those opposed to transracial adoption insist that because white adoptive parents are not black and cannot experience minority black status they will rear a psychologically defenseless individual, incapable of understanding and dealing with the racism that exists in our society. Amuzie Chimuzie articulated this position when he emphasized the fear of black social workers and other experts in the child-rearing field that black children reared in white homes will not develop the characteristics needed to survive and flourish in a predominantly white society. After first observing that children tend to acquire most of the psychological and social characteristics of the families and communities in which they are reared, Chimuzie added, "it is therefore possible that black children reared in white families and communities will develop antiblack psychological and social characteristics."[13]

Some black professionals argue that there is a major bottleneck in the placement of black children in black adoptive homes because child welfare agencies are staffed mainly by white social workers who exercise control over adoptions. That these white agencies are in the position of recruiting and approving black families for adoption causes some blacks to argue that there is institutional racism on the part of the whites. In contrast, there have been several instances where concerted efforts by black child welfare agencies to locate and approve adoptive black families resulted in the adoption of comparatively large numbers of parentless black children.

The above position was strongly argued by Evelyn Moore, executive director of the National Black Child Development Institute.[14] In an extensive interview on the child welfare system, published by the National Association of Social Workers (NASW) in April 1984—a significant portion of which dealt either directly or indirectly with TRA—Moore said that 83 percent of all child welfare workers in the United States are white, whereas 30–40 percent of their cases deal with black families. This skewed ratio, she contends, is one of the reasons there are so few cases of black inracial adoption (IRA). "The adoption system in this country was established to provide white children to white families. As a result, most people who work in the system know very little about black culture or the black community."[15]

Moore also argued that "white middle-class standards" are largely responsible for the rejection of lower-class and working-class black families as potential adopters; instead, they are encouraged to become foster parents: "while black children under the age of 19 represent only 14 percent of the children not living with their birth parents" (e.g., in foster care or institutionalized).[16]

Two studies conducted by the National Urban League in 1984 are cited by those opposed to transracial adoption as further evidence of the likelihood that institutional racism is one of the primary reasons that more black children are not given to prospective black adoptive families.[17] These studies reported that of eight hundred black families applying for adoptive parental status, only two families were approved—0.25 compared to a national average of 10 percent. Another study concluded that 40–50 percent of the black families sampled would consider adoption. An acceptance rate of 0.25 percent becomes somewhat more dramatic when compared to black inracial adoption rates of eighteen per ten thousand families. (The figures for whites and Hispanics are four and three per ten thousand families, respectively.)

In a 1987 Ebony article entitled "Should Whites Adopt Black Children?" the president of the NABSW was quoted as saying: "Our position is that the

African-American family should be maintained and its integrity preserved. We see the lateral transfer of black children to white families as contradictory to our preservation efforts."[18]

In 1986 the founder of Homes for Black Children—a successful black adoption agency in Detroit—issued the following statement:

> I believe it was the convergence of these two diverse movements, the transracial adoption movement and the one on the part of Black people to affirm our ability to care for ourselves and our children ... that resulted in the clash.... For those of us who are Black, the pain has been the fear of losing control of our own destiny through the loss of our children.... There is real fear, in the hearts of some of us who are Black, as to whether a child who is Black can be protected in this society, without the protection of families who are most like him ... [A] Black child is especially endangered when agencies or programs that are successful in finding Black families are not available to meet his need.[19]

The winter 1989 newsletter of Homes for Black Children carried a response to the above statement, written by a member of an Ohio organization called Adopting Older Kids: "Nowhere in this statement is there acknowledgment of the adoptive parents whose love transcends racial boundaries.... Nor are there suggestions about the future of those minority children, already waiting for families, who will be denied loving homes because agencies refuse to consider transracial placements."[20]

How can one explain the discrepancy between the apparently widespread desire to adopt among blacks and the dearth of approved black homes for adoption? First, blacks have not adopted in the expected numbers because child welfare agencies have not actively recruited in black communities—using community resources, the black media, and churches. Second, there is a historic suspicion of public agencies among many blacks, the consequence of which is that many restrict their involvement with them. Third, many blacks feel that no matter how close they come to fulfilling the criteria established for adoption, the fact that many reside in less affluent areas makes the likelihood of their being approved slight.

In 1987 the Council for a Black Economic Agenda—a group dedicated to advancing social welfare policies relevant to the black community—met with President Ronald Reagan to discuss what they and other black groups see as unfair practices on the part of adoption agencies. Urging that eligibility criteria for adoption such as marital status, income, and adoption fees be reexamined with an eye toward more black-oriented standards, they said, "The kind of standards that are being applied by these traditional agencies discriminate against Black parents."[21]

At the annual meeting of the Black Adoption Committee for Kids on 8 November 1991 another former president of the National Association of Black Social Workers, Morris Jeff Jr., stated: "Placing African-American children in white European-American homes is an overt hostility, the ultimate insult to black heritage. It is the creation of a race of children with African faces and European minds. It is a simple answer to a complex situation. It causes more problems than it solves."[22]

The Child Welfare League of America (CWLA) holds the position expressed in its "Standards for Adoption Service," which states:

> Children in need of adoption have a right to be placed into a family that reflects their ethnicity or race. Children should not have their adoption denied or significantly delayed, however, when adoptive parents of other ethnic or racial groups are available.
>
> … In any adoption plan, however, the best interest of the child should be paramount. If aggressive, ongoing recruitment efforts are unsuccessful in finding families of the same ethnicity or culture, other families should be considered.[23]

Another example in which transracial adoption is the second choice to inracial placement appears in a statement made by Father George Clements, a noted black clergyman and founder of "One Church, One Child," a national plan whereby one family from each black church would adopt a black child. After stating that inracial adoptions were preferable to transracial adoptions, Father Clements added, "But you cannot always have the ideal, and in lieu of the ideal, I certainly would opt for an Anglo couple, or whatever nationality, taking a child in."[24]

By the end of the 1990s the major arguments against TRA by those opposed to it are (1) that more than sufficient numbers of black families would be waiting to adopt all available black children were it not for racist adoption practices that prevent them from doing so; and (2) that black children adopted by white parents would develop into racially confused adults, no matter how sincere their white adoptive parents were, no matter how hard they tried to instill in their adopted children a sense of black pride, and no matter what research said to the contrary.

It also appears that the major child welfare and adoption organizations remain strongly committed to the idea of recruiting minority adoptive parents for similar children. Organizations such as the National Association of Black Social Workers continue to argue that race should be the primary determinant of a child's placement, even if the child has already been placed with and integrated into a family of another race.

The arguments supporting transracial adoptions are based primarily on the results of empirical work that have been conducted over more than thirty years. Those studies are summarized in the next section.

Review of Empirical Studies

The work of Lucille Grow and Deborah Shapiro of the Child Welfare League represents one of the earliest studies of transracial adoption. Published in 1974, the major purpose of *Black Children, White Parents* was to assess the success of transracial adoptions.[25] Their respondents consisted of 125 families.

Based on the children's scores on the California Test of Personality (which purports to measure social and personal adjustment), Grow and Shapiro concluded that the children in their study made about as successful an adjustment in their adoptive homes as other nonwhite children had in prior studies. They claimed that 77 percent of their children had adjusted successfully and that this percentage was similar to that reported in other studies. Grow and Shapiro also compared the scores of transracially adopted children with those of adopted white children on the California Test of Personality. A score below the twentieth percentile was defined as reflecting poor adjustment, and a score above the fiftieth percentile was defined as indicating good adjustment. They found that the scores of the transracially adopted children and those of white adopted children matched very closely.

In 1977 Joyce Ladner—using the membership lists of the Open Door Society and the Council on Adoptable Children (COAC) as her sample frames—conducted in-depth interviews with 136 parents in Georgia, Missouri, Washington, D.C., Maryland, Virginia, Connecticut, and Minnesota. Before reporting her findings, she introduced a personal note:

> This research brought with it many self-discoveries. My initial feelings were mixed. I felt some trepidation about studying white people, a new undertaking for me. Intellectual curiosity notwithstanding, I had the gnawing sensation that I shouldn't delve too deeply because the findings might be too controversial. I wondered too if couples I intended to interview would tell me the truth. Would some lie in order to coverup their mistakes and disappointments with the adoption? How much would they leave unsaid? Would some refuse to be interviewed because of their preconceived notions about my motives? Would they stereotype me as a hostile black sociologist who wanted to "prove" that these adoptions would produce unhealthy children?[26]

By the end of the study, Ladner was convinced that "there are whites who are capable of rearing emotionally healthy black children." Such parents, Ladner continued, "must be idealistic about the future but also realistic about the society in which they now live."[27]

To deny racial, ethnic, and social class polarization exists, and to deny that their child is going to be considered a "black child," regardless of how light his or her complexion, how sharp their features, or how straight their hair, means that these parents are unable to deal with reality as negative as they may perceive that reality to be. On the other hand, it is equally important for parents to recognize that no matter how immersed they become in the black experience, they can never become black. Keeping this in mind, they should avoid the pitfalls of trying to practice an all-black lifestyle, for it, too, is unrealistic in the long run, since their family includes blacks and whites and should therefore be part of the larger black and white society.

Charles Zastrow's doctoral dissertation, published in 1977, compared the reactions of forty-one white couples who had adopted a black child to a matched sample of forty-one white couples who had adopted a white child.[28] All the families lived in Wisconsin. The two groups were matched on the age of the adopted child and on the socioeconomic status of the adoptive parents. All the children in the study were preschoolers. The overall findings indicated that the outcomes of the transracial placements were as successful as the inracial placements. Zastrow commented:

> One of the most notable findings is that TRA parents reported [that] considerable fewer problems related to the care of the child have arisen than they anticipated prior to the adoption.... Many of the TRA couples mentioned that they became "color-blind" shortly after adoption; i.e., they stopped seeing the child as a black, and came to perceive the child as an individual who is a member of their family.[29]

When the parents were asked to rate their overall satisfaction with the adoptive experience, 99 percent of the TRA parents and 100 percent of the IRA parents checked "extremely satisfying" or "more satisfying than dissatisfying."

And on another measure of satisfaction—one in which the parents rated their degree of satisfaction with certain aspects of their adoptive experience—out of a possible maximum of 98 points, the mean score of the TRA parents was 92.1 and that of the IRA parents was 92.0.

Using a mail survey in 1981, William Feigelman and Arnold Silverman compared the adjustment of fifty-six black children adopted by white families to ninety-seven white children adopted by white families. The parents were asked to assess their child's overall adjustment and to indicate the frequency with which their child demonstrated emotional and physical problems. Silverman and Feigelman concluded that the child's age—not the transracial adoption—had the most significant impact on development and adjustment. The older the child, the greater the problems. They found no relationship between the adjustment and racial identity.[30]

W. M. Womak and W. Fulton's study of transracial adoptees and non-adopted black preschool children found no significant differences in racial attitudes between the two groups of children.[31]

In 1983 Ruth McRoy and Louis Zurcher reported the findings of their study of thirty black adolescents who had been transracially adopted and thirty black adolescents who had been adopted by black parents.[32] In the concluding chapter of their book, McRoy and Zurcher wrote: "The transracial and inracial adoptees in the authors' study were physically healthy and exhibited typical adolescent relationships with their parents, siblings, teachers, and peers. Similarly, regardless of the race of their adoptive parents, they reflected positive feelings of self-regard."[33]

Throughout the book the authors emphasized that the quality of parenting was more important than whether the black child had been inracially or transracially adopted: "Most certainly, transracial adoptive parents experience some challenges different from inracial adoptive parents, but in this study all the parents successfully met the challenges."[34]

In 1988 Joan Shireman and Penny Johnson described the results of their study involving twenty-six inracial (black) and twenty-six transracial adoptive families in Chicago. They reported very few differences between the two groups of 8-year-old adoptees. Using the Clark and Clark Doll Test to establish racial identity, 73 percent of the transracially adopted identified themselves as black compared to 80 percent for the inracially adopted black children. The authors concluded that 75 percent of the transracial adoptees and 80 percent of the inracial adoptees appeared to be doing quite well. They also commented that the transracial adoptees had developed pride in being black and were comfortable in their interactions with both black and white races.[35]

In 1988 Richard Barth reported that transracial placements were no more likely to be disruptive than other types of adoptions.[36] The fact that transracial placements were as stable as other, more traditional adoptive arrangements was reinforced by data presented in 1988 at a meeting of the North American Council on Adoptable Children (NACAC) focusing on adoption disruption. There it was reported that the rate of adoption disruptions averaged about 15 percent. Disruptions, they reported, did not appear to be influenced by the adoptees' race or gender or by the fact that they were placed as a sibling group.

In 1993 Christopher Bagley compared a group of twenty-seven transracial adoptees to a group of twenty-five inracially adopted whites. Both sets of adoptees were approximately 19 years old and were, on average, about 2 years old when adopted. Bagley concluded his study with the following statement: "The findings of the present study underscore those from previous American research on transracial adoption. Transracial adoption ... appears to meet the psychosocial and developmental needs of the large majority of the children involved, and can be just as successful as inracial adoption."[37]

In 1994 the Search Institute published *Growing Up Adopted*, a report that describes the results of interviews with 715 families who adopted infants between 1974 and 1980. When the survey was conducted in 1992–93, the adoptees' ages ranged from 12 to 18. A total of 881 adopted children, 1,262 parents, and 78 nonadopted siblings participated in the study.[38] Among the 881 adoptees, 289 were transracially adopted, of which the largest single group comprised 199 Koreans, who made up 23 percent of the total sample. The Search study reported that 81 percent of the "same-race" adoptees and 84 percent of the TRAs (of whom 68 percent were Korean) said, "I'm glad my parents adopted me."

Various "tests" of "mental health," "self-esteem," and "well-being" were given to the inracial adoptees and the TRAs. The results are shown in tables 2 and 3.

On attachment to their families, the Search study found that transracial adoptees are more likely than same-race adoptees to be attached to their parents: 65 percent for Asians, 62 percent for all TRAs, and 52 percent for same-race adoptees.

In the words of Elizabeth Bartholet:

The evidence from empirical studies indicates uniformly that transracial adoptees do as well on measures of psychological and social adjustment as black children raised inracially in relatively similar socio-economic circum-

Table 2 Percentage of Adolescents with High Self-Esteem

	BOYS	GIRLS
National sample*	51%	39%
All transracial adoptees	55	51
Asian TRAs	53	53
Same-race adoptees	63	53

* National sample of public school adolescents; N = 46,799.

Table 3 Four Measures of Psychological Health for Transracial and
Same-Race Adoptions

MEASURE OF PSYCHOLOGICAL HEALTH	RANGE	SCALE AVERAGE		SCALE AVERAGE (COMPARED TO SAME-RACE GROUP)
Index of well-being	0–16	All TRA	11.23	No difference
		Asian	11.40	No difference
		Same-race	11.08	
At-risk behavior	0–20	All TRA	1.80	No difference
		Asian	1.55	No difference
		Same-race	1.78	
Self-rated mental health	1–5	All TRA	4.10	No difference
		Asian	4.07	No difference
		Same-race	4.11	
Achenbach	1–120	All TRA	44.63	No difference
		Asian	43.94	No difference
		Same-race	42.29	

stances. The evidence also indicates that transracial adoptees develop comparably strong senses of black identity. They see themselves as black and they think well of blackness. The difference is that they feel more comfortable with the white community than blacks raised inracially. This evidence provides no basis for concluding that, for the children involved, there are any problems inherent in transracial placement.[39]

The Simon-Altstein Longitudinal Survey

In 1971–72, as part of the Simon-Altstein Longitudinal Survey, Rita Simon contacted 206 families living in the five cities in the Midwest who were members of the Open Door Society and the Council on Adoptable Children and asked whether she could interview them about their decision to adopt nonwhite children.[40] All the families but two (which declined for reasons unrelated to the adoption) agreed to participate in the study. The parents allowed a team of two graduate students, one male and one female, to interview them in their homes for sixty to ninety minutes at the same time that each of their children, who were between 4 and 7 years old, was being interviewed for about thirty minutes. A total of 204 parents and 366 children were interviewed.

The number of children per family ranged from one to seven; this included birth children as well as those who were adopted. Nineteen percent of the parents did not have any birth children. All those families reported that they were unable to bear children.

Sixty-nine percent of the first-child adoptions were of children less than 1 year old, compared to 80 percent of the second-child adoptions. One explanation for the greater proportion of younger adoptions the second time around is that adoption agencies were more likely to provide such families—who had already proved themselves by their successful first adoption—with their most desirable and sought-after children than they were to place such children in untried homes.

In 1972 only a minority of the families had considered adopting a nonwhite child initially. Most of them said they had wanted a healthy baby. When they found they could not have a healthy white baby, they sought to adopt a healthy black, Indian, or Korean baby—rather than an older white child or a physically or mentally handicapped white child or baby. They preferred a child of another race to a child whose physical or mental disabilities might cause considerable financial drain or emotional strain. About 40 percent of the families intended or wanted to adopt nonwhite children because of their own involvement in the civil rights movement and as a reflection of their general sociopolitical views.

During the first encounter with the children in 1972 (adopted and birth) they were given a series of projective tests including the Kenneth Clark doll tests, puzzles, pictures, and so on, that sought to assess racial awareness, attitudes, and identity. Unlike all other previous doll studies, our respondents did not favor the white doll. It was not considered smarter, prettier, nicer, and so forth, than the black doll either by white or black children. Nor did any of the other tests reveal preferences for white or negative reactions to black. Yet the black and white children in our study accurately identified themselves as white or black on those same tests. Indeed, the most important finding that emerged from our first encounter with the families in 1971–72 was the absence of a white racial preference or bias on the part of white birth children and the nonwhite adopted children.

Table 4 Self-Esteem Scores

CATEGORIES OF RESPONDENTS	N	MEDIAN	MEAN	STANDARD DEVIATION
Black TRAs	86	17.8	18.1	3.49
Other TRAs	17	18.0	18.3	3.66
Birth children	83	18.1	18.0	3.91
White/adopted	15	18.0	18.5	3.16

Table 5 Family Integration Scores

CATEGORIES OF RESPONDENTS	N	MEDIAN	MEAN	STANDARD DEVIATION
Black TRAs	86	15.4	15.4	3.66
Other TRAs	22	15.3	15.2	4.27
Birth children	83	14.7	15.4	3.17
White/adopted	15	15.5	16.7	4.00

Over the years we continued to ask about and measure racial attitudes, racial awareness, and racial identity among the adopted and birth children. We also questioned the parents during the first three phases of the study about the activities, if any, in which they, as a family, engaged to enhance their transracial adoptee's racial awareness and racial identity. We heard about dinnertime conversations involving race issues, watching the TV series *Roots*, joining black churches, seeking black godparents, preparing Korean food, traveling to Native American festivals, and related initiatives. As the years progressed, especially during adolescence, it was the children, rather than the parents, who were more likely to want to call a halt to some of these activities. "Not every dinner conversation has to be a lesson in black history" or "We are more interested in the next basketball or football game than in ceremonial dances" were comments we heard frequently from transracial adoptees as they were growing up.

In the 1983–84 phase, all the children were asked to complete a "self-esteem scale," which essentially measures how much respect a respondent has for her- or himself. A person is characterized as having high self-esteem if she or he considers her- or himself to be a person of worth. Low self-esteem means that the individual lacks self-respect. Because we wanted to make the best possible comparison among our respondents, we examined the scores of our black TRAs separately from those of the other TRAs and from those of the white birth and white adopted children. As shown in table 4, the scores for all four groups were virtually the same. No one group of respondents manifested higher or lower self-esteem than the others.

As shown in table 5, the lack of differences among our adolescents' responses was again dramatically exemplified in our findings on the "family integration scale," which included such items as the following: "People in our family trust one another"; "My parents know what I am really like as a person"; "I enjoy family life." The hypothesis was that adopted children would feel less integrated than children born into the families. But the scores reported by our four groups of respondents (black TRAs, other TRAs, white birth children, and white adopted children) showed no significant differences; indeed, the three largest categories were almost identical: 15.4, 15.2, and 15.4.

In 1983 we had asked the respondents to identify by race their three closest friends; 73 percent of the TRAs reported that their closest friend was white. Among the birth children, 89, 80, and 72 percent reported, respectively, that their first, second, and third closest friends were white. In 1991, 53 percent of the TRAs said that their closest friend was white, and 70 percent said their second and third closest friends were white. For the birth children, more than 90 percent said that their three closest friends were white. A comparison of the two sets of responses—those reported in 1983 and those given in 1991—shows that TRAs had shifted their close friendships from white to nonwhite and a higher percentage of the birth respondents had moved into a white world.

The next portion of the interview focused on a comparison of the respondents' perceptions of their relationship with their parents at the present time and when they were living at home during adolescence; on their reactions to their childhoods; and—for the TRAs—on how they felt about growing up in a white family.

Respondents were asked the following question: "When you were an adolescent—and at the present time—how would you describe your relationship with your mother and with your father?" The data indicate that, for both the adopted and birth children, relations with both parents improved between adolescence and young adulthood. During adolescence the TRAs had a more distant relationship with their mothers and fathers than did the birth children; but in their young adult years more than 80 percent of both the TRAs and the birth children described their relationship to their mothers and fathers as very close or fairly close.

We asked the TRAs a series of questions about their relationships to family members during their childhood and adolescence, many of which focused on racial differences. The first such question was this: "Do you remember when you first realized that you looked different from your parents?" to which 75 percent answered that they did not remember. The others mentioned events such as "at family gatherings," "when my parents first came to school," "on vacations," or "when we were doing out-of-the-ordinary activities," and "immediately, at the time of adoption." The latter response was made by children who were not infants at the time of their adoption.

The next question was this: "How do you think the fact that you had a different racial background from your birth brother(s) and/or sister(s) affected your relationship with them as you were growing up?" Almost 90 percent of those who had siblings said it made little or no difference. The few others were divided among those who said that it had a positive effect, a negative effect, or that they were not sure what, if any, effect it had.

We continued with this question: "Was being of a different race from your adoptive family easier or harder during various stages of your life?" Forty percent responded that they rarely found it difficult; 8 percent said they found early childhood the easiest; and another 8 percent said that they had a difficult time throughout their childhood and adolescence. Twenty-nine percent said that people of the same racial background as their own reacted "very negatively" or "negatively" toward them during their adolescence. The other responses ranged from "neutral" (37 percent) to "positive" (10 percent) and "very positive" (15 percent).

We asked the birth children how they felt about living in a family with a sibling of a different race. Only one respondent reported having "somewhat negative" feelings, and this same respondent felt that his parents had made a mistake in their decision to adopt a black child. Thirty percent acknowledged that at times during their childhood they felt out of place in their families—for example, when their families participated in "ethnic ceremonies" or attended black churches. But when asked, "How do you think being white by birth but having nonwhite siblings affected how you perceive yourself today?" all but 13 percent answered that the experience "had no effect." The others cited positive effects such as "it broadened my understanding" or it "made me think of myself as part of the human race rather than part of any special racial category."

Among those children whose parents lived in the same community, all the TRAs and birth children said that they saw their parents at least two or three times a month; most saw them almost every day or a couple of times a week.

On the 1983 survey we asked the children a modified version of the following question: "If you had a serious personal problem (involving your marriage, your children, your health, etc.), who is the first person you would turn to, the second person, the third?" Two other problems were posed: that concerning money and trouble with the law. In 1983, 46.8 percent of the TRAs chose a parent or a sibling; 45 percent of the birth children chose a parent or sibling; and 25 percent of the white adoptees chose a parent or a sibling.

In 1991—eight years later—we again asked the children who would be the first, second, and third person they would turn to with a serious personal problem. Again we found no evidence that TRAs were less integrated into their families than the white children. The TRAs were as likely, or more likely, to turn to parents and siblings as were the birth children or white adopted children. In almost all instances, however, children in all three categories said that they would first turn to their adopted parents or birth parents. For the

TRAs, a sibling was named as the next person. For the birth children, spouses and/or girlfriends or boyfriends constituted the second likely choice. The birth children and the white adoptees were older than the TRAs (a median age, respectively, of 26 and 25 versus 22), and this may explain why they were less likely to turn to their parents for help or advice.

We believe that one of the important measures of the parents' unselfish love and concern for their adopted children may be found in their responses to the question about the children's birth parents. In 1983 approximately 40 percent of the parents told us that their children expressed interest in learning about their birth parents. Of those, 7 percent also wanted to locate and meet one or both of their birth parents; an additional 10 percent of the parents had already provided their adopted children with whatever information they had—even before, or in the absence of, the children's request. Of the 40 percent whose children asked about their birth parents, only three parents were sufficiently threatened by the child's interest to refuse to provide the information they had.

Looking at the issue from the adoptees' perspective, we found that 38 percent of the TRAs had already tried or were planning to try to locate their birth parents. The others said that they had not decided or did not plan to try to find them. The most typical response was: "I am happy with my family. My other parents gave me up." Most of the adoptees did not have deeply rooted feelings about their reasons for wanting to locate their birth parents; curiosity seemed to characterize most of their feelings. Many said, "I would like to see what I will look like when I'm older." Those for whom the issue was more traumatic were children who were adopted when they were three or more years of age, had some memory of a mother, and felt a sense of abandonment or betrayal. They expressed their feelings in this rather muted phrase: "I'll feel incomplete until I do."

In the 1991 phase of the study the transracial adoptees, who, by this time, were young adults, were asked how they felt about the practice of placing nonwhite—especially black—children in white homes, what recommendations they might have about adoption practices, and what advice they might offer white parents who are considering transracial adoption. We also asked the respondents to evaluate their own experiences with transracial adoption.

We opened the topic by stating, "You have probably heard of the position taken by the National Association of Black Social Workers and by several councils of Native Americans strongly opposing transracial adoption. Do you agree or disagree with their position? Eighty percent of the adoptees and 70 percent of the birth children disagreed with the NABSW position. Among the latter, 17 percent agreed and 13 percent were not sure. Only 5 percent of the transracial adoptees agreed with the NABSW position. Others were not sure how they felt about the issue. The reasons most often given for why they disagreed were that "racial differences are not crucial," "TRA is the best practical alternative," and "having a loving, secure, relationship in a family setting is all-important."

One black male adoptee said, "My parents have never been racist. They took shit for adopting two black kids. I'm proud of them for it. The Black Social Workers' Association promotes a separatist ideology."

Another black female commented, "It's a crock—it's just ridiculous. They [the NABSW] should be happy to get families for these children—period. My parents made sure we grew up in a racially diverse neighborhood. Now I am fully comfortable with who I am."

Another commented, "I feel lucky to have been adopted when I was very young [24 days old]. I was brought up to be self-confident—to be the best I can. I was raised in an honest environment."

In response to the question, "Would you urge social workers and adoption agencies to place nonwhite children in white homes?" 70 percent of the TRAs and 67 percent of the birth children said yes without qualifications or stipulations. Almost all the others made some stipulations, most commonly that it should not be the placement of first choice, that a search should be made to find appropriate families of the same racial background as the children. The second most frequently mentioned stipulation was that the children should be placed with those white families who are "willing to make a commitment to exposing the child to his or her native culture."

We then shifted to a more personal note and asked, "How do you think being black (or Korean or Native American) and raised by white parents has affected how you perceive yourself today?" One-third of the TRAs thought the adoption had a positive effect on their self-image, one-third thought it had no effect, and one-third did not know what effect the adoption had on their self-image.

One male adoptee said, "Multicultural attitudes develop better children. I was brought up without prejudice. The experience is fulfilling and enriching for parents and children."

Our next question was this: "All things considered, would you have preferred to have been adopted by parents whose racial background was the same as yours?" Seven percent said yes; 67 percent said no; 4 percent said they were not sure or did not know; and 22 percent did not answer. When asked why they held the position they did, most said, in essence, "My life has worked out very well"; "My parents love me"; or "Race is not that important."

One female black adoptee believed that she "got the best of both worlds.

I can be myself and have black and white friends. I don't look at people for their race."

Another said, "The transracial adoption experience gives us an open view of the world. Prejudice comes from ignorance."

When asked what advice they would give to parents who have the opportunity to adopt a young child of "your racial background," and about how she or he should be reared, 91 percent largely advised that such parents be sensitive to racial issues; 9 percent advised that they reconsider.

One of the transracial adoptees who agrees with the position of the NABSW said, "I feel that I missed out on black culture. I can sit and read a book about Martin Luther King, but it is not the same." His advice to white parents who adopt black children is this: "Make sure they [the TRAs] have the influence of blacks in their lives; even if you have to go out and make friends with black families. It's a must—otherwise you are cheating them [the TRAs] of something valuable."

NOTES

1. Ellen Goodman, "The Orphanage Option," *Washington Post*, 24 April 1994, C6; and "Who Has the Rights to Black Children," *Baltimore Sun*, 7 December 1993, 19A.

2. Packard Foundation, *The Future of Children: Adoption* 3, no. 1 (spring 1993): 63.

3. Ibid.

4. Ibid., 29.

5. William T. Merritt, Speech presented to the National Association of Black Social Workers National Conference, Washington, D.C., 1972.

6. Ibid.

7. U.S. Senate, Committee on Labor and Human Resources, Excerpt from testimony by William T. Merritt, president of the National Association of Black Social Workers, June 25, 1985.

8. North American Council on Adoptable Children, "Barriers to Same Race Placement," (St. Paul, Minn., 1991).

9. Sandy Barnesky, "The Question: Is It Bad for Black Children to Be Adopted by Whites?" *Baltimore Sun*, 28 May 1975, B1.

10. Leon Chestang, "The Dilemma of Bi-racial Adoption," *Social Work* (May 1972): 100–105.

11. Ibid., 103.

12. Ibid., 105.

13. Amuzie Chimuzie, "Transracial Adoption of Black Children," *Social Work* (July 1975): 296–301.

14. Evelyn Moore, "Black Children Facing Adoption Barriers," *NASW News* (April 1984): 9.

15. Ibid.

16 Ibid., 10.

17. Ibid., 11.

18. Morris Jeff Jr., "Should Whites Adopt Black Children?" *Ebony* (September 1987): 78.

19. Homes for Black Children, Statement in *Homes for Black Children*, newsletter, Detroit, Mich., 1986.

20. *Homes for Black Children* (winter 1989).

21. Council for a Black Economic Agenda, Press release on meeting with President Ronald Reagan, Washington, D.C., 1987.

22. Morris Jeff Jr., "Interracial Adoptions Wrong, Says Official," *St. Louis Post Dispatch*, 9 November 1991.

23. Child Welfare League of America, *Standards for Adoption Service* (New York, 1988).

24. "Statement of Father George Clements," *The National Adoption Report* 10, no. 3 (Washington, D.C., May–June 1989).

25. Lucille J. Grow and Deborah Shapiro, *Black Children, White Parents: A Study of Transracial Adoption* (New York: Child Welfare League of America, 1974).

26. Joyce Ladner, *Mixed Families* (New York: Archer, 1977).

27. Ibid., xii.

28. Charles H. Zastrow, *Outcome of Black Children-White Parents Transracial Adoptions* (San Francisco: R&E Research Associates, 1977).

29. Ibid., 81

30. William Feigelman and Arnold Silverman, *Chosen Child: New Patterns of Adoptive Relationships* (New York: Praeger, 1983).

31. W. M. Womack and W. Fulton, "Transracial Adoption and the Black Preschool Child," *Journal of American Academy of Child Psychiatry* 20 (1981): 712–24.

32. Ruth McRoy and Louis A. Zurcher, *Transracial and Inracial Adoptees* (Springfield, Ill.: Charles C. Thomas, 1983).

33. Ibid., 130

34. Ibid., 138

35. Joan Shireman and Penny Johnson, *Growing Up Adopted* (Chicago: Chicago Child Care Society, 1988).

36. Richard P. Barth and Marian Berry, *Adoption and Disruption* (New York: Aldine de Bruyter, 1988), 3–35.

37. Christopher Bagley, "Transracial Adoptions in Britain: A Follow Up Study," *Child Welfare* (June 1993): 149.

38. Peter L. Benson, Anu R. Sharma, and Eugene Roehlkerparrain, *Growing Up Adopted: A Portrait of Adolescents and Their Families* (Minneapolis, Minn.: Search Institute, 1994).

39. Elizabeth Bartholet, "Where Do Black Children Belong? Politics of Race Matching in Adoption," 139 *University of Pennsylvania Law Review* 1163 (1991).

40. Rita J. Simon and Howard Altstein, *Adoption, Race, and Identity: From Infancy Through Adolescence* (New York: Praeger, 1992); and Rita J. Simon, Howard Altstein, and Marygold S. Melli, *The Case for Transracial Adoption* (Washington, D.C.: American University Press, 1994).

PART II

SIBLINGS TELL THEIR STORIES

INTRODUCTION

THE MEN and women whose opinions we elicit in this third volume in the series are the siblings of the twelve men and twelve women whose experiences of having been adopted across racial lines were explored in the first volume, *In Their Own Voices*. At the time of the interviews the twelve women ranged in age from 22 to 28. Eight were adopted at age 3 months or younger. The other four were 1 year, 18 months, 2 years, and 6 years old, but the 6 year old had been living with the family as a foster child since her birth. Rhonda, adopted when 2, had been in foster care with an African American couple, who may have wanted to adopt her but were disqualified because of their age. Rhonda was abandoned by her birth mother, taken directly from the hospital to the black foster family, and then was finally adopted into a white family. Five of the twelve describe themselves as "mixed," the others as black. Kimberly, one of the five who describes herself as mixed is married to a white man and is the mother of two sons. Two of the mixed respondents are married to black men, another is unmarried but has a son who is two and a half, and the fifth is unmarried and has recently moved back to her parents' home. Eight of the women have at least a bachelor's degree, one is working on her Ph.D., one has an MS in speech communications, and one is working toward a master's degree in social work. One graduated from high school and had taken college courses but was not currently working toward a degree.

Of the twelve male participants, eight were adopted before they were 6 months old, one was adopted when he was 2, two were adopted when they were 5, and one lived with a white family in a southern, rural Virginia community from 1954 to 1959, from 13 to 18 years of age. Four were born and raised, respectively, in Iowa, Michigan, Illinois, and Oregon. The other eight were born and reared on the East Coast in Connecticut, Vermont, Massachusetts, New York, Maryland, and Virginia. Eleven of them, when interviewed, ranged in age from 23 to 31. Lester was 57. Six are married: three to white women, one to a Haitian woman, and two to American black women. Four have children; one adopted a black child when the child was 6 months old. One is a single father.

The careers of the respondents varied greatly. There was a professional athlete and Olympic Gold Medal Winner, a minister, a property manager, a ninth-grade teacher, an aspiring screenwriter, a student, a stockbroker, an actor, a police officer, a technical writer, and a retiree from the Department of the Army. Eight of the participants held at least bachelor's degrees. At the time the interviews were conducted most of the respondents lived in small or medium-sized cities.

The adoptees' stories reveal their thoughts on family, adoption, and self-identity issues from their perspectives now as adults. While *In Their Own Voices* substantiates the claims that were empirically demonstrated by traditional researchers (from the mid-1970s to the early 1990s) working primarily in the social work and child development fields, which is that love and stability are essential in establishing healthy families, including families established through transracial adoption, the stories also push readers to ask this critical question: Is love (and stability) enough? Must parents of transracial adoptees make radical changes in their lives on matters such as the neighborhoods they live in, the churches they attend, the friends they have?

The second volume reported the parents' reactions to adopting across racial lines. *In Their Parents' Voices* picks up where *In Their Own Voices* leaves off, this time drawing from the personal accounts of the adoptive parents, many of whom had the opportunity to read about their sons' and daughters' intimate discussions on their adoptive experiences. The parents reflect upon their choice to adopt and raise black and biracial children against the backdrop of the civil rights movement and the controversy over transracial adoption. In volume 2, parents representing sixteen families introduced in volume 1 talk candidly about their reasons for adopting, the adoption process, the challenges and triumphs they encountered in raising their children, and the relationships they have with their adult children, and, in many cases, with their children's spouses and grandchildren. The parents express their opinions on transracial adoption, the opposition by certain groups in the early 1970s to transracial adoption, and they offer advice to other adoptive families in the process of raising children of color.

Similar to the research design of *In Their Own Voices*, the authors interviewed participants for *In Their Parents' Voices* primarily over the phone (with the exception of two couples and one parent). The interviews lasted one and a half hours, on average, and were transcribed and mailed to each participant for review and consent before it appeared in the book.

In Their Siblings' Voices takes readers full circle in our series on transracial adoption. This volume gives voice to twenty of the (adult) children who were born to the parents in the second volume and are the white non-adopted siblings to the adoptees in the first volume. Some refer to this group in the adoption literature as the "invisible voices."

It may be argued that white non-adopted siblings in these veteran families did not participate in the decision their parents made to adopt a child of color, nor were they subject to the controversy over the validity of transracial adoption, but the authors contend that these siblings nevertheless have a definite voice in promoting the understanding of transracial adoption. These individuals were affected (and continue to be) by the adoption whether they asked for it or not. Growing up with siblings who were adopted from different racial and cultural backgrounds almost certainly transformed their identities. But to what degree? Has the transracial adoption experience hurt or helped white non-adopted siblings? Have their experiences with transracial adoption visibly shaped their views as adults about race, adoption, and their own identity? Do they think transracial adoption is good policy for families? What can researchers, foster care and adoption professionals, adoptive parents, adoptees, and the public learn from the experiences of this important group about the intended and unintended consequences of transracial adoption in the long term?

In Their Siblings' Voices highlights the stories of eight men and twelve women representing eleven of the sixteen families from the second volume. Four families from that same volume did not participate in the siblings study because they did not have children born to them. Another family was not represented because the only non-adopted sibling chose not to participate in the study owing to a busy work schedule. In this volume, seven of the siblings interviewed were born after their parents had adopted at least one non-white child, and thirteen siblings were born before their parents adopted transracially.

The eight men interviewed for the current volume range in ages from 29 to 40. All but two have bachelor's degrees, and most of them earned advanced degrees (master's degree, Ph.D., and Jurist Doctor). The two men who only had high school diplomas and some college courses pursued entrepreneurial ventures. The careers of the respondents the authors interviewed included an electrical engineer, investment researcher, elementary school administrator, attorney, academic faculty member, founder of a technology company, CEO/owner of manufacturing companies, and a senior manager for a large corporation. Five of the eight men are married, and three of the five have children. Of the three single men, two have never been married. The third divorced and has a child. The married men all have Caucasian wives with the exception of one who has a Japanese wife. All of those married with children chose to have their own children. Two of the men interviewed, however, have expressed interest in adopting. The majority of the male respondents identified themselves as Protestant, one identified himself as Jewish, and another did not identify with any religion. Most of the men, like the adoptees in the first volume, live in small or medium-sized cities.

The twelve women interviewed for the current volume range in age from 28 to 54. Eight earned their bachelor's degrees and some went on to take graduate courses; only one of the women completed her master's degree. Of the four women with only high school degrees, most of them have taken at least a few college courses. The women's career choices included a program director of a wound healing center, a travel agent, an artist/stay-at-home mom, a project manager of a utility company, a minister/entrepreneur, a manager for a telecommunications company, a nurse, a stay-at-home mom/ business owner, a laboratory technician, an employee of a medical billing company, and a customer service representative. Six of the twelve women are married, two are divorced, and four never married. Nine of the twelve women have children. All the children are Caucasian, except for one multiracial child. None of the women respondents chose to adopt. The majority of the women interviewed identified with the Protestant faith. Three women indicated that they had no religious affiliation, or it was "still to be determined." Most of the women, like the men respondents, lived in small to medium-sized cities.

The research design used in the first two volumes in the series is consistent with that used in this third volume. All the participants were interviewed by phone; the interviews lasted one and a half hours on average; and the interviews were then transcribed and mailed to each participant for their review and consent before appearing in the book.

Understandably, the interviews solicited for the first volume were more challenging to obtain, given the "hidden voices" of black and biracial adult adoptees throughout the country. Locating these adoptees was difficult, as was earning their trust so that they felt comfortable telling their stories publicly, especially given the sensitivity of the subject. The lengthy process also required that we, as authors, continually reassured the participants that their stories would be used appropriately and with integrity. Helpful, perhaps, was that one of the authors had been adopted transracially and was willing to be interviewed for project.

In the subsequent volumes the authors were able to obtain the interviews from family members more easily. In fact, some family members told the authors that they, too, wanted their voices heard. The authors attribute this response to the success of the first project and the adoptees' initial experiences in participating in the work. It must be said that all the participants in this series believed strongly that their voice had value and should be included in the adoption literature, and that the honest discussion about transracial adoption, as it touches families throughout this nation in increasing numbers, must continue.

THE WHITE NON-ADOPTED SIBLING

In the first two volumes of the series on transracial adoption the authors presented both sides of the transracial adoption controversy, which heightened in the early 1970s. The debate, as many readers know, primarily centered on whether black and biracial children could grow up to become healthy individuals and productive citizens if raised in white families. One concern of the opponents in the debate was that these children would grow up without a strong sense of being black, and they would be separated from their racial and cultural communities of origin and be unprepared to function in a "racist society" as African American adults.[1]

The fact is, however, that much of the research generated in the twentieth century, especially in the early 1970s through the early 1990s, argued that transracial adoption was good policy for families because they focused on the social development and self-esteem of these children of color living in white homes. Many of the social scientists engaged in that research conducted interviews mostly with white adoptive parents and asked them about their perceptions of their adopted child's/adolescent's assimilation into their family and their child's/adolescent's level of self-esteem.[2] In some cases, the researchers asked the children/adolescents themselves about their own racial identities and self-esteem.[3] The findings in these studies reinforced the premise that love was enough when raising these children in white homes. On the other hand, little information from these traditional studies revealed how the white non-adopted siblings reacted to the transracial adoption phenomenon.

What do we know about the white non-adopted siblings in these families from the traditional research? The Simon-Altstein longitudinal study from 1971–91—the only study that tracked this segment at all—reported that among the 104 Midwestern families they interviewed, the birth children indeed reacted to the transracial adoption experience throughout the study. In the early years Simon and Altstein reported siblings' occasional expressions of annoyance and anger at how much time and energy the parents were devoting to their adopted child: "Our family life has been turned upside down since 'D' came home" or "'M' gets all the attention." But these remarks were rare. In most of the families, the black adoptee was "my brother" or "my sister"—to be cared about, played with, and, if necessary, protected. Race had receded into the background.[4]

There is still much more knowledge to be gained from the experiences of the white non-adopted siblings in transracial adoptive families moving into adulthood. We must ask them if adoption was good for them. Did they have to take on added responsibilities because they had a black or biracial brother or sister in their family? Does the transracial adoption change how they think of themselves as white individuals in society? We must learn from the past by looking at these veteran families, including the white non-adopted siblings, so that we can better inform and prepare our social work students, adoption professionals, and families in the twenty-first century about how to most effectively build racially integrated family structures where every member has a voice and is equally valued.

One of the few available resources that examines non-adopted children in transracial adoptive families is a dissertation written by the scholar John Raible, titled *Sharing the Spotlight: The Non-Adopted Siblings of Transracial Adoptees* (2005). In his study he interviewed twelve white non-adopted adults who grew up with a transracially adopted brother or sister. He divided their stories into five categories, based on five different types of siblings: safe siblings, responsible siblings, moral siblings, aware siblings, and, finally, the ultimate transformation, what Raible terms "transracialized" siblings. He defines "transracialization" as the unusual and creative ways to enact new racial identities. Raible argues that transracialization transcends the normal ways in which we learn to see the world in racial terms, including the ways that we understand ourselves and others as "raced" beings. In concluding his study, he reported mostly positive outcomes and experiences among the siblings: "All of the sibling participants expressed deep affection and love for their adopted brothers and sisters." He added, however, that "[still] others shared heartbreaking stories of suicide, estrangement, trouble with the law, and so on."[5]

Perhaps through Raible's study and now the publication of *In Their Siblings' Voices*, we can gain a deeper understanding of transracial adoption from a different angle, through the eyes of white non-adopted adult siblings. It is essential to hear the voices of these individuals before we make assessments and generalizations about their experiences within the discussion of transracial adoption.

NOTES

1. William T. Merritt, chair of the committee on transracial adoption, speech to the National Association of Black Social Workers National Conference, Washington, D.C., 1972, quoted in Rita J. Simon, Howard Altstein, and Mary Gold S. Melli, *The Case for Transracial Adoption* (Washington, D.C.: American University Press, 1994), 40; and Leon Chestang, "The Dilemma of Bi-racial Adoption," *Social Work* (May 1972): 100–105.

2. Charles H. Zastrow, *Outcome of Black Children-White Parents Transracial Adoption* (San Francisco: R&E Research Associates, 1977); William Feigelman and Arnold Silverman, *Chosen Child: New Patterns of Adoptive Relationships* (New York: Praeger, 1983); Joan Shireman and Penny Johnson, *Growing Up Adopted* (Chicago: Chicago Child Care Society, 1988); and Rita J. Simon, Howard Altstein, and Marygold S. Melli, *The Case for Transracial Adoption* (Washington, D.C.: American University Press, 1994).

3. Simon, Altstein, and Melli, *The Case for Transracial Adoption*; Ruth McRoy, Louis A. Zurcher, Michael L. Lauderdale, and Rosalie E. Anderson, "Self-esteem and Racial Identity in Transracial and Inracial Adoptees," *Social Work* 27 (1982): 522–526

4. Rita J. Simon and Howard Altstein, *Adoption, Race, and Identity*, 2nd ed. (New Brunswick, N.J.: Transaction, 2002) 222–223.

5. John Raible, "Sharing the Spotlight: The Non-Adopted Siblings of Transracial Adoptees," Ph.D. dissertation, University of Massachusetts, 2005.

SHECARA'S SIBLINGS

FROM *In Their Own Voices* we learned that **Shecara** (pseudonym) was born in Indiana in 1970. That same year she was adopted into a large family where she was raised in the predominantly white college town of West Lafayette, Indiana. Her parents were devout Roman Catholics, but they had stopped going to church because they disagreed with certain aspects of the doctrine. Still preserving their strong morals and values, they raised their eleven children with guidelines that would help them live a productive and responsible life.

Shecara was the only biracial-adopted child in her family. She had a good childhood and enjoyed spending time with her older siblings. It was apparent in her teenage years, however, that her allegiances to the white and African American communities were divided. Needing, from her point of view, to be "accepted" by persons who physically resembled her, she pursued relationships primarily with black students in her school and at the local university. She said that it was "her way of getting in touch with her blackness." Yet many of the cultural views and traditions she believed in were different from those maintained by her black friends.

The road she took to understanding her ethnicity and to feeling a part of a group led her to leave college and move to a predominantly black neighborhood in Indianapolis. Her experience there was tumultuous and potentially dangerous. She returned home to live with her parents. During that period she gave birth to her daughter, India. In 1996 Shecara earned her nursing degree and married her husband, Arsale (pronounced A-r-l-e-e). In *In Their Parents' Voices*, Shecara noted that she and Arsale are the proud parents of two more children, Kiya, age 5, and Alexis, age 3 (India was then 16, and their son Asante was 9). Shecara recognizes the value of exposing her children to their ethnicity but, most important, she realizes that children need love most of all. That is the lesson she gained from her parents.

The following interviews are with the two youngest children of this family of thirteen. Unfortunately, by the time the book went to press we were unable to solidify interviews with the older tier of the family.

DAN BAKER

AUSTIN, TEXAS
AUGUST 2007

Dan Baker is 32 years old and the second youngest of eleven children. Shecara is five years older than Dan. Earning both his B.S. degree and M.S. degree in electrical engineering at Purdue University, Dan gained an excellent foundation to pursue a career in engineering. Dan and his wife, Kristy, have been married for nine years. Although they do not have children yet, they very much want to build their family through adoption. Dan and his wife are Protestant. They indicated that their economic status is middle class. Regarding his relationship with Shecara growing up, Dan reports that they had a close and positive relationship as children. In his words: "She was a role model for me." Today Dan describes their relationship as positive and moderately close.

How would you describe the place where you grew up, and what was it like to be part of a large family?

West Lafayette, Indiana, where I grew up in the seventies and eighties, was a reasonably small town of about thirty thousand people, but it was near a university so it wasn't like typical small towns, it was very nice. It was kind of weird growing up in a family with lots and lots of brothers and sisters, especially ones who were particularly creative because you learn very early how to be creative, how to work with mechanical things, how to work with electrical things, how to design a variety of things. I remember being in second grade and I was particularly bored one day and my dad had this little engine, I think from a piece of lawn equipment, maybe a chain saw or something. He said, well if you're bored (remember I was in second grade here) take the whole engine apart and figure out what all the little pieces do, and then put it all back together again. It was just the type of thing that we got to do as children. That's one of the reasons I ended up being an engineer I think, is just because of those sorts of experiences. I remember we didn't have a ton of money to go around so if you wanted something, you'd find a way to build it yourself, pretty much. So we'd build all sorts of things, from musical instruments to go-carts, and putting engines on skate boards and everything in between.

What was your relationship like with the older tier of your siblings compared to the younger tier of your siblings?

I really didn't know my oldest brothers and sisters very much, being number 10 of 11. There was a twenty-year span start to finish, to within a week. So the older three or four I really didn't get to know particularly well until I was a teenager or even in my twenties. At first it sort of felt like they were aunts and uncles. Of course, later in life I've gotten to know them well, but mostly I was pretty close with everybody from maybe number 5 or 6 on to 11.

What was your relationship with your sister, Shecara, who was interviewed in the book *In Their Own Voices*?

Shecara was five years older than me. I think we had a really good relationship as kids. One of the things I remember most about Shecara was she understood social issues pretty well. My mom was quite busy and there were some things that just kind of went without notice, like even basic things like learning how to dress well, or how to comb your hair, and Shecara was always there to help me … she kind of looked after me to make sure that I was learning social skills I needed to have. I think you sort of have that in a big family, where the older brothers and sisters take care of the younger. Early on I remember Shecara was sort of my image of what it was to be cool. She had lots of friends, and she seemed like she did well on the social scene; and so I wanted to imitate her in a lot of ways in terms of figuring out how to fit in socially.

All of your siblings are white and not adopted, except for Shecara. Do you remember any conversation that you had with either Shecara or your parents about the difference?

I really don't. Not with them. No. I always thought it was pretty neat that I had an adopted sister. Not only was I from a special family but it was kind of an extra special family because I had a sibling that was adopted.

So your parents didn't talk to you about adoption? It was more of what you observed?

I do remember growing up; we would celebrate Shecara's adoption day. I think if I remember correctly we had this special candle for her that day. I am sure there were conversations about it but I just can't recall them at this point in time.

What about the type of relationship that you had with Shecara? In your opinion did she feel comfortable with you enough to talk about what was going on in her life and did you feel comfortable enough to respond?

I think we were very comfortable conversing. Really nobody in my family talked much about how they felt about anything. I wouldn't say that I had any different conversations with her compared to anybody else.

Did your friends or did people in your neighborhood approach you about the physical differences between Shecara and other family members?

It certainly wasn't normal. Any family with 11 children is not normal in America. But I tended to think it was pretty cool and I think that most of my friends and people I knew at school also thought it was cool. I don't remember, even a single time, being teased about having a big family or having an adopted sister. I don't think there was anything like that. I think most people respected our family.

Is it fair to say that your siblings had many different interests?

Yes. I would certainly say so. Quite a few of us ended up being engineers, so to some degree our interests were sort of similar, but there were other artistic interests and musical interests, of course. I'm also a musician and several of my brothers are as well.

As you reflect on the influence of your family, did the fact that you had a sister of a different race/ethnicity and that you came from a family with varying interests shape you for the better or the worse?

Definitely for the better. Specifically, with regard to my sister being of a different ethnicity I think that it has certainly made me much more comfortable around people of different ethnicities than myself. In fact, I remember growing up that any time I was in a situation where there was somebody who was African American or there was someone who was talking about somebody who was African American I felt sort of a sense of connectedness.... hey, I have a sister who's African American. And if somebody was telling a racially charged joke, for example, I'd be like, you better not joke about that. The good thing was meeting somebody who was African American, if something came up like that; I'd know how to relate because my sister was African American. It was kind of a neat feeling of connectedness that I wouldn't have had any other way.

That is something I am trying to understand. If a family, or family members, don't necessarily discuss race and adoption, why do you think you instinctively stand up against that mind-set when a racially derogatory statement is said about a black person?

It is not only that, but there are a lot of other things that are implied in families that are passed down without specific instructions. A really easy example is what kind of grades you're going to achieve in school. My mom never sat me down and said, listen, I know you're capable of getting all "A's," that's what I expect from you. But if I came home with a "C" I knew I had done less than I was capable of, even though she had never said that. I think there are things that are implied and passed down by nonverbal communication, if you will, just through conversations that aren't specific, but you get the gist of it.

I think that is what happened with my sister, is that we may not have ever had a big family meeting where we're going to talk about what adoption is, and what race is and so forth, but you get it. It's like when you see your parents loving this adopted person unconditionally, treating them with the same amount of love that they treat you, specific to the situation, then you get it. This person is just as deserving as I am of anything. I'm going to treat them with equal respect that I treat myself, and you start to get the picture that that's how you should treat all human beings.

Did society ever "get in your face" about the differences between you and your sister, Shecara? I ask that question, because, in Washington, D.C., where I grew up in the 1970s and 1980s there wasn't, I don't think, a lot of room for me to just blend in with my family because somebody would be in my face or the faces of my family members. I was asked many times: Why are you black? Why are you in this white family? Why do you talk this way? So that's why I ask the question ... where you lived in Indiana, were you ever as a white male approached by anyone that made your situation more up-front and personal?

Yes. There were a few people that I worked with through my high school jobs that sort of acted along those lines ... antagonistic, quite questioning of any sort of racial mixing, if you will. But I would say where we grew up in Indiana it was few and far between, and I probably credit that to the fact that the university was such a large influence on our town and there was such a huge foreign student population at the university that it is pretty common that people who aren't white are walking around town. Twenty miles out in the country perhaps it would have been a different story or in another small town of equal size but without the university there it might have been a different story, but I personally attribute that to the university influence that you have there. I think the whole town ... because basically on our side of the river at least, the town was about the same size as the university so the university had a significant influence on the city. On the other side of the river it was a little bit more divided and that's where I ran into a few people who were antagonistic.

That is a good point. As somebody who is Caucasian and considered by society to be privileged, from your perspective, what are your views on race relations in this country? By that I mean, when it comes to transracial adoption, do you think that it works having black children raised in white families? Do you think there are stresses?

Let me see if I can answer your question based on what my wife and I are addressing right now. We are in the stages of considering adoption. Actually we're planning on adopting one or more children ourselves, and we've had to talk through all these race issues. For the various places you can adopt domestically and internationally, there is a variety of races that are options for adoption, and we've sort of had to talk through them all and decide well, can we do this? Can we do that?

I think one of the conclusions we've come to is you sort of have to take it on a case-by-case basis in terms of what the parents are capable of. I don't think there are any hard and fast rules in terms of Caucasian parents, African American children, Asian children, Hispanic parents, etcetera. It really comes down to what those parents can handle and what the children can handle. I do feel that you cannot rob children of their heritage and you can't rob them of how they are going to fit into society, because you are not just raising a child, you are raising that child to become and exist as an adult. For example, if I would consider adopting an African American child, the question I would ask is this: Given that there is a pretty well established African American culture in America, can I accurately represent that culture myself, given my personality and my wife's personality and my home and where we live? Can I do that justice? And if I can't do that justice, then I am probably better off not bringing that child into my house and should instead pick a different ethnicity that I can do justice to. But if I can do that justice, if I feel like I can relate very well to that culture, that I could help the child not only experience my culture but whatever aspect of the African American culture they are going to need to know when they are an adult and living in America, then by all means I think transracial adoption will work.

You have admitted that cultural heritage is important. Do you think that, in the family you grew up in, justice was done in exposing your sister Shecara to her racial/cultural heritage?

You have to keep in mind that being five years younger than Shecara there was a lot going on that I didn't see. I can certainly remember specific application points that I would like to highlight. I know that there was a center in Lafayette across the river called the Hannah Center, and I don't remember much about it but I do remember my parents, I think, worked hard to get Shecara involved at that center. My understanding was that there were people that one would consider to be strong role models of African American cultural descent in that center. So my parents said obviously we're not African American role models for our child, we're Caucasian role models, but maybe we can find some African American role models as well, so that she can see that aspect. I think it was my parents' idea to get her hooked up with some people over there to try to build some other role models. I remember going to some dances and some cultural experiences that we probably wouldn't have gone to if we didn't have a sibling of that cultural descent. That said, I know that Shecara really had to learn how to walk that line of living in a white family and knowing that someday she was going to have to leave home and go out into the world where people were just going to see her as being African American. She knew, I think, that she had to learn to live in both cultures.

I think it was pretty challenging for her, honestly. I give my parents credit for what they did. I think if they didn't have ten other children they might have done more, but I think in the end you could say it worked out well. Along the way, there were times where Shecara had sets of friends that I don't think any of us were too thrilled about, but she needed to explore that angle just to see what was out there.

Do you think when it comes to transracial adoption it would be beneficial for the adoptive parents to develop and establish relationships with people from their child's ethnic community?

I think so. By doing that, parents would have a chance to help pick who they want to be mentors or role models within their child's ethnic background. You have to assume that's going to be the case, right? By the time you get to a point that the child recognizes, wow, I have a different skin tone than my parents, and they then see somebody who has the same skin tone, they are going to pay attention to that person that looks like them. They're going to go, huh … that person looks kind of like me, what are they doing? What's going on with them? That's why I think that if parents can have established friends who they trust and admire and of a similar ethnic background to their transracially adopted child then I think it would be only beneficial in the long run, especially for the child.

I think you make a very good point.

Yes. My wife and I spent considerable time talking through that, even to go as far as to say what are the types of foods we really enjoy eating, and what are the types of exercise we really enjoy and generally which cultures fit well with the sorts of things that fit well with us that we could most easily adapt to?

Do you and your wife also think about the neighborhood you live in when considering the racial and ethnic background of the child you want to adopt?

Yes.

That is impressive. Back in the seventies and eighties, many parents didn't go through that mental process that you and your wife have already gone through and continue to go through. To what do you and your wife attribute your awareness, willingness, and ability to do that?

To some degree we are both particularly analytical people. We took six months to pick out a stove. So we want to make sure we really make the wisest decision possible. To another degree, you have one chance at this life and you want to do the best you can with it so when you make a decision like this it is very powerful in your life and in somebody else's life, and anything you can do to make that decision as best as possible is just going to pay off dividends in the long run.

Tell me what motivated both of you to think about adoption.

A few things ... my wife has really been interested in adoption for quite some time, probably at least five years, maybe even going back to before we were married, ten years ago. I have always been sort of proud of the fact that I have an adopted sister, because that was a very good experience for me and from that I was certainly open to it. Becoming a Christian and reading more from the Bible about how much God really cares for the orphans and widows and people who don't have anybody else caring for them, I just get this sense when you adopt God smiles big. You just kind of feel His arms loving you as you are loving that child. So both of us probably as much as five years ago were like, we're going to do this; we're going to have to do this. So that's really kind of where it all stems from.

I think that speaks a lot to your experience and the impact family and adoption has had on you.

I would never have had the experiences that I have had, had my parents decided to birth another child biologically ... because that child wouldn't have been black, period. So it is an experience that only came because my parents decided to adopt a child. I wouldn't trade that for anything now.

Today, what is your relationship with Shecara and her husband, Arsale?

I would say I am moderately close with them. Since they moved to St. Louis we certainly see a lot less of them, and since we moved to Texas we've seen a lot less of them. We pick it up pretty easily where we left off when we do get to see each other, which is probably once a year, I would say.

Do you connect specifically with Arsale, and vice versa?

I would say moderately well, yes. I don't think there was any time that I would just call him up and say, hey, let's go hang out for a few hours, but we'll play basketball together and go to various sports events together. We connect moderately well.

Is it fair to say that the relationship that you have with Arsale and your sister, as well as their children, has helped you in your search to adopt?

It probably has. I would have to think about it. My response would be initially that it hasn't, but now that I think about it a little bit more I would say, well, probably it has. I really get to see Shecara in her environment with her family. This is the life that she lives everyday when she gets up. This is her husband and her kids. When my parents decided to adopt her as an infant, they were raising her to be an adult—and this is what that adult turned out to be. So you can see the effects of all the things my parents worked with her on, showing up now that she is a mom, and wife, and so on. There are benefits to seeing her in her environment, just to recognize that the child that my wife and I will adopt will become their own adult at some point in time.

Is it challenging to establish relationships with people outside your own race, given that you live in Austin, Texas?

Austin is kind of a unique place, again because we have a university here, the University of Texas. We also have very high-tech industry here, and so there tends to be a fair amount of cultural diversity because of the high-tech nature. Myself, personally, what I notice is that once I really get to know somebody I completely forget, or I tend to forget their ethnicity. I have a friend at work, for example, who when I sit back and think about it, I realize he's Indian-American, he came from India originally. Normally when I'm talking to him it's just like my friend at work. It is not the first thing that pops into my mind. Before I got to know him, I remember seeing him and going, oh there's a guy who must be from India. Initially, before you get to know somebody, you just sort of see the whole person, you don't focus on their face and their features and the way they smile or blink their eyes. After you get to know them, you start to notice their features more and their color less.

You and your wife have done a lot of research in the hopes of adopting a child. Do you think that there are good resources out there on adoption?

Definitely. We have been buying books on adoption. They sort of come in two varieties, at least what we have been able to find so far. The first variety is sort of the nuts and bolts of how to go through an adoption, paperwork you need to fill out and the options for where you can adopt from, and so forth. The second variety sort of recaps the stories. There's a variety of stories that you can read, but there you are sort of left to draw the conclusions yourself; and there are good conclusions you can draw.

Finally, what types of books would you like to see more of on adoption?

I would encourage more books to be written about how to raise transracially adopted children to become adults, to establish their own sense of identity, and to decide effectively how to pick friends and role models and people of their own cultural ethnicity.

TOM BAKER

WEST LAFAYETTE, INDIANA
JULY 2007

Tom Baker is Shecara's younger brother and the youngest of eleven children in his family. At 29 years of age and only with a high school education, Tom is the owner of a technology company. His economic status is upper middle class. He indicates no religious affiliation and has no children. He reports that, when growing up, both he and Shecara had a great relationship. As he put it: "She's a hell of a lot of fun." Today Tom says that they get along well and have a strong adult relationship.

For starters, what are you doing professionally?

I started a business with a buddy of mine manufacturing outdoor laser tag equipment. I would say we are in competition for the top spot of laser tag makers in the world. There are three top companies and we are one of the top three. I have five employees and we're making money.

When I was a teenager I realized that college wasn't going to work for me. I think I'm a smart guy and that I received a good education but I am also the type of guy who needs to learn something and then move on. That is why I knew that college was going to be tough for me, because of how regimented it is. It is interesting. Everybody decides what they need to do, whether that is to go to college, whether that is starting your own business. In our family there seems to be a lot of starting your own business. That is where I got the background to work from, so it was kind of a natural next step for me.

I put all of my time and energy into growing my business. Therefore I don't spend energy on dating right now. I may consider more of that in the future. In the meantime, since I am not establishing another life somewhere else, I am still living with the folks. They are getting older, and I am in a position where I can help them out a lot … and they help me out a lot with things like cooking dinner, etcetera. That relationship is working out real well. It is co-beneficial. As a result I get to see a lot of the family. Family is very important to me.

Let's go back to your childhood, your foundation.

Basically growing up in a large family here in a university town, West La-fayette, Indiana, let's just say we all kept each other very busy with having so many kids around. All of us had our own interests, so some of the kids hung out with some of the others, and some you basically didn't see at all because they were out doing their own things. We had enough money to get along, but most of it went to food and clothes. We have two great parents; you've talked to them a lot.

Our parents raised us all with this mentality that you've got to work your way through life, nothing's given to you. But on the other hand they would tell us that you can make things easier on yourself by working with people as opposed to being an independent that forsakes everybody. As a result, we ended up with very strong family connections.

You give such a unique perspective because you are the youngest of 11 kids, especially given the twenty-year age range between you and your oldest sibling.

That's right.

From your perspective, growing up in your family, what were the benefits and downside of being the youngest?

Some things were easier and some things were harder, because the folks had figured out a lot on how to raise kids by the time they had me. But being the youngest you always got picked on the most, you had the least amount of control; you didn't have anyone under you to pick on. That said, I'd have to say I had an easier time because a lot of my siblings had moved out; therefore the house was less crowded and it was easier just to get around.

What did you do to have fun?

I had a lot of friends in the neighborhood so I would go out and play Frisbee in the street with them, and ride bikes all around. Being that there was a bunch of boys in our family we also had a lot of fun coming up with interesting things to do like set foot traps in trees, out of cartons and stuff like that. Then we'd go out and hit a baseball around, play tennis. Primarily it was, "Do as much outdoors as possible." The parents, while they didn't put strong restrictions on how much TV we could watch, they made sure that we were outside [rather than inside] as much as possible.

Your sister, Shecara, who was interviewed in *In Their Own Voices*, is the only one in your family that was adopted. How did you reconcile that?

Shecara was adopted before I was born, so it was a complete non-issue to me. This was just how life was. It didn't matter whether she was black or white or Asian or anything. She was just another sibling. It really was a color-blind situation. The only time I had to pay attention to race at all was when someone would ask, "Is that your sister?" I would then explain that she was adopted. As a young kid, it was just not even noticed, because when you're a kid you accept everything as it is around you. There was none of this barrier of we're white, she's black.

Then when you got older ...

As I got older, basically when I was ten, Shecara was in high school, something along those lines, and so she was starting to try to learn what it meant to be black in this town. She was picking up a lot of the sort of styles of speech, styles of clothes, styles of acting that were more black. As a result it was kind of fun because ... you know when you've got siblings you never let them get away with much. So if they're acting different than they used to, you have so much fun poking holes in them. That's fine you're talking like that, but you start making fun of them for trying to strike out and do the "black thing." Shecara was what I would consider a very real person even when she was a teen-ager. For instance, she'd blow me off when she didn't want the little brother around. She would give me a hard time when she didn't want to be dealing with a situation. You could come to her and talk to her about stuff and she wasn't going to rat you out to the parents because she just knew what things were like. I always felt very comfortable around her during those times.

Did you ever have a conversation with Shecara about race, especially given that you lived in a predominantly white community?

No, race I don't think was an issue for either of us. I'd talk to her like I would talk to another sister. As a result, there wasn't any sort of real discussion about race, because in my mind at my age it was irrelevant to me.

As a family that had someone of a different race, it was not discussed—it was a moot point?

It wasn't that we were not going to talk about it. Rather, it was that there was just no reason to talk about it because we were all just human beings. Things changed slightly as Shecara got older and as I got older. It seemed like any eligible black guy in the city was trying to track her down. Then race became more visible to me, because the blacks that I saw were blacks who had been raised black, basically. They had different ways of acting, different ways of speak-ing, different ways of whatnot. Many of the black guys that I saw with her were football players. They were very intimidating to me. I was young at this point. I just would say "Hi" to them and move on. The thing of it was that even in those circumstances, our parents still just treated her like a daughter. They wanted to make sure that she was treated right and ultimately got to the right place in her life. They showed the same treatment to the rest of their children.

Did you ever think, if the tables were turned, and if you were someone who was African American in a white family, that it would be difficult?

Oh, yes. I've always thought it was hard for my sister. I always thought that she would have a lot of issues, mostly because we were out in a small town. It's kind of like there are a very … there's a very low population of blacks in this city and she was trying to find her identity and all of us white non-adopted siblings knew our identity. We all considered her to be part of our identity and we didn't need to make that effort to try to find the rest of our identity. It was difficult for Shecara, we all knew that. It just didn't affect our lives. When you have that many kids in the family it is sort of that you can recognize that someone is having trouble in school, or is having racial trouble, or just getting married, but no one really takes all those issues on themselves because there are so many of us.

There were references in the first book in this series, *In Their Own Voices*, where Shecara mentioned that at times she broke away from the family, particularly when she was older, to explore her black identity. I believe she went to a black community.

Yes, Indianapolis.

And then she said that a couple of her siblings had to come and get her. Do you remember that? I know you were young then.

Yes. This is later on in life, past her childhood and teenage years. We move forward a couple of years and she is just basically off on her own. The folks wanted, of course, to make sure she was OK but also they knew that she was going to have to figure this out on her own. But basically she was hanging out with a lot of people who she admits now in retrospect was just a bad idea.

What is life without learning? You're not going to learn unless you try, right? Shecara was just doing these things the best she knew how. I personally wasn't involved in the details. My older siblings got more involved. I was still worried about what was going on in my life right then. It may sound callous, but there are so many people that you just have to let subgroups create themselves within the family. You have to say this person and this person work together well and watch out for each other more, and this person and this person have a tighter bond. But once she came back home, I was the one that just sort of hung out with her and chatted with her at her normal level. For example, when she came back and she said, "Hey, Tom, I'm pregnant." I'm like OK, well, all right. You kind of go on with things. It's her life, and she's who's going to figure out what she needs to. Shecara was a very independent person during that period of her life. There was nothing to do besides say, "Oh, OK." You may not always feel that way when it is actually happening, but put through the retrospect of that time, you can view this thing with a slightly more rational sense than emotional.

Has this experience of having a black sister impacted you as a person and as a business owner? Has it given you some type of awareness about people who look and act differently than you?

Oh yes, certainly. Having Shecara in our family has been a tremendous asset for me, just in my life because I think there is a human tendency to not cross race barriers. In my opinion, if you are not exposed early on to people as people, as opposed to people of another race, then no matter how much one denies it there is a certain internal kind of scared reaction towards someone of another race. You just don't know who they are, how they are going to act. I think it is kind of just a base level reaction that the human brain has.

Here's the scenario: Let's say I'm playing basketball outside on the basketball court and there is a group of white guys playing on one part of the court and a group of black guys playing on the other side of the court. Given my family experience I can make the transition between the two groups.... I can go over and hang out with the black guys because I don't have that much of a hurdle to cross between the two, to make that internal race transition. If you are able to say, wait, I have a sister who's black and I've hung out with a lot of black people, it becomes a gateway to be able to start having a conversation or interaction with a person that you would otherwise be too uncomfortable to approach.

Shecara is married to an African American man and they have children who, of course, are also African American. How do you feel about having added racial diversity within your family?

I think it is great. Whenever they come to visit, whenever she is here for one of the big family parties, it is a lot of fun. We have the young white kids and the young black kids playing side by side together.

Shecara's family is going to be able to say, you know, I don't really necessarily have so many prejudices against white guys, because I know them. Even our Grandma and Grandpa are white. They're in my family. It is a really good experience for everybody in the family because my nieces and nephews who are white can hang out with my nieces and nephews who are black and vice versa and they get to experience that same sort of racial acceptance that I did because of growing up with Shecara. It is the same process happening just on a large scale with more people.

What about your extended family, your aunts and uncles? Did they accept Shecara in the same spirit as you did?

Yes, for the most part everyone accepted Shecara like I did. Maybe one or two people in our extended family tried to egg her on but it doesn't have a chance to fester in our family because there are so many people who create positive feelings that it just overruns any of the negativity.

Are you supportive of transracial adoption, particularly if a white family adopts a black child and lives in a predominantly white community?

Well, certainly. I think transracial adoption is a very good thing, a very healthy thing. Personally, I think that the only way society can advance when it comes to eradicating racism is to have more understanding, and understanding comes with living with someone who is different than you; I wouldn't say that it is easy on the minority though. Unfortunately, I think that is just one of those struggles the minority person would have to face in that situation.

Doesn't that put Shecara or anyone who is transracially adopted in a precarious situation?

I wouldn't say Shecara is any worse for coming through a white family. I'd say that she has experienced a lot more this time around in life in terms of being able to advance herself spiritually; she is able to understand the interactions between people better. She is such a character ... she is such a great people person. She has so many pools of people she can tap into so easily, whether black or white, whatever city they're in.

So what would your words of wisdom be for parents who are adopting transracially?

I would say treat these children just like any other kid in the family. In our family we didn't even care that she was adopted or of another race. There was no distinction between adopted and non-adopted in our family. To this day, I kind of have to think back and say, oh, yeah, she was adopted. As long as you make sure to treat the adopted child like everyone else, I don't really think that there's anything to worry about. You can get hung up when you put too much emphasis on special treatment of the adopted child. Will they get beat up in school because they're different? Sometimes yes, but you know people get beat up because they're stupid or ugly or for some other reason.

Do you think, now that you reflect on it, that seeing how Shecara struggled with her identity issues, that it would have helped her had she been more exposed to her ethnic community when she was growing up or if your parents—

I think her problems with her racial identity were so tightly tied up with her teenage years, her hormones and boys that it was hard to separate out race education from bringing the wrong boys around. These boys would have been the wrong boys whether they were white or black. Shecara had a tendency to go after guys who did not treat her like a real person, guys who were out there only to "play the field." As a result, she was pulled into an environment of lower-class people, regardless of race. I think that it made her search for her identity from the ground up. So you've got more drugs, more slums, living hand to mouth, more stealing, just bad situations for anybody regardless of race, and that was kind of her starting point of creating her identity of what it meant to be black. Shecara lived that experience for a few years as a teenager/young adult and then pulled herself out of that situation. She recognized, in my opinion, that the people she was around were creeps, even though they were black; and that she needed to find other black people that would treat her respectfully. She was able to do that and make a family. Today, I think Shecara has a very distinct understanding of the range of what it means to be black. She has seen black people who are good people, educated, and holding good jobs. She's seen people who go through the whole gamut. So, to answer your question, I think it is hard to say that Shecara had trouble just with figuring out what her race was. It was also her needing to figure out who her companions in life were going to be.

In your situation as a white individual raised in a white middle-class community you have naturally been exposed to white people who are edu-

cated, achieving good jobs, and so on. So you saw them as models. You were able, perhaps, to discern by example that these are good choices over here, bad choices over there. But in your sister's case, she didn't get to see that early on.

I would disagree with that. I would say she got to see a lot of role models, but she didn't see very many black role models.

That is what I am referring to, that your sister did not see many black role models early on.

Right, and so it has taken her many years of her life to figure out what it is to be the type of black person she wants to be. I agree with your point completely. I also have to say, though, that there is a certain amount of rebelliousness involved with knowing, on the one hand, that there are good role models around regardless of race, and, on the other hand, abandoning certain levels of one's upbringing in pursuit of doing what you want to do anyway. Shecara has returned to the values that our parents instilled in her, but I feel that she rejected a lot of those values for a while in an attempt to figure out what it meant to live in a black community. Everybody does that in life. I know too many white guys who were raised in a middle-class family who throw their life away by making bad choices. I see it in this town, which is nearly all white, people engaging in destructive behavior even though they have plenty of white role models. Yes, I think if Shecara had more positive black role models during her childhood, it would have made her life easier, but a portion of it simply has to do with personal choices and not adoption.

Recently your parents celebrated their fiftieth wedding anniversary. Did Shecara and her family come out for that?

Yes. About a week before their fiftieth wedding anniversary, my dad got sick. It seemed like the flu but it went on for a week of absolute misery until he ended up in the emergency room. It was in the emergency room that we were told that his gallbladder was bad. So then, on my parents' fiftieth anniversary, my dad had surgery to remove his gallbladder. We had everybody in town all the way out from Texas, Shecara from Missouri. It was kind of nice having everyone there so that everyone felt like they had a chance to see Dad.

He's now up and doing great. He is feeling better than I am these days. Shecara got to come then. It's funny, because her nurse's training always seems to kick in on these things. She was a great help and pointed things in the right direction. The reunion, of course, was not as we had planned, but people still got together and chatted with one another and had lots of fun anyway.

If you were to recommend transracial adoption to a white family, would there be any caveats you would add, or would you just say it's a great thing?

It is hard for me to answer that question. Since I was younger than my sister, Shecara, this was my experience as it happened. I didn't have any preconceived notions going into this. It was 100 percent normal for me.

Did you ever feel that you were in a position where you had to defend your sister or defend other people who were African American who perhaps had been unjustly treated?

The fact that my sister was adopted into our family certainly made me more open to recognizing unjust treatment of other races. Other, older people in my family were more in the defensive position for Shecara; and there was always something going on with her being black. But the flip side is that my best friend was Indian, from India, and growing up he got just as much crap as she did. We live in a university town where there are a lot of Asians, but there weren't as many Indians growing up there, so the Asians kind of got some of the crap but not very much, the Indians got more, the blacks got more. So it is kind of like everybody had to deal with something, but it certainly made me more aware of how ignorance leads to some really god-awful behavior.

Is there anything you want to say that we haven't discussed?

I'd underscore that transracial adoption has made my life a lot easier. I think that everybody in the family probably feels the same way … that we have all significantly benefited from the experience because those barriers to other races are that much easier to get past. That is not to say that this experience has been easy for Shecara, not as it relates to our family … her living in a white community, I don't think that was always easy for her.

What do you mean by that?

Shecara's husband was a Purdue football player. He is very strong, seldom says a word, and is of dark complexion. If Shecara hadn't been my sister, I never would have had a conversation with him because he would have scared me too much. I think the basis of most racism is fear. Shecara helped take down that barrier by introducing us to her husband, Arsale. We now know this person, we talk to him, he's the father of her kids, and he's part of our family. Culturally, he's still very different than we are. He doesn't always hang out at the same parties and talk to the same people as we do. So what? We now have our connection established. Granted, he still has his environment that he feels comfortable in, which is very different than our environment growing up, so our families don't have tremendous things in common. Yet we have more in common the more time goes on, because we have more contact with each other. If that contact didn't exist, then there would be a little more racism in the world.

I really do appreciate your honesty and your outlook on this.

But the thing is I didn't have to do anything about it. This was not something that I had to say, "I'm going to break down some racial barrier." I grew up in this family, and it happened automatically. So other people have done hard work, but I still don't think it is as hard work as it would have been if people had to do it without that initial forced contact of growing up together.

When you do decide to date, are you open to dating someone of color?

I am open to it, but it is only if I am attracted to the person intellectually. I'm not terribly attracted to blacks physically. It's not something that I care about one way or another; I just have a tendency to be attracted to white women. There are always exceptions. When it comes to life and love, nothing is set.

Tell me about your relationship with Shecara now.

It's a great relationship. She's a hell of a lot of fun. We get along real well now, and we have a good, strong adult relationship.

Something interesting is that I may think I am comfortable around blacks, but when I go drive through the black part of St. Louis, I'm like, "Okay, lock the doors!" It's amazing how you just don't think you're prejudiced or biased or racist … how uncomfortable you can feel when it's not just I'm a white and here are some blacks, rather, I am the *only* white in a couple of mile radius around here. It is amazing how your brain has some sort of reactionary thing that says I'm not in Kansas anymore. Shecara has to deal with this all the time … you're not black enough or you're not white enough, what are you? You talk like a white but you look black. She has to deal with so much judgment from the black community, but now she's got kids who have dark complexions so that buys her some space, but she always has to go through that mind processing. I'm sure you know what that's all about.

So what is the neighborhood like where your sister and brother-in-law live?

They live in a suburban area; not downtown. It's just a nice, comfortable neighborhood. But you can go four or five blocks in one direction and get into older, more ghetto parts, or four or five blocks in the other direction and get into more upscale communities. The kids have a nice area to grow up in—not too much traffic, nice house. They have a yard to play in, and sidewalks to ride their bikes up and down. It's quite similar to how Shecara grew up in West Lafayette.

Is the neighborhood they live in predominantly African American?

It is predominantly mixed.

I'm sure when you arrive at their home after driving through parts of St. Louis, given your experience, you want to run up and hug your sister once you see her.

I tell you it's kind of one of those things you don't want to admit. You don't want to admit that you're scared because you're like I'm not supposed to feel this way. I'm not supposed to feel that I'm intimidated by blacks but, as I said before, I think that there's some part of the human brain that says these people aren't quite like me. It creates an automatic division in your brain, which I don't think is fair, because very few people would intellectually make themselves racist. But I think there is a strong tendency to say I recognize people that are like me and I don't like people that don't look like me. I don't know why we have that in ourselves.

The thing of it is: knowledge of the individual person transcends this kind of built-in racism that we have. If you just see someone you don't recognize on the street—like if I didn't recognize Arsale, I would be scared stiff to go up to meet him. But having knowledge of that person, knowing the person, not the package he's in, then we see him and the fear doesn't exist and I think that is what … what still has to be done. You grow up in an interracial family and you still have to deal with racism but you've got a leg up, you're one step closer to being able to work with people from different races and backgrounds.

LAURIE'S SIBLING

ACCORDING TO *In Their Own Voices*, **Laurie Goff** was born in Seattle, Washington, in July 1970. That same year, the Goffs, a Jewish family residing in Seattle with their two biological sons, ages 3 and 5, adopted Laurie. Laurie's parents remained in Seattle while her father completed his medical residency and fellowship. Soon after, the Goffs moved to Sierra Leone, Africa, where her father was a physician with the Peace Corps and her mother volunteered as a teacher in the local African school. By the time Laurie was a teenager, she had lived in countries in the Middle East, Africa, and Central America.

Along with their strong conviction to work toward social justice in the United States and overseas, the Goffs made it a priority to raise children of good character. Reared in the Jewish tradition, Laurie learned the value of family, the importance of cause-oriented work, and the need to appreciate persons from different ethnicities and cultures. Education was also emphasized within the home. Through reading culturally diverse literature, Laurie took great pride in the significant contributions African Americans made to society.

Laurie describes herself as a self-assured, goal-oriented, fun, and "no-nonsense" person. Undoubtedly her personality was influenced by the love and commitment of her family. Perhaps the strong foundation her parents gave her proved to Laurie that she could overcome hurdles in her life. As a child she suffered from attention deficit disorder and dyslexia. Plagued with these learning disabilities, Laurie confronted the ironies of being black and Jewish in a white family, and at times, in foreign lands. She faced the tension of racial bias in the U.S. and often saw where equality was defined in black and white. Refusing to ignore these issues, Laurie fought them head on.

Laurie has a bachelor's degree from Evergreen State College in Olympia, Washington. After working as a production assistant in animation for Steven Spielberg's Dreamworks Productions and holding various jobs in the non-profit arena in California, Laurie left California to move back to Washington

State to be near her adoptive family and close friends. She no longer maintains ties with her biological family.

Laurie has two siblings, both older than she and born to her adoptive parents. We interviewed Adam, the younger of her two brothers, who had been about two years old when his parents adopted Laurie.

ADAM GOFF

SEATTLE, WASHINGTON

2006

Adam Goff, 38, is Jewish and is married to Aki, who is Japanese. Adam received his B.A. from Vassar College and his M.A. from the University of Washington Stanley School of Language. Currently he is director of research at the Frank Russell Investment Company. As children, Adam says, "she [Laurie] and I had a reasonably good relationship." Although he conceded that they didn't share many of the same friends when growing up or confide in each other, he attributes that to his having gone abroad to a boarding school at age 13. Regarding Laurie's personality and his interactions with her, Adam says, "Laurie can be overwhelming, and sometimes it just drives you crazy."

The following interview was conducted by Rita Simon.

How many years of schooling have you had?

I earned an undergraduate degree and a master's degree in International Affairs, with a focus on Japan, from the University of Washington. I've also taken finance courses.

What sort of work do you do now?

I work in an investment firm and manage an investment team.

Where are you located?

Tacoma, Washington.

You are married, is that correct?

Yes, to Aki who is Japanese.

Do you have any children?

No.

You are currently living in Tacoma, Washington?

No, I'm living in Seattle, working in Tacoma.

How old were you when your parents adopted Laurie?

I must have been right around 2.

So they didn't discuss their decision to adopt Laurie with you?

They may have.

Do you remember your first reaction when Laurie came into your house?

I don't remember that much. I was a spacey little kid. I don't have very much more than vague almost impressionistic memories. I have no memory of when she was first there.

How would you describe your relationship with Laurie as the two of you were growing up? Was it close? Distant?

She was a little sister. She was the baby of the family and she was a loveable sister, she was equal part cute and attention seeking. She and I had, I thought, a reasonably good relationship throughout her childhood. Laurie has always been very full of energy, and when she was a child she was always very needy for lots of attention. I think ... I could deal with that because my mode of living, at least as I remember it, was fairly spaced out, where I think she and our brother Michael probably had more problems with each other.

Did you and Laurie share any of the same friends as you were growing up?

No, we didn't share friends, but we both hung out with each other in our family; and there were family friends who had children and Laurie and I both hung out with them.

Did you have any of the same interests in music or sports or anything? Did you share any common interests?

Sort of. Laurie developed an interest in soccer a little later on, but that was pretty late.

And you were interested in soccer, I take it?

I was in soccer from a very young age.

Did you spend a lot of time together as you were growing up ... before you went off to school? Did you talk to each other a lot?

We talked to each other some, but I don't think we saw each other as confidants.

Do you think having a sister of a different race affected how you perceived yourself? Did it change your sense of your identity?

What affected me more was that we were living in all these different countries. I was constantly in the minority wherever I was. Probably I've reflected on it more as I've become an adult and continued to live all over the world. I think that's always been a valuable experience in the sense that when I've lived overseas I certainly did not feel in the majority culture. And what I mean by that is not that I have any sort of big disadvantages but I just feel off center from where the society is.

Even if I understand what they are saying, the culture has not really targeted me, and when I came back to the states I never felt like I was snapping back into the majority. Frankly, being Jewish, is something that, particularly when I was back in the states on the East Coast, is something people picked out that made me different. The sister was sort of another layer of that, of saying, well, OK, there is something a little different about my family.

When I asked if having a black sister affected how you saw yourself, what about your family? Did you think of your family differently now that you had a black sister and obviously a white brother? Did it affect your perception of your family in any way?

I was aware that it was unusual for my parents to have chosen to adopt someone of a different race.

As you got older, did you talk to your parents about that, about why they adopted transracially?

Yes. It was sort of, every family has their own creation. They would tell me, well, we really, really wanted a girl and race was not as important. Also my father having gone to Howard University, a historically black university located in Washington, D.C., and being very strongly affected by the civil rights movement, race was not something that I think he allowed to be a reason not to adopt, and it wasn't.

Did you and Laurie have the same quality relationships with grandparents, aunts, and uncles? Did you feel that you were both treated the same by other relatives in the family?

Yes. I did feel that we were treated the same. I've never felt differently. In fact, as we've gotten older, I think Laurie's relationships, if anything, have been better with our relatives. Not that mine have been negative, but it was probably because I've been so far away geographically.

You were living in Japan for a while, is that right?

Yes, since I got out of college, I've lived two years in Japan, one year in Thailand, and about six or seven years in Seattle, which is still pretty far away from my grandparents, and then back to England and Japan. So I've spent more than half my life after college out of the states, and certainly more than half my whole life overseas.

Was your relationship with Michael, as you were growing up, closer than your relationship with Laurie? Describe how you related to each of your siblings.

They are both such individuals. I don't think I could say that one was closer than the other because basically Mike was a little prickly, a tough guy to get close to. When Mike and I went to boarding school we spent more time together, but even then I didn't feel particularly close to him.

At what age did the two of you go to boarding school?

I was 13 and Michael was 16. We went to boarding school for two years together. That is the other thing to remember. When I left home I really did not live with Laurie for an extended period after that.

And you and Michael were not particularly close growing up and are not now, as I understand it.

Teenage years were very tough for him, and, as I said, I guess the best word to describe it would be that he was a little bit of a prickly character. But we were kind of close. We did a couple of trips in Southeast Asia together, but I don't know how well you know Mike.

I don't know Mike well, unfortunately.

He's not the kind of person who has sought tremendous closeness in the family. I am more likely now to call up Laurie and chit chat than I am to call Mike.

When you left to go to college, Laurie was still at home, right?

Yes. I went straight from boarding school to college. Laurie stayed home all those years.

While you were at boarding school and at college, did you and Laurie write or phone each other?

No, Laurie and I stayed in touch mostly by occasional calls. It wasn't a relationship where we would write long letters to each other, or even short letters.

When you started dating, and I take it maybe Laurie may have started dating, did either of you date people of different races? Did you date any black women or Asian women?

When we were in Bangladesh, I dated a couple of women who were Vietnamese, and in college I dated one black woman. I don't remember whether Laurie dated or dates white men at all. She hasn't done that much dating I think.... Maybe she dated a Native American.... I don't know. You'd have to ask her.

How would you characterize your relationship with Laurie today?

Laurie is a huge personality. We are happy to have her nearby, but we sort of are bracing ourselves, because she can sort of overwhelm you with her personality.

Are she and your wife, Aki, close at all?

They are very close. Even Laurie and I talk fairly frequently; in fact, I would say that over the last couple of years we're pretty close. Laurie visited us when we were in London, and we actually paid for her to come to Tokyo once and we paid her way to go to Hawaii and meet us there once. She's had a lot of interest in our lives, and she's been very supportive of both me and my wife. I talk with her as frequently or more than I do with my father. She talks with him more frequently than she does with me. We stay in pretty close touch, and I am pretty aware of what is happening with her.

And now that she is coming to Seattle, I imagine that the three of you may see a good deal of one another.

I kind of feel we will see each other occasionally. I wouldn't be surprised if we go for walks and have her over for dinner and all that sort of stuff, but in a while. But she calls up occasionally and we call her up occasionally.

Going back over the years, how do you think transracial adoption affected your family life? Do you think it made a big difference in your family life, the five of you?

Trying to isolate the adoption part is difficult, because there are a couple of different factors I can think of: first of all, my parents' decision to have a third child; second, the fact that Laurie has ADD and a couple of other things which made her somewhat hyperactive at times. These two factors have nothing to do with the fact that Laurie was adopted.

The fact that she was black, did that change things in your family? Did your parents do things they would not have done if Laurie had not been adopted, that is, did your family seek out new friends or seek out black friends or move into a different neighborhood?

I don't think it worked that way. My sense is the same sort of influences that made it completely OK and natural for them to adopt someone of another race made it perfectly natural for them to live in Africa for several years and have black friends, etcetera. That is not a causal factor. Again, her being adopted and given that she's had things like ADD and other problems …

What other problems did she have besides ADD?

Dyslexia.… And I think that created some challenges for her and my parents. My parents had to figure out how to help her and work with her. I don't know if you can separate the dyslexia from the adoption.

WERE THERE times during your childhood that you were jealous of Laurie … was she getting too much attention from your parents or other relatives?

There were times when I was angry with Laurie. I don't think jealous is the right word. Laurie is not someone who inspires indirect feelings like that. She's in your face at times, as an adult and as a child she's not very good with boundaries, and she can be very overwhelming and sometimes it just drives you crazy. I understand, based on my own relationship with my parents and a lot of independent confirmation from people, that I was a pretty spacey kid. I was up in my own little dream world. People were shocked that not only am I doing well in a financial firm but that I have a job at all. And I think from that point of view, I would get annoyed by things that were happening around me. Frankly, when I went to boarding school when I was thirteen, my mother was very upset. She was very conflicted. At the time, I don't think I probably recognized the importance of what was happening around me. I went, and I made the best of it, and I think that probably characterizes my way of working with Laurie. When she directly drove me crazy, then I was not pleased.

What were some of the things that drove you crazy about Laurie?

She was in your face. She sometimes has trouble assessing a situation, figuring out the best way to deal with the situation ... sort of being able to think it through. She has gotten a lot better, and I think she recognizes that as well as she's grown older. As a kid she was always focused on her point of view and what she was thinking and feeling at that moment. I think that has to do with the ADD. I've noticed a definite improvement since she started taking the medicine.

Would you encourage white families to adopt black children? Do you think basically it is a good idea?

Yes. I certainly wouldn't discourage them. My wife and I are looking at adoption at the moment. I don't know if we're going to do it, frankly. I'm sure you've heard from Laurie, there were challenges for her of a greater magnitude than the challenges that I had moving back and forth from country to country. And because of that, that's a lot to ... you just have to really support the child ... and understand no matter where you live, and no matter how much you travel or if you don't travel at all, there is going to be some sort of bridging issues and some conflicts between perception and how people are perceived and how they have been actually raised that can be difficult. I think for the adopted child, it can be very challenging. I wouldn't choose to adopt lightly unless I really felt I could do that.

Where are you in your thinking about adopting? Might you adopt, and, if you decide to, does it matter what the race or ethnicity of the child is, or the age or gender?

I think from our point of view we would be looking first at the Japanese kids.

Does age or gender matter?

Not really. We have small preferences, but they wouldn't rise to the point of saying one gender or the other. At this point we're coming out of a long bout of infertility.

How long have you been married?

We've been married ten years.

Have you talked with Laurie about the whole business of adopting?

We've talked about it some. She is very encouraging.

All things considered, are you glad that your parents adopted a child of a different race? Are you glad that they adopted Laurie, in particular?

I guess I would say yes to the latter, and I'm not really sure I even want to answer the question.

Did I miss anything, or is there anything else you want to say about the whole experience.

Did you get in touch with Mike?

No, not yet. We will continue to try.

I don't know how he will talk about it, and I will leave that to him. But I think Mike and Laurie over the years have never really gotten along that well, so that should be a very interesting conversation. I don't know what he'll put it down to: whether it's Laurie being someone who he doesn't get along with, or her being adopted.

Well, Laurie and your father went through some rough times, but it was a marvelous interview that he agreed to do.

But there is a difference between my father and Mike …

We'll see. But the fact that Laurie has opted to move to Seattle indicates that she has some faith that the two of them will get along.

You never know. I think, as much as anything, Los Angeles was just sapping her strength, and she has lots of friends here, and we're here and my father is close by.

CHANTEL'S AND NICOLLE'S SIBLINGS

WHEN INTERVIEWED for *In Their Own Voices*, **Chantel Tremitiere** played professional basketball for the Women's National Basketball Association (WNBA) and was the founder/CEO of Assist One, an adoption-related foundation based in Sacramento, California. She believed that children who are blessed with stable and nurturing homes have a strong shot at a bright future. That is why she partnered with adoption organizations, community leaders, and celebrities to help encourage adoption in order to provide homes for children who otherwise would be left in foster care or neglected.

Chantel's passion behind promoting opportunities for children comes from the fact that she herself benefited from adoption. Born in 1969, Chantel was placed directly into her adoptive home. Bypassing the ethnic differences of her siblings, Chantel says she focused on the laughter within her family. To her, laughter was the force that unified and strengthened the Tremitiere family.

Now retired from the WNBA, Chantel Tremitiere continues her commitment to community and to children, especially those in need of homes. In 2005 Chantel was the guest speaker at the annual conference of the North American Council on Adoptable Children. She has also done charity events and participated in other activities designed to offer children domestic support. Chantel appeared in a Disney movie called *Double Teamed* (2002) and was in negotiations to have her life story made into a movie.

A main focus of her time today is her young company, BLANK Entertainment, in Louisiana, where Chantel, as CEO of the company, oversees the development of commercials and music videos. BLANK Entertainment also houses a recording studio. Her business influence has been recognized by the Association of Business, Engineering, and Science Entrepreneurs, which hosts a Louisiana Tech "Top Dawgs" Business Plan Competition designed to give students experience as entrepreneurs. One message about adoption that Chantel wants to make known is that thousands of children in the United

States are waiting desperately to be adopted. If more funding and attention were devoted to these children, she believes they would have homes. Instead she fears that adoption is becoming a fad because of the current media frenzy about celebrities adopting children abroad. In her view, stories about adoption should be focused on everyday people and what they go through to adopt and provide a good home for that child.

In the first volume of this series, *In Their Own Voices,* it was apparent that **Nicolle Tremitiere Yates**'s undaunting character and faith in God were the underpinnings that gave her the liberty to discover who she really is. She was born in Huntington, Pennsylvania, in 1969, and was in foster care there for eighteen months before she was adopted. Nicolle's adoptive parents were active supporters of the civil rights movement in the 1960s and believed that children, regardless of race or ethnicity, deserve stable homes. Within ten years, her parents, in addition to their three biological children, adopted twelve children who were Amerasian, Korean, African American, and Vietnamese.

Nicolle grew up in York, Pennsylvania. Throughout her elementary and high school years, she attended ethnically diverse public schools. She then went to Kutztown University, where she earned her bachelor's degree in sociology in 1992. She became interested in seeking out her African American heritage. Certain books, especially *Their Eyes Were Watching God* by Zora Neale Hurston, helped Nicolle to identify with her inner self. In her spare time she spoke publicly on transracial adoption issues and was a "listening ear" for other transracial adoptees.

Nicolle has divorced since being interviewed for *In Their Own Voices* and, after a stint in Colorado, is now living back in York, Pennsylvania, with her daughter, Azariah, 14. Nicolle is working toward a master's degree in social work at Temple University, where she has a 4.0 average. This is an especially significant accomplishment for Nicolle, as she had experienced serious academic difficulties throughout her K–12 and college years. In 1997 Nicolle was finally diagnosed with dyslexia and spent two years "relearning how to read" with a reading specialist. Her experience with dyslexia is one focus of her graduate studies, as she prepares herself for developing an intensive adult training program for adults with untreated dyslexia who want to complete postsecondary education or vocational training. Grounding Nicolle through all this is her faith in God, which she sees as central to her core identity. Transracial adoption is a part of Nicolle's history and familial reality, but it no longer defines her. She focuses on being a good parent, and on her professional preparation and growth. Nicolle maintains a close connection to her adoptive family and continues to support transracial adoptions when they are well thought out for children who do not have access to an appropriate parent who shares their cultural identity.

The following interviews are with Scott Tremitiere and Michelle (Tremitiere) Zech, siblings of both Chantel and Nicolle.

SCOTT TREMITIERE

DENVER, COLORADO
MAY 2007

Scott Tremitiere is the youngest of three biological children in his family. He has twelve adopted siblings, including Chantel and Nicolle, and all of them came into the family after he was born. He is 40 years old. Divorced in 1994, Scott continues to co-parent his fifteen-and-a-half-year-old biracial son, Jake, with his former wife whom he met after college. Scott is a Born-Again Christian. He currently works in senior management in consumer retention with American Express. He describes his economic status as upper middle class. Regarding his relationship with his siblings, Scott says, "My relationship with my siblings is not as deep as I would like it to be and a lot of that is because of the geographical distance. I try my best to keep in touch with as many of my siblings as I can, but it is hard when you live so far away. Whenever my business travel allows, I try to see them."

Scott, where are you living right now?

I live in Denver, Colorado. I moved to Denver from York, Pennsylvania, in 1990, only a few months after I was married. Pretty much everybody in my family lived in York back then. My sister, Michelle, moved to Florida about the same time that I moved out here.

What led you to Denver?

I moved here because the company I was working for, which was a tele-marketing company, asked me to open an office in Denver. So we relocated here. My wife and I had our son, Jake, but later we divorced. I ended up becoming president of the company and nine years later, at the end of 1999, I kind of semi-retired. I put a lot of money into the stock market at the wrong time in 2000, and so I had to go back to work.

Tell me about your next professional step.

American Express actually called me, out of the blue (it was "God's favor"), and offered me a position. What's nice about this position is that I work virtually out of my house. It is important because in the early years of Jake's life I wasn't really around that much because I was traveling and running the telemarketing company. It is nice now to be able to drop him off at school and pick him up at school. As long as I'm not traveling—though I do travel some—I can be part of his life. Jake lives with me from Wednesday to Sunday every week and with his mom Sunday through Tuesday every week. We exchange him at church on Sunday.

How old is Jake, and what type of activities do you do with him?

Jake is almost 16. One thing we do almost religiously is play basketball. Yesterday we had ten kids over here playing basketball in the driveway. But Jake's passion is rapping. He was up late last night practicing. In fact, Jake and I turned the spare bedroom in our house into a recording studio for him and a bunch of his friends who rap. They actually have all the software and the "mikes" here, so they record for hours at our home a lot of times.

What kind of lyrics does Jake write and rap to?

They're positive lyrics. Jake didn't want to be classified as a Christian rapper, because it is almost a death sentence in a music store. You know what I mean? Nobody goes searching for the Christian rap section. But his lyrics are very positive…. It's all about dreams, about positive stuff. I could send you an example of one of his songs, but there are no negative references to "rims" or "shorties" or talking about women, money, and cars.

How did he get into this profession? He seems pretty well advanced.

Jake raps as a profession because he feels it is his calling and so he actually puts an undue amount of pressure on himself. He feels this is what he was born to do. His defining moment was when he was in fourth grade. He woke up one night with a bunch of lyrics on his mind and wrote them on post-it notes. He stuck the post-it notes to his forehead so he wouldn't lose them. Those words became his first song … called "Mile High," which he used to perform in the fourth and fifth grades. Ever since then, he just knew that was what he was meant to be, a rapper. My sister, Chantel, who was interviewed in *In Their Own Voices*, was and continues to be a big influence in getting him interested in the business. In her career she has produced a couple of platinum beats.

In addition to his aunt Chantel, does Jake have other role models?

Jake has a lot of role models. From the music side, he doesn't look up to just one person because a lot of different musicians, not just rappers, have influenced him in different ways. He likes different things about many of them. Most of them are alive now, but, of course, in that business not all of them are. Even he'll refer to Tupac Shakur (1971–1996), who is arguably one of the most prolific rappers of the twentieth century, in a lot of his songs as one of the first guys that really hit the level that Jake believes he could obtain. The problem is how hard it is to get into that business.

How is it to be a white father of a son who is a rapper?

The only time I ever think about it is when he does a lot of stuff down in Louisiana. If I go to a rap concert where he is performing I feel a little uncomfortable, not for myself but for him. I don't think that I'm the prototypical dad that's going to be hanging out at a rap concert. I just don't want my image to impact him negatively but to this point it hasn't. I'm sure that it wouldn't but sometimes, when I am in the environment, I'm thinking I'm a forty-year-old white guy—I'm not the typical person to listen to rap music, although I do enjoy a fair amount of it especially when the lyrics are good. I listen to hip-hop probably more than any other type of music now because of Jake and because we spend a lot of time together.

Tell me about your childhood and where you grew up, particularly given your open-mindedness.

This goes back to the late 1960s. Initially I grew up in the suburbs, and I remember stories about the KKK. I don't know if they threw a brick through our window or what the case was, I'm sure my mom can tell you all about that. But there were definite pressures of living in the suburbs, especially for an ethnically diverse family like ours. The area we lived in was a racially tense area. There were race riots to the level that the National Guard was called in. So the decision to move into York was obviously a good one. From my recollection of my mom's stories, the decision to move was based on my parents wanting all of their kids to have role models of individuals in their same race rather than sitting out in the suburbs and living some different kind of lifestyle.

From the time I was about four we lived in the city. So I was always around a diverse group of people. My best friend from kindergarten was black and I didn't … I never even really thought about it. It was just the way that it was. I know my comfort level with people who looked different than me was normal and it carried through to my adulthood years. It's interesting that, when I went to a mostly white college, I remember that the environment made me feel fairly uncomfortable; even when I started working for the telemarketing company, which was also predominately white, I felt very uncomfortable.

In contrast, the church my son and I go to now has ten thousand members and it is multicultural. It is probably one of the very few churches in the world that is mixed to the degree that it is. I have decided that the places where I feel the most comfortable are diverse areas. Even when I was in Utah, watching my sister Chantel playing basketball with the WNBA, I found it very uncomfortable even to go to the movies or some other activity there because the environment was basically all white.

Were you more uncomfortable going to a movie in Utah than to a rap concert in Louisiana?

Yes, because everybody looks the same in Utah, generally speaking, and the worst part is not only do they all look the same but they all look like me. And I'm around me twenty-four hours a day, you know what I mean? I don't need to be around me, I need to be around people who are different than I am.

That is a very good point. How come most white men (and women) don't get that in this society?

I think because they never had a taste of it; and if they did have a taste of it, it was in an environment that was not comfortable for them, where they felt threatened or in a situation they did not expect to be in. Today in America, I think more so than ten, fifteen, or twenty years ago, individuals and companies have to think about everything, every situation that could be potentially racially or culturally charged. For me it never became more obvious than when I was the president of the telemarketing company. The company was sued for racial discrimination. It was one of the most bizarre accusations ever, and when it went to the EEOC [U.S. Equal Employment Opportunity Commission] they threw it out because it was so ridiculous. This "claimant" was essentially trying to get money from the company. It was when the EEOC began looking into this case that I first realized that because of my experiences and personal qualities, my attitude and perspective on this situation was much more different than those around me. It was very evident that the claimant didn't realize my background and apparently assumed that anybody who is white and owns the company is fair game.

So the claimant underestimated you?

Underestimated the situation, for sure. There are a lot of individuals out there that try to sue as many employers as they can because somebody is going to settle rather than fight it. But this person underestimated the fight that would be in me if he accused me of something that I'm the opposite of. If anybody promoted minorities, it was me, and I gave everyone the opportunity to succeed.

Going back to your childhood, was it hard to see increasingly more adopted siblings coming into your family, and did you find that you had to shift gears or was it simply a natural progression for you?

It seemed natural to me, but I'm sure every child ... especially when you get to be a teenager ... becomes very self-centered, even the best of kids with the best intentions. When I was a teenager I remember a few times when all the changes were upsetting to me. I remember only maybe once or twice, though, ever even thinking we don't have as much as we would have if there was only the three of us. But to address your question, the evolution in our family was gradual, it was consistent. It just kept happening and happening, and to me it was mostly a blast. We had plenty of hard times, don't get me wrong, and there were plenty of growing pains trying to integrate all those personalities, particularly the ones that were older when they were adopted, like Bob and Kevin, and Kris and Laura. Those cases were different, because now you're bringing in somebody that's my age and I am already in fifth grade and now there's this other guy there. That was different than bringing in the twins and all those that came in when they were real young, i.e., babies. I think when you take care of little kids like that you create a different kind of bond with them. It's not the same as when you bring in a nine year old or a ten year old. The ten year old needs a home more than anybody, so I'm very glad that my parents adopted older kids, too. But those were the most challenging situations.

Did your parents ever talk to you about what was going on?

I don't remember. I know we got together as a family on Sundays after church and had a family council. If I remember right, that was often the time my parents handed out job duties, but it seems to me that they kind of opened up the floor if us kids had anything to discuss. But when you're a kid you don't know what's important and what's not important and you just kind of go with the flow. That's why kids are so resilient and can bounce back from divorces and a lot of other things. I know I never gave it much thought that this transracial adoption was something that we needed to discuss.

Did you ever have to defend any of your siblings because of race?

Oh, most definitely.

How did you do that exactly, and was it hard or frustrating for you?

It was eye-opening and extremely frustrating, because even in the city there still were a lot of people that were prejudiced or saw color instead of seeing the person. There is really no other way to say it. Here's a very real situation: One of my black brother's girlfriend was white, and apparently her parents didn't know or approve of their daughter dating a black guy. So I would have to go once or twice, as I recall it, to pick up my brother's girlfriend so that the both of them could go out together. My brother would be waiting in the car. I also had friends who were black that I would have to do the same thing for. You think about that ... the whole theory that the father or the mother of that girl already decided that you weren't good enough for their kid because of the color of your skin; that left a big mark on me.

How is your relationship with your siblings today?

My relationship with them is not as deep as I would like it to be; and a lot of that is because of the geographical distance. I try my best to keep in touch with as many of my siblings as I can, but it is hard when you live so far away. I would rather live somewhere where our lives become entangled. Whenever my business travel allows, I try to see them. I work in New York, so once in a while when I am there I will see some of my siblings. The last time I was in New York I took a train down to see Steve and Steph. I saw Michelle last week because I had business in Fort Lauderdale. Still, it is very hard to stay in contact with them on a regular basis. I spend eight hours a day on the phone and on the Internet answering e-mails, so the last thing I like to do at night is pick up the phone or e-mail people. However, I think of them constantly.

Do any of your siblings call you just to ask you your opinion professionally or personally?

Yes, they have but not so much personally. I'm probably not the poster child for relationships ... actually people who are divorced are probably better sources to get information from. You know, some people learn from their failures more than from their successes. I think I learned a lot from my divorce, relationship-wise. And I am only not remarried now because it is easier for me to help Jake with what he needs until he graduates from high school and I am also able then to put more time into the work that I do.

You were married to Jake's mother who is Cuban. Was it hard for you being in an interracial marriage?

To give you some background information, I met my former wife, Mercedez, in York, Pennsylvania, shortly after I had attended Bucknell University, a predominately white college. My best friends were probably the only three black guys there. I'll never forget, it wasn't until Mercedez and I went there for a formal dance (or whatever it was) that I had even thought about any challenges of a biracial marriage or raising biracial kids. Actually more than one of my friends pulled me aside, and said, "Are you prepared for how hard it is, to be in a biracial marriage?" That was the first time I ever thought about it. I brushed it off like, no ... I'm like, why would it be any harder than ... marriage is hard, period, even if I married a white girl. Yes, my eyes were opened, but I remember thinking if people had a problem with my dating across racial/cultural lines, that's their problem, not mine. But to answer your question, my challenges in a biracial marriage would be in integrating cultures and trying to get the most out of each culture, but not in just the fact that she is a different race than I am.

I know that you live in a suburb of Denver, but is the community that you live in diverse ethnically and racially?

Yes. It wasn't so much when we first moved here, but it is very diverse now. In fact, in my cul de sac there's a Korean family, a couple of African American families, a couple of Mexican families, a couple of white families, and a family from Australia. And when the neighborhood kids are playing in the driveway, just about everybody is represented. The school that Jake attends is very much like the school that I went to growing up, so it is very diverse.

A question that white parents who have adopted transracially often ask is how do you find that kind of diversity?

Right in this area there are three high schools that kids on our block go to where very easily you can find diversity, because they have open enrollment here. Two of the high schools I wouldn't want Jake to go to, not because of the whiteness of the schools but because of the affluence of the schools. So if you don't get a BMW when you are 16, there's something wrong with you. That's the lifestyle that I didn't want my son to grow up in. It just so happens that these two schools are also predominantly white. Now the middle-class environment that Jake lives in is completely different than where my brother Steve lives and where my sister Michelle lives. They both live in very affluent areas, and their kids do have to deal with that affluence. And although I'm in a nice house, in a nice middle-class neighborhood, it is also an integrated middle-class neighborhood and it is not where everyone is driving Rolls Royces and Bentleys around.

How did you go about seeking out that diversity?

I didn't really think too much about it, honestly.

Are you saying it just happened?

When I moved into this neighborhood, I didn't know who lived in any of the houses. So it wasn't like I said, ah, there's where I want to live or anything like that. I knew that the school was integrated, and pretty big, kind of like the one I had grown up in, so you make a natural assumption that the neighborhoods are that way. But at the time I was looking to purchase a home it was when the housing boom was on, and so you had three hours to decide if you wanted the house. Nowadays you probably could do more research on the type of neighborhood you want to live in, but back then you literally had to decide right away, so I didn't really think about it too much. I pray about everything, so I believe that I am put where I should be. One good way is to attend a talent show at the local high school. If the talent is diverse, the school will be. The talent show normally reflects not only the population of the school but how the administration embraces diversity.

Would you have moved had you found out that you were living in an environment that wasn't racially mixed?

I would love to say yes with no hesitation, but I think that if it meant I was going to lose $20,000 on the house.... I don't know. I'd love to say I would, but I just don't know. Fortunately, I didn't have to make that decision.

Scott, are you supportive of transracial adoption?

I am, but I also understand the challenges for the kids who are adopted. I understood my sister Nikki's article that she wrote a while ago in *Essence* magazine called "Black Children Should Have Black Parents," especially about the reality that there are culturally different things that could be very hard for the adoptee to deal with. But I think that being transracially adopted is better than not being adopted at all, and so in that scenario I do feel that transracial adoption is a great option for kids. I also think it is great for the adoptive parents and for the homemade siblings to learn about other cultures and to learn about how different people interact with one another. I think that we, the biological family members, get a lot more out of it probably than the adoptees do. I would like to stress one thing here; I feel that it is our obligation to pass not our acceptance but our celebration of other cultures down to our children. Those of us who have been fortunate enough to experience the beauty of mixed cultures should do everything we can to ensure that the next generation is able to enjoy the differences the way we were able to.

Please explain that.

When the transracial adoptee comes into a white family … let's just say Nikki, for example, there are certain things that are part of who she is that she is going to have to look for elsewhere, just like she says in her piece in *Essence*. The easiest example is her hair. My mom had no clue how to handle an African American girl's hair.… In fact, she ruined most of their hair by putting rubber bands in it and different things that most white girls do to their hair when they're little. I remember my sister, Monique, just screaming when my mom would take the rubber bands out of her hair at the end of the week. It wasn't until finally the mother of my best friend, the guy I talked about from kindergarten, stepped in and said, "Let me take care of their hair, *please*, for their sake." That's what you need. You have to be smart enough as a parent to know that it's not a negative against you that you can't provide everything that in this case your black child needs. You have to understand that there are just some things that you don't understand and you have to be willing to look for assistance from other adults that are of the same race as your child so that these knowledgeable adults can help with these things. So in that scenario, I believe transracial adoption can be a great thing. I would rather they be adopted than left in foster care.

Do you agree or disagree with the premise of your sister's article, "Black Children Should Have Black Parents"?

In the scenario where you can find black parents for black children, I agree. Good parents, not abusive ones. If you can find a good loving black family to adopt a black child, I think that is a good scenario, because the child is going to be able to relate to a lot of things that I probably wouldn't be able to relate to.

I wouldn't hesitate to adopt a black child into my home knowing that, number one, if it was a child that was hard to find a black home for, then I'm all for it, and, secondarily, I am going to go outside and look for help to raise that kid. I wouldn't assume that my knowledge would be enough to be able to help that person come up to full speed because I am a huge believer in nature vs. nurture. And although my family did nurture several things in my life and created a lot of the things that I am, I believe that when you're born, you're born with a lot of it. The reason I believe it so strongly is that I have seen it. It is easier to believe things that you see.

Please explain what you mean by that.

My sister, Chantel, is a perfect by-product of her birth father and mother. Her father would have been in the NBA [National Basketball Association] had he not suffered a serious car accident. That is her basketball side. Chantel is also a great volleyball player and a world-class musician. Well, her mom was an all-state volleyball player and a concert pianist and also played the trumpet. Chantel did all these same things never having met them. We, the Tremitiere family, probably influenced her to some degree to achieve as much as she could, but the ability that she had and the things that are part of her makeup, I believe, is in her nature. That said, I would think that it would be easier for black parents to raise black children. But that option is not always available. I think it wasn't available in the 1970s when my parents were adopting.

Do you think adoption policies have improved since the 1970s, or are we still not promoting adoption enough in this society?

I have limited experience with this, but I think, largely because of what I've seen and the people I know who adopt, that there's a lot of people going to other countries to adopt kids and bring them into this country. That could be because of the infatuation caused by the stars or by sympathetic cases. I have several friends, in fact, who are in the process of adopting overseas right now. My concern is that right in our own country there is a ton of African American kids, I'm sure, who are up for adoption and could be adopted, and I don't see enough focus on kids in our own country that are in need; the focus worldwide is pretty much there.

Why do you think Angelina Jolie or other celebrities do not consider the opportunity of adopting domestically?

I think they probably do think about it. But I think that when celebrities travel to other countries and see this stuff firsthand that's when it touches their heart. These same people most likely don't travel to inner-city Detroit to see this need. I think that if someone like Angelina Jolie were to travel to Detroit and see some of the things that are there, i.e., poverty, homelessness, it very easily could touch her. And had that happened first, it might have been the path that she took. But I just don't think that the stars go into downtown LA, to Compton, and see how these kids live, the need. These kids are not necessarily in one "orphanage" or one place like some places overseas. I think the goal in America is to try to put parentless children in the foster care system, so you can't go look at them in one place like you do when you go to the orphanages overseas. We need to place more attention on the children in this country who are in need of homes.

Are you able to articulate how transracial adoption has helped you as an individual?

Yes. This may go back to the nurture thing we talked about. In my family the nuances that I like about the different races is that it helped mold me. I think I was born with leadership qualities, but this experience has helped me to be a better leader because of my growing up in that environment. It has shown me the necessity to pursue the best way to manage people of all cultures. It gave me sensitivity and a vision that diversity can be accomplished effectively. I believe it is a huge part of who I am.

I would think that a lot of white men, particularly CEOs, don't get that, or don't necessarily see the incentives of finding that ethnic diversity that you're talking about. Perhaps, for some, the costs outweigh the rewards. How do you make that shift?

That is why I like where I work now, for American Express. Ken Chenault who is the CEO of American Express is African American. To get to your point, there is an incredible amount of talented people in our country from other cultures. I think the strength of America is that we don't rely on one culture or one race and the benefits of that one race. And the other side of that, like you said, the risk … you have to balance out the risks and the rewards. The risk side of that is that we do have problems that other countries with one culture probably don't have as well, so you have to decide which is better. I think that—and this comes down to men and women as well—there is a lot of benefit to finding the people that can lead regardless of their race or gender. I believe strong companies are built because they have strong leaders throughout the organization. Therefore, a smart CEO like a Ken Chenault will look at that and say I embrace the cultures but mostly I'm just looking for leaders. I don't care if you're white, brown, purple, yellow, red, it doesn't matter to me. The goal is to be a strong leader and to intersperse your entire organization with strong leaders — and this is how I ran the telemarketing company I oversaw that is successful today. Strong leaders determine the strength of the company; pretty much nothing else really matters because you can teach people job functions and you can teach people missions and visions and everything else, but you have to have strong leaders, regardless of where they come from. That's what I would tell anybody that I am face to face with that has not embraced that portion of it.

And it doesn't affect your ego if the strong leaders happen to be people of color or of a different gender than you?

It doesn't affect my ego at all. I would marry a woman that was a stronger leader than me, and making ten times as much money as me, if I found that person. I'm not sure I'll ever find that person, but that would be great. Ego is the biggest distraction in both business and in sports. People's egos hold them back more than anything else. I have seen egos destroy companies, because the owners of the companies won't give up on their own ego. In fact, in 1986 a Russian cargo ship crashed into a cruise ship killing 398 people. The weather was perfect, and all instruments were working properly. The problem was that both captains refused to change course, believing that they were in the right, and expecting the other captain to shift course. Thanks to their egos, 398 people lost their lives. I am sworn to learn from others' mistakes rather than repeat them.

So how is your ego?

I have a very strong ego. I won't say that I don't. I just try every day not to let it get in the way of success.

MICHELLE ZECH

NAPLES, FLORIDA
APRIL 2007

Michelle Zech, who is 43, is the only girl among the Tremitiere family's biological kids. She is also the oldest child of all her fourteen siblings, both adopted and biological. In 1985 Michelle and her husband, Brian, were married, and they now have three children: Jordan, 17; Kyle, 15; and Garrett, 10. She holds a B.A. in business administration and has completed graduate courses. She is Protestant. Currently Michelle is a program director at a wound healing center, where she specializes in addressing injuries such as bed sores and crush injuries. She describes her economic status as upper middle class. When asked about her role in the Tremitiere family, she says, "My role in my family was more of a mom figure than a sister or a friend since both my parents worked."

You spent much of your childhood growing up in York, Pennsylvania. Please tell me about that experience.

Actually I was born in San Antonio, Texas, and then my parents moved up to York when I was about 4 or 5, so I started school there. We lived in a little ranch house when we first moved there. And that's when my parents started to adopt the kids. We didn't quite fit in, in the suburbs, so we moved into the inner city. I'm glad that I had that opportunity because I know with my kids down here in Naples, Florida, where there is not a lot of ethnicity, it really changes your thought processes.

So there's a significant demographic difference between where you and your family are currently living in Naples compared to York where you were raised?

Yes. My kids tend to be around Caucasians more than people of other ethnic backgrounds. I think my kids seek out the ethnicity down here because of the family that I have which is kind of neat. In York, most of my friends were black or of different nationalities. It's weird now because I always say to people who know me; you know I grew up in a family where my two biological brothers and I were the minority in the family. We were the only white kids in the Tremitiere family. The people I tell that to seem to think that's pretty funny. Back when I was growing up, our house was like the open house for neighborhood kids. We always had kids in our house, kids who were having trouble or who just found our house the place to hang out. I am glad I had the opportunity to grow up the way I did in York because it really taught me a lot.

You are the oldest child. When your parents decided to adopt children who needed homes, did they talk with you about it at any time, especially regarding why they decided to move from the suburbs to the city?

I don't remember us ever having a conversation about moving until later on. I just figured we needed a bigger house. But I was pretty young when my parents started adopting kids. I do know that we had the conversation that we were going to bring other kids into the family. I remember my parents saying to me that these kids didn't have a home. I just knew I had to share my room, and I wasn't too thrilled about that! My brothers had shared a room, but I never had to do that. So when we first adopted Doug, he went into the boys' room; then when Chantel was adopted, she came into my room. It was hard for me at first, but since my parents started to adopt when I was young I just thought it was the natural thing to do. And living in the inner city was less difficult than living in the suburbs.

Can you elaborate on that?

I think, for me, it would have been awkward living in the suburbs where everyone was Caucasian. Having brothers and sisters of a different color you just didn't see that there. My husband actually grew up about five miles from where I lived in the suburbs, and there wasn't even one black kid in his high school. In fact, when we met, it was a big change for him to see my family. I think it would have been a lot tougher to explain or to fit in because of the diversity of our family if we didn't live in the inner city.

As someone who was a minority in your own family and probably also a minority in the community where you were raised, what situations were most confrontational when you were growing up and how did you navigate through them?

I was not confronted because I was white. The question I tended to get from people was more like, "Why did your family adopt?" I remember going out to eat with my family, and people in the restaurant thought we were a baseball team or something; they certainly did not believe that we were a family. Even now my son, just last night when we were talking, said Chantel was "not my real aunt"... and I asked him, "Why would you say that?" He didn't really have an answer. My response was to tell him that "Chantel is your real aunt, and she's my sister. She's part of our family. She's my sister; it's just like you and your brother."

So I don't think being white had anything to do with it; it was mainly just navigating through questions about why my family chose to adopt. And I think my explanation to them was what my mom had told us, "they, my adoptive brothers and sisters, didn't have a family, but they're part of our family now; they may have had people who cared about them but maybe couldn't take care of them."

That's a very good response.

Thank you. I think by saying that it helps other people understand the situation better. In the city we also had an adoptive family across the street from us most of the time we were growing up; so our block was filled with biracial families. I think that once our neighbors got to know us they could see that we were a good family. A lot of them actually pitched in to help. One of our neighbors was the guardian for a couple of my siblings. I could tell right there that they cared enough to help, especially when my parents clearly had a lot on their plate.

When you were growing up did you feel comfortable to date across the color line?

Yes. I actually dated a black guy in high school who was a really super nice guy. When I was dating him, even in the inner city school, it was kind of frowned upon. It's like I tell my kids, it's just an outside color. You have to find somebody who you are compatible with and are comfortable with. If we were compatible I would have married him. To me color means nothing except that person has a suntan and I don't. My son was just saying to my husband and me, "There's a hot Peruvian chick." And we didn't think anything about it. Now, my in-laws could have a problem with that. My cousin married a black guy, and she had trouble with her parents, and I said to her, "You have to do what feels right, it's your life. And you have to realize that regardless of what may transpire with your family, it is ultimately your life and you have to live the rest of *your* life if you want to be happy with the person your with." I tell my kids the same thing.

Did you have conversations with your siblings growing up about race or adoption?

No, I don't think it really was an issue at that stage. My role in the family was more of a mom figure than a sister or a friend since both my parents worked. That's probably why I am not as close to the four of my adopted siblings that graduated together, or those that grew up after I was out of the house. We're just starting to build some of those relationships as adults. Back when I was growing up I had to make dinner; and I was responsible to make sure that my siblings had their chores done. Once I started driving, I normally drove them around to their practices and activities. So there wasn't really an issue for me about race or adoption, or that they didn't feel comfortable talking to me about that. We had discussions about when some of them might want to find their birth parents, and how that would affect how they saw our mom and dad. They said that it wouldn't change their feelings, because mom and dad are the ones who raised them. And I think that is true. I think all of us just melted into the family. My siblings may have questioned their adoption, but I never heard anything to that effect.

As your adopted siblings became young adults, did race and adoption matter to them, as far as you know?

I know that as my siblings got older they would talk about possibly missing things in their backgrounds—if they were black, missing African American culture. Now they get that in their own way, through their friendships and through their relationships with people of their background, but they still have love for our core family.

What have you learned about transracial adoption? Having grown up in such a unique family, and now as an adult, have you carried over any of the lessons you learned into your professional career and your family life?

I honestly believe that the person I am today is the result of how I grew up. I don't see people for the color of their skin, I see them for what they can do, their abilities, and how we get along. A black girl assists me at work, and an Asian physician also works in our office. Had I not grown up in such an ethnically diverse family, I think I would have racial biases today, especially down here, in Florida, against Haitian or Mexican people.

If somebody has the abilities and qualities that I'm looking for in a given position, I'm going to hire that person. The experience has also helped my kids as well, because they have aunts and uncles who are of a different race and we've talked about that. When they were old enough to understand, they would say,

"Hey, Uncle Mark's black, why is that?" And then we would have a discussion. Actually, if we had a larger home I would like to adopt a little girl ... a little girl of a different color. I think it would be difficult to think along those lines if you don't come from a racially and ethnically diverse family, where everybody is different. I believe that my experience in my family has shaped my perspective on life, in a good way.

How has your husband, Brian, viewed your racially diverse core family, especially since you mentioned that he came from a background with no ethnic diversity?

I think that it changed his thought processes totally. When I first met him, the guy I was dating in York brought Brian over to the house just because our house was on his way back home. My brothers and sisters were playing outside and all around the house. Now that could have scared off some people! My brothers, Mike and Dan, were very small, and Nicolle wasn't very old either. They were hanging all over Brian. Then, surprisingly, the next night he called to ask me out. I was totally shocked and could not believe that this guy who is from way out in the suburbs found me interesting ... and here I am with my family that is not normal. He just took to it. From my standpoint, it really didn't change his philosophy about me, but he looks at things differently now. For example, he doesn't have a problem with our kids dating someone of a different color. Now Brian believes the same thing that I stand by when it comes to relationships, that it just depends on what that person has on the inside, and how you get along, that is what matters the most. I don't think he would have said that based on the way he grew up.

How has the diversity of your family impacted your relationship with your in-laws?

At first I think my in-laws were shocked. It's funny now, because when Chantel was in the paper a lot for basketball or whatever, they would cut out the articles and send them to us. They've been to a lot of our family events. Are they totally as comfortable as Brian with it? Probably not. But it has taught them that people with different ethnic and racial backgrounds are O.K. too.

Given your background and that you are the only white female sibling in your family, are you able to feel confident as a white woman today?

Yes. I'll joke around about being the only white girl. Even when I introduce one of my brothers or sisters to somebody else, they give me a really strange look.

And I know my biological brother, Scott, experiences the same thing. We'll say to a few people, for example, "Hey, this is my brother, Dan." And they'll look, and we'll smile and ask them, "Don't we look alike?" "What's your problem?" Scott interjects, "Yes, he is my twin! Don't we look a lot alike?" And we always joke about that because people just look at us so funny. It's just like with Chantel. My boys are always bragging about Aunt Chantel, and people are looking at them like, what? She's your aunt? They're like yeah, "Don't we look alike?" They're picking up on that, too.

As an adult, does it ever bother you that you have to offer an explanation?

No. I look at it as being pretty cool, because I actually have something to explain. There aren't too many people out there that have something to explain about their family, especially the way their families look. I'm proud of each and every one of my siblings; there aren't many families that have fifteen kids, none of whom has really ever had a bad issue. Most of them are college-educated and are in the business community and have really done well, so I'm very proud of them.

Obviously your parents did quite a few things well for the sake of their children. What do you think were some of those things?

For one, just having the heart to decide that adoption was a good thing to do. I always say that my parents looked through the Sears catalog and picked out the ones they wanted. It's sort of like what we do now online, click and choose; add it to your shopping cart. But they had a big enough heart and the wherewithal to know that it would be tough for them to take these kids and raise them when they didn't have a lot of outside support. Those kids would have been stuck in the foster care system or out there and never would have been able to experience family. That's what I see.

So it took heart.

Yes, it had to be heart because they didn't have any money! I remember crock pot dinners, when my mom would throw the rest of whatever she had in the pantry in the crock pot, and we would all turn up our noses at it, but little did we know that that's all she had to feed us. We used to go to a place like Costco in York, but at this place the canned goods were often damaged, and you'd have to take your own boxes for your food items, knowing that that wasn't the coolest thing, but that's how we could make ends meet. My parents didn't have any help from the government, nor did they want it. That to me means that the heart was there. It wasn't for the money. Some people look at adopting or fostering as a money maker, which is a shame. Really, it is all about heart.

They obviously made some conscious decisions such as moving from suburbia to the inner city. Do you think they were able to do that because of their heart?

Oh, I do. Much of what they had to decide on and confront was difficult. Even in the city we lived right around the corner from a Ku Klux Klan guy and I remember the KKK burned a cross on our front yard. You have to be able to take a lot of adversity to be able to do what my parents did, and explain to your kids why such acts are happening.

How did you feel when you realized that there was this Ku Klux Klan guy down the street from where your family was living?

I was six at the time. But I could not understand why somebody who has the same bone structure, same inside as you but just looks different on the outside deserves to be treated so horribly. And especially how can anybody want to harm kids or a family that was trying to help others? How could anybody do something so mean? I was mad.

Did you ever have to defend your siblings because of their race?

Yes. Some people did not understand our situation. As I said earlier, people would think we were a baseball team. Others questioned why there were black kids in our family. I said the same thing then as I do now, that we're a family.

I admire you for that. Too many of us, whether we are employers, fellow employees, or neighbors, don't know how to stick up for people when they have been judged wrongly simply because of the color of their skin.

I agree. That's why I think, when you have to deal with someone of a different race or family, you act very differently when you've grown up in a transracial adoptive family as opposed to not growing up in one. That's why I think that if everybody had that opportunity to have people in their family from different racial and ethnic backgrounds the world would be a different place.

What would you say to other families who are looking to adopt interracially?

That it is probably the best thing they could ever do. I think it teaches us that we are all really alike. I know a lot of people adopt from China now, but there's a ton of kids in our country who need homes, kids who are of a different color than us. Every child should have the opportunity to have a home.

RACHEL'S SIBLINGS

BORN IN Chicago, **Rachel** was raised just a few minutes away, but worlds apart, from the predominantly white, Dutch community of South Holland where she was delivered into foster care at birth into the home of a forty-something couple with three biological daughters. The couple ultimately adopted Rachel, making her and her subsequently adopted Lithuanian sister unique exceptions among the thirty-five foster children who have passed through their home in the intervening years.

Rachel and her siblings were raised in the Protestant Dutch Reformed tradition pervasive in that area. Consistent with that tradition, her father worked as a carpenter and her mother was a full-time homemaker. Neither parent had pursued a college education.

In *In Their Own Voices*, Rachel emphasized her difficulty in accepting her dark skin, kinky hair, and African features in the context of being part of a white family within the bastion of white society. How does someone who is black and adopted into a white family decide his or her own worth in our society? Rachel continues to struggle with this question today.

Rachel's racial identity and self-esteem have strengthened over the years, as she attested to in *In Their Parents' Voices*. Recently married to Robert, a young African American man, Rachel hopes to complete her bachelor's degree in elementary education and music.

The following interviews are with Rachel's three sisters, all born to Rachel's adoptive parents and all much older than Rachel.

KATHY MULDER

SCOTTSDALE, ARIZONA

JULY 2006

Kathy Mulder, 54, is the oldest sister of the five Anker girls. The Ankers gave birth to three biological children and then adopted two children; Rachel was the youngest. Kathy was married in 1971 and no longer lived at home when Rachel was adopted. The relationship between Kathy and Rachel was more like that between aunt and niece. Kathy's son, Mark, 29, is only two and a half years younger than Rachel. Kathy and her husband, Ross, have two other children: Phil, 26; and Jon, 24. Kathy is a travel agent and has completed some college courses. Her and her husband's economic status is upper middle class. They are raising their family in the Protestant faith.

Tell me about your life now—your family, your children, where you live.

My husband, Ross, and I both grew up in the Chicago area and raised our children there. About four years ago we moved to North Scottsdale, Arizona. Our oldest son was working out here. We would visit him, and would visit him again the following year and stay a little longer, and finally we asked ourselves, why do we live in the cold and the snow? My husband was retired, so we finally made the move out here to North Scottsdale. We love the desert and the Arizona weather. Ross traded in his snow shovel and lawn mower for a new rake. He now rakes the stones, every now and then.

And are you still working professionally?

I was a travel agent for about fifteen years in the Chicago area, and when my husband retired I thought maybe it was time for me to retire, too. We moved to Scottsdale in May 2002, and by July or August I was ready to work again. It took me a couple of months to get acclimated, get the house where we wanted it, etcetera. But once those things were done, I realized that I had too much free time on my hands, which was not good. Luckily I found a job close to home.

What was it like being raised in South Holland, Illinois, in the 1960s? And what was your family like?

We had a great family. South Holland was a great place to grow up as a kid. South Holland was a middle-class town … you could ride your bike from one end of town to your friend's house. My parents never worried … nowadays you just wouldn't let your kids ride their bikes three miles from the house. We would ride our bikes into town to go to the bakery on a Saturday morning, or the Ben Franklin store to get candy. If you wanted something, you'd get on your bike and go get it. Mom and Dad didn't drive us all over. We were involved in school and after-school activities. Almost everyone in town knew one another either through school or work or church. It was a close community. It was a great place to raise kids, it really was.

Given that you were the oldest child in the Anker family, you experienced the influx of foster kids and adoptive kids in your home. How was that for you?

Yes. It didn't seem like a big deal. My mom took in foster children instead of choosing to work outside the home. I think she worked before she got married, or when they were first married, but she's not a 9:00 to 5:00 type person. My mom is open and loving. I think she felt that if she was going to be a stay-at-home mom that she wanted to contribute in some other way, too. And she loved babies … she just didn't want to keep having them! Teenagers weren't her favorite. That would not be what she would do, foster teenagers. My mom always said a baby can't talk back, can't walk away or get in the car. She loved having babies around.

I imagine you did a lot of babysitting?

Oh yes. I remember my mom having to run to the grocery store. On her way out the door she would say, "The baby is sleeping right now, he should stay sleeping but if he wakes up change him, I'll be back in a little bit." It's normal for any older sister to babysit. You help out … not if you're 8 or 10, but if you're old enough. I think I was 11 or 12 when the first foster child came to live with us.

Do you remember what you thought about that?

Not really. I feel like it was my mom and dad's decision, and they talked about it. I don't remember having specific thoughts for or against them foster parenting. My mom was set on doing this. I recall the first foster child was two and a half and an abused child. She was very timid and very quiet. She was especially afraid to go into the tub. When my mom put her in the tub, she would cry so much and the only thing they could figure out was that maybe she had been abused in the tub. They had this little one for about … six or eight months. The next one was Kimmy. We thought this was just going to be short-term, too. Then after a few weeks my parents found out she was deaf, so she would not have been as adoptable. Then Kim just kind of stayed with us.

What is her ethnic background?

I think she's Lithuanian and something else … she's white. I know her [birth] mother was Lithuanian, I don't know about her [birth] father's ethnic background.

How old were you when Rachel was adopted?

I was already married and out of the house. In fact, I was already married when Rachel first came to our home as a foster child.

So you were out of the house …

I got married when I was 19. The first foster baby came when I was 11, so Kimmy was just little when I got married, maybe 6 or 7. Rachel was born in

1974, and I got married in November of 1971, so I had been married for three years when Rachel was born.

What was the relationship like between you and Rachel as Rachel was growing up and you were out of the house married and raising your own children?

I had my son Mark in 1977, so he and Rachel are almost three years apart. Basically I am old enough to be Rachel's mother. At first she was just another one of my mom's babies. She was so cute when she was little. And she had these little pig tails and a beautiful smile. She was fun to play with, but she had a lot of physical problems when she was first born so my mom was real busy with her. I was working full-time. It's hard to say, but at first she was just another foster child.

When did your parents decide to adopt her?

Rachel was about 7 when she was adopted. Rachel had been in our home since she was born. But by then it was different; Rachel wasn't another one of my mom's foster babies, where she'd only have the babies six or eight weeks. It's amazing my mom could remember each one of them; but I couldn't even remember their names, since they were only around for such a short period of time.

Do you remember any discussions your parents had with you about adopting Rachel?

I remember a little about the discussions. I think one of the main reasons my parents chose to adopt Rachel was that there was another family seriously thinking of adopting her; and after having Rachel seven or eight years my parents just couldn't let her go. Rachel was a part of our family. I think Rachel has always been part of the family, whether the adoption papers said "yes you were" or "no you weren't."

It just kind of transitioned in. At that time in the early 1980s I remember my mom telling us there's a family that might want to adopt a child that has physical problems. And we just said, "What, oh my goodness, what are you going to do?" I think my dad felt the same way, I remember him saying one night, "We can't keep collecting them." At that point they had adopted Kimmy, and I think Rachel was the last foster child they had. My mom and dad were grandparents then. My dad strongly believed that if they were going to adopt Rachel, then this had to be it. By then, I already had my sons Mark and Philip, and my sister Lynn had her son Eric. My parents had to decide: Do we want to help our kids with the grandchildren or continue to raise children of our own?

Is that when your parents started thinking that they should stop fostering?

Right—after "umpteen" years. And I think they felt like it was time to be helping out with the grandkids. And we were all local, we were nearby.

Even though you were out of the house with your own family, you were still in the same community as your parents and other siblings. Did you have a relationship with Rachel in those early years?

I've always had one. She's always been my sister, but I think I mentioned before, I would take care of her sometimes if my mom and dad were doing this or that. "Can Rachel stay with you?" they would ask. For me it was like having a niece or nephew around, and yet it wasn't… the feeling was different with Rachel than with my other nieces and nephews. Kendra is Kimmy's oldest daughter, and she is 18 and we have fun with Kendra but it is not the same type of relationship that I had or have with Rachel. It's funny, once Rachel became a little older and was a senior in high school, my son was a freshman. He would come up to her and say, "Hi Auntie Rachel." And he was five or six inches taller than her! Yet she was my younger sister. Sometimes I'd ask Rachel who she was going out with, as if I was talking to a sister. But her age in relation to mine made her more like a very close niece.

Did Rachel ever talk to you about personal struggles in her life?

Like an older sister? No, not so much when she was younger. I think that we have talked more in the last few years since she's been out of college and is now an adult.

What was the relationship like between you and Rachel when she was out of college?

We talked more regularly, but I was really busy with my kids … one in junior high, one in high school, and one in college. I had three boys and they were all in sports … baseball, swimming, and golf. Granted, we just lived a mile and a half down the street from each other. Rachel was living with our parents then, but she was always busy herself, including taking additional college courses. I'd talk to Rachel or stay updated by my mom.

Looking back on your childhood/adolescent experiences in South Holland, do you think that race was an issue, especially when it came to how people perceived your family with a black child? Was it a good thing, a bad thing?

At first, there were occasions when Rachel and I would walk in a store together and, of course, people would look surprised. Occasionally I would explain that Rachel was my younger sister. People in town also saw my mom with this little black baby or a 2 year old in the grocery store and other places; I could not help thinking that they were wondering whether my mom was babysitting or if this child was hers. Even today if I see a white lady with a black baby I stop and think … I wonder if she's taking care of this infant or if the baby is adopted. Yet, because South Holland was such a close-knit town, most people knew the situation and learned to accept it. So later when my parents adopted Rachel, it was not a surprise for the community. Nobody in town believed that my mom and dad would do anything less than that. Rachel was already such a part of our family.

How has the fact that you had a large family growing up, made up of foster children, adopted children and biological children, impacted your life as a mother?

I think it raised my awareness. When we were growing up we were a middle-class family. I got a job when I was 15 or 16 working at the local drive-in as a waitress. It was expected that I had to earn money to pay for extra things that I wanted. With my first paycheck from my job I bought a sewing machine so I could make my own clothes.

I remember sometimes when I was a teenager thinking that maybe if we didn't have so many babies in the house all the time ... maybe if we weren't always buying diapers and formula ... and baby food ... maybe we could afford to have and do more things. Now that I look back on my childhood, I never really lacked for anything, and if I did I didn't know it. There was always food on the table. I always had decent clothes, I didn't have designer outfits, but most people in South Holland really didn't either. We also took family vacations.

I heard that on one of your family vacations you were accidentally left behind for a few hours at a restaurant. Does that ring a bell?

No. I don't remember it that way exactly.

My understanding, as one of your siblings told it, is that it actually turned out being fun for you. You ended up with soda pop and dessert while you waited for your parents to return for you.

Oh, yes, that could have happened. It was like, "You got the baby, you got the diaper bag? Yea, but leave your eldest behind!" I don't remember it happening at a restaurant though ... you know that was forty some years ago and I pushed that memory way back there some place.

Your sister, Rachel, was married since the time she was interviewed in *In Their Own Voices*. Tell me about your impressions of her wedding.

I thought the wedding was very nice. It was Rachel. It was exactly what she wanted. Rachel likes to keep things low key and simple. There were a lot of family and friends there, even though some of Robert's, Rachel's husband's, family couldn't attend.

Your family comes from a different racial/ethnic/religious background than Robert's family, correct?

Right. His family, I believe, is Jehovah's Witnesses, and therefore I think his mother has very strong opinions about who her son should have married. In my opinion, Rachel is the one who has to live with him and be married to him; and if there are going to be issues and problems, then the two of them have to work that out. If there is an issue in my marriage I don't expect Rachel to address it; that's my responsibility. Robert is a great guy, he really is. I think he's a little intimidated by our family sometimes. The first few times he came to our family gatherings, the poor guy just sat in the chair, wide-eyed, looking around. And I just said to him once, "You have no idea what you are getting into, do you?" And he just politely smiled and didn't answer one way or the other.

It sounds like he's really willing to try to fit into your family because of Rachel. He must really love her.

Yes, he does love Rachel … and that's all that matters. It doesn't matter what color skin he has. If Rachel had married a white guy, a Hispanic guy, a black guy, it wouldn't have mattered. What matters is that Rachel and Robert are happy together.

When Rachel was younger, a few times people would look at my mother and me and Rachel because she was racially different than the two of us. You could see the wheels in their minds going; but this was twenty-some years ago, too. And things are different now. Back then, people would look at our family, some would smile, especially at Rachel, and would strike up a conversation, "Oh, how cute, how old is she?" They were just looking at a cute little girl who would smile back at everybody. But other people would look and would turn to say something quietly to the person next to them. My mother didn't care that Rachel's skin was different than ours. And every time I was with my mother when that happened, I think a little bit of her attitude rubbed off on me. You learn something from your parents not always by what they say but how they respond to a situation.

You mentioned earlier that having siblings from different backgrounds and foster children in your home helped make you more aware. How has that translated into your adulthood years as it relates especially to your perception of people of color?

Those experiences definitely have helped me when it comes to my perception of people from different racial and ethnic backgrounds. But the fact that I am a Christian person has affected my perceptions, too. I don't judge somebody by the color of their skin or how they walk or how they dress … I try not to. I try to stay very open-minded. If I don't care for somebody or if I want to avoid somebody, it's going to be more about how they've acted toward me or what they've said to me; if they've been very rude to me then I may not be as friendly back to them, but it would not be based on the color of their skin.

Would you recommend transracial adoption to other families who may be living in predominantly white areas?

I think that the decision is up to the person who is thinking about adopting transracially. Based on how I've grown up and my relationship with Rachel and what my mom and dad experienced, I don't see any problem with transracial adoption. South Holland was a great environment to raise children, to have friends, to have family, and to have a church family. I can't speak for someone else, but I have no problem with it. I believe it is a personal decision. You do have to be prepared to handle it, though.

If you think it will bother you if people look at you funny, then maybe you should reconsider—because that will definitely happen! If you are secure in your own decision and your own beliefs and your own attitudes toward adopting a child from another race, then it shouldn't be a problem. I don't think it was ever a big problem for us. If someone didn't like it, I never heard about it. I don't remember having racial slurs or threats hurled at us. But here was this cute 2- or 3-year-old little girl. She was no threat to anybody. But I wonder if my mom and dad had taken in an older foster child ... say a 16-year-old boy from the city ... maybe things would have been different. Maybe other people in the neighborhood, in town, in church, would have seen that more as a threat. I don't know. To our family it didn't happen that way, so it wasn't a problem.

MARY ANN PALS

CHESTERTON, INDIANA

JULY 2006

Mary Ann Pals, 51, is the second oldest Anker sister of five. She is nineteen years older than Rachel and was 23 when Rachel was adopted. Mary Ann is married to Randy, and they have two children: Michael, 22, and Jill, 16. Mary Ann has a B.A. in elementary education and has completed graduate courses. She has played many roles, including stay-at-home mom, elementary school-teacher, private tutor, and artist by trade. It was she who took care of the details of Rachel's wedding.

Please tell me a little bit about yourself—what you do, where you live, and where your children are now.

I am married to Randy, and we live in Chesterton, Indiana, which is up by Lake Michigan. Randy and I have two children. Currently I am an artist and a private tutor. My family is Christian, and we attend a Protestant church.

How far is Chesterton from South Holland where you were raised?

It's about thirty-five minutes away.

Is South Holland where you were raised from the beginning?

I was actually born in Lansing, which is right next door to South Holland, and then when I was starting first grade, we moved to South Holland. South Holland is a southern suburb of Chicago. When we moved there it was basically a white community with a lot of Dutch people. When I was in third grade, my parents started fostering children.

What was that like?

Oh, it was fun and exciting. We got a little 2-year-old girl for the first foster child, but she came with a lot of built-in fears and problems from her previous life experiences. It was difficult for our family because we were all dealing with this child and we didn't know what would set her off into being really afraid. She would curl up into a shell emotionally and sometimes not want to interact with us. She was only with us for a few months. After that experience, my parents decided that they'd rather just have infants come into the house because it would just be easier on all of us emotionally to deal with infants rather than these foster kids who came with their own bundle of problems.

Shortly after that, my parents started taking in newborn foster babies right from the hospital. That was so much fun. I absolutely loved it. I grew getting positive strokes from helping to take care of all those babies. I was the babysitter of the community. Everybody knew that Mary Ann could take care of the baby because I had been doing it since I was in third grade. Every weekend my schedule was filled with babysitting jobs when I was a teenager. And I loved it. I absolutely loved kids, and it made me even more convinced that I wanted to go into elementary education when I got into college.

Your parents adopted both your sisters Kimmy and Rachel.

Yes. They adopted Kimmy ten years before they adopted Rachel. Kimmy was a baby also when she came to us. It just sort of evolved into adoption, mainly because none of us knew that she was deaf. That's the sort of thing that's difficult to know when a baby is really tiny. It was when she was a few months old that my dad was noticing that she just wasn't responding to loud noises like other babies do. My parents had her tested, and, sure enough, she was hearing-impaired. The adoption agency changed her status from "normal child" to "handicapped child," which meant that she would not be adopted.

Then, ten years later, your parents adopted Rachel?

Yes, and, there again, when Rachel came to us, she was only 2 or 3 days old. Then suddenly she had this hip problem, and it turned out to be a staph infection in her hip. It stunted the growth of the top of her leg, and so right away she was labeled "handicapped" because she would need future surgeries on her leg. And because of that, she wasn't adopted. After my parents took care of Rachel for four or five years they applied to adopt her. I don't think that my parents were going to let her go to somebody else. It just wasn't even a question, "Should we adopt?" I guess it was in my parents' mind, but yet in a way it wasn't. It was like, "Of course, we want to adopt her!"

How old were you when your parents adopted Kimmy and then later Rachel?

I was probably about 13 when they adopted Kimmy, and I was 23 when they adopted Rachel.

Did your parents discuss their thoughts about adopting these two girls with you?

As far as Rachel's situation, I think that hers was a bit more involved. Of course, I was 23 years old when they adopted her. So, yes, they were discussing it with me and my sisters. But it was obviously because of the racial situation that they were discussing Rachel's adoption. Both my mom and dad were wrestling with the question of how this was going to work out. They were not wrestling with the question, "Can we handle this?" I think there are two important questions to consider when you're considering biracial adoption. The first one is: Can we give this child unconditional love? Is anything holding us back from giving this child our unconditional love, just like we do with our other children? My parents had already answered that question years earlier when they started caring for foster children of other races. So that question never really came up because it had already been answered ... answered in my parents' actions all those years they took in, and loved, foster children. But the second question you need to ask is this: How will the adoption affect this child? Will he or she be able to lead a normal life socially? That was the question my parents wrestled with much more so with Rachel than with Kim.

Do you think your parents wrestled with these questions because of the geographical location in which they were living?

Yes. At that time some blacks were moving into South Holland, but prejudices ran higher than they do now. And there was a little bit of white flight going on, with whites moving out of the community because they saw that blacks were moving in. But my parents talked to a number of people about it ... people who would give them honest answers about what Rachel would face as she got older. I think that was very helpful to them. Ultimately they decided, because of the proximity of South Holland to Chicago and because more blacks were moving in, to take that gamble and that it would be OK. I think Rachel is very well adjusted socially. She has more friends than I will ever have. She's just the sweetest person, and I don't think she felt out of place when she was young.

In your family, did you discuss her African American heritage? Did you as a family bring attention to potential African American role models that both she and the rest of the family could interact with?

I don't remember specific conversations, but there might have been an occasional conversation about her African American heritage.

What was your relationship like with Rachel as you were growing up, particularly given that you were 23 when she was officially adopted?

I was delighted to have Rachel come into our home at first because she was another African American baby to help take care of. I got my strokes taking care of babies. She was just another one to love. I was in college most of that time when she was tiny, but I was home every summer. I think because Rachel and I both have gone into elementary education and interact with and love children, there is a bond between us; it has always kept us really close. She calls me at least once a week still to this day. She and I have just always clicked.

And, growing up, was there that closeness?

Yes, there always was.

Did Rachel talk to you about issues of identity or race?

Not much as she was growing up. Rachel and I would talk about the same things any two sisters would talk about, but it usually wasn't about race.

Not until about six years ago did she start talking more about her whole identity situation, when she went through the process of finding her birth mother. That was a difficult process for her in a lot of ways. She needed to talk to somebody about it, and she talked with me. She talked to my mom some, but you know how it can be between mothers and daughters sometimes, and so she felt more open talking to me about it.

Rachel had big expectations about what her birth mother would be like. Every young girl probably does, of finding her mother and what that's going to be like. And Rachel had these high hopes, unrealistic expectations, I guess. After she met her birth mother for the first time, she was depressed for a while. She said, "I don't even know what I was expecting, but this isn't what I expected." You put your mother on a pedestal all those years in your mind because you have nothing else to go on. So that was really difficult for her to go through.

Did you give her advice as she was going through this process?

I encouraged her to take everything she was learning about her biological heritage and birth family in small bites. For example, her birth mom wanted Rachel to go to a family get-together. This was not the first event that she wanted Rachel to attend with the family. Rachel did not know what to do. I urged her to go but to stay for an hour if that's all she could handle. I told her that she needed this like she needed water and air, but she needed to take it in small bites. And so she did. She started to get to know her half- sisters and half-brothers. She even started to like one half-brother a lot. I encouraged her to stay in contact with him and if she got an invitation to go to his house, to go, even if it was just for a short visit.

Having Rachel as a sister, how has that affected you?

I guess I don't know life any differently. It is not a matter of change because I never knew life differently. People are people, it doesn't matter what color they are, what race they are, they're all people. And that's how I look at them.

When I first started teaching school, I taught second grade in a southern suburb. It was in an integrated community, about two-thirds white, one-third black. Halfway through that first year of teaching, an acquaintance of mine, who I knew was racist, said to me, "So I hear you're teaching in Chicago Heights." Chicago Heights is known to be a rather tough integrated community. Racial violence is common. Then he asked me, "How many darkies do you have in your class?" I was fuming inside, but I decided simply to answer his question. What surprised me was that I hadn't thought about that before, the racial background of my students. I had to literally go through every row of desks in my mind and start counting on my fingers the number of whites and blacks, and when I ran out of fingers, I said to him, "I can't tell you. I don't know. I would have to see my class list." He could not believe that I did not know. But isn't it wonderful that I didn't even know?

If you didn't have the influence of foster children and the ethnic diversity of your siblings, would you be a different person?

Probably. Well, somewhat different. Though I think that most of what you have, what you feel about people of other races, you catch from your parents. You're not taught it, you catch it. It just sort of comes through the air. And I think with my parents' openness to treating all people as people no matter what color they are or what their culture, I would have probably caught that anyway, even if my parents hadn't done foster care.

Is your relationship with your adopted siblings similar to that of your biological siblings?

I am closer to Rachel than I am to my other two biological sisters.

You talked a bit about going to college. When you went to college, did you see African American students?

I went to Northwestern College; it is a Reformed Church college located in northwest Iowa. I went from a high school of 750 graduating students to a college of 750 students. It was a big change. Northwestern College was in a rural area. Primarily the college was all white. The only African students on campus were foreign exchange students from Africa.

Would you have been open to the idea of dating someone outside your race?

I think so. I was good friends with some of the African guys, but you know it was like, what's the point? They intended to go back to Africa, and I didn't want to live in Africa. I didn't look at it as, no I don't want to date an African guy. I looked at it practically. I was good friends with them, but I didn't want to have a heavy, serious relationship with any of them; they all had intentions of going back to their own country.

Your sister recently married an African American young man. Tell me about the wedding and how that was for you.

Their wedding was so special. I was the wedding coordinator. I took care of all the details. I tend to be a detail person, and Rachel didn't want to have to worry about the logistics so it worked out nicely. The more Randy and I got to know Rachel's then fiancé Robert, the more we thought he was a gem. For Rachel it was quite a switch, because Robert comes from a traditional black family, and Rachel, of course, was not raised in that environment. She's basically a white person with black skin, so that was quite a culture shock for her. But the wedding was neat. I'm just so happy for them. I was busy before the wedding running around and taking care of details, and as soon as I saw her come down that aisle, I just burst into tears.

Did the guests interact with one another?

Yes. It was interesting because at the reception there were tables of Robert's African American family members, but then there was a table or two of Rachel's African American biological relatives. In fact, that table was right next to where Randy and I were sitting, and I went over and met Rachel's birth mother for the first time. No one had to introduce her to me—I knew she was Rachel's birth mother the minute I laid eyes on her at that reception. The two of them look like twins. I walked over to her and introduced myself. I could tell that she was trying to place me in relation to my other sisters. Once I told her that I was "Moe," which is my nickname, she said, "Oh, you're Moe!" She knew right away because Rachel and I talk about each other a lot. Later on, during the reception, I was able to take a picture of Rachel, her birth mother, and my mom standing together. Rachel was so touched by it. She said it was one of the most special pictures taken on her wedding day.

Would you recommend transracial adoption to other families?

Absolutely, but they would have to wrestle with the question of how this would affect the child they are adopting.

Do you think that transracial adoption affected Rachel in any way?

I think Rachel did fine. You know, it could be that if she had come to my parents as an older child, it might have been a much harder decision for my parents. I think growing up right from infancy on in my family where she was loved unconditionally, no strings attached, I think that made all the difference in the world as to her adjustment to growing up in a white family.

Do you think it also prepared her to navigate in a black community?

Yes. Unconditional love is great; it can just buoy you up in many situations. It cuts across race and culture. Rachel knew that she'd get a listening ear in me and whoever else in the family she needed to talk with when she went back to finding out about her roots. That helped her weather many storms she went through.

Is there anything else you would like to add?

A kind of litmus test for me and my biological sisters when we were dating is whether a guy who we wanted to marry would be a good fit for us and our family, particularly whether he would be able and willing to handle the whole racial situation on our home front. It's not like nobody knew about Rachel, a little black girl in a white family in a white community. Everybody knew Rachel. Everybody knew our situation. And the guys who were at all racist just didn't "come calling," and that was a good thing.

I dated this one guy in college—that was when Rachel was tiny, an infant—and he was also in elementary education. He was a nice guy. I didn't know where the relationship would go, but he really wanted to have a serious relationship with me. Well, he's from northwest Iowa, not far from where I went to college, and he didn't have any experience with black people whatsoever. He thought it was so cool that our family was caring for all these children of other races and backgrounds. He hung on to our relationship until the end of our freshman year, when I finally invited him to spend four or five days at our house. We're talking six hundred miles away … he flew out to my home and stayed for a few days, and just about the entire time he was there, he spent time playing with Rachel! He was just so enamored of her; she was 10 or 11 months old at that time. First thing in the morning she'd get up and come into the kitchen and he'd be eating breakfast and she would crawl up into his lap and sit there and smile at him. She was content to sit on his lap and do nothing. They were best buddies the minute they laid eyes on each other. And he'd hug her and he'd talk to her and then he'd play with her, and I'd be like, "Hello, remember me?" Sadly, we broke up during that visit, and he admitted to me the next year at school that he knew our relationship was coming to a dead end during the previous school year, but that he really wanted to meet Rachel. This little girl had such an impact on him. After that summer, he went out of his way to befriend many of the African foreign exchange students on campus. And years later, after he married and had his own children, I found out that he named his firstborn daughter Rachel.

We don't always know the far-reaching effects our loving actions will have on the lives of others. Raising a child, any child in love is not a small thing—it's huge! Its effects radiate in all directions, like sunbeams.

LYNN MILLER

MUNSTER, INDIANA
JULY 2006

Lynn Miller is 47 years old and is the youngest of the birth siblings in the Anker family. Regarding the impact her sister Rachel has had on her, Lynn says, "The biggest lesson I learned growing up with Rachel and from my relationship with her is that I don't see color." She also notes that Rachel describes herself as a "black Dutchman." When Robert, Rachel's husband, first moved out of his family's home to strike out on his own, he lived in Lynn's house for a year and a half. Lynn is single now but had been married. She has two children: Eric, 24, and Joshua, 22. Lynn is a project manager of a utility company. She describes her economic status as middle class. She is Protestant.

Lynn, where do you live now, and what has been going on in your life?

I live in Northwest, Indiana, which is still considered "Chicago-land" so I am not a Hoosier. I grew up, obviously, in South Holland, Illinois, where my parents lived and still currently live. I married at 19 and started having babies shortly thereafter. I have two boys ages 24 and 22, Eric and Joshua. Eric has completed college, and Joshua has one year to go.

In 1994 my sons' father passed away. It was very difficult for both of them. They were only 10 and 12 years old. Both sets of grandparents and my sisters kicked in and played a huge role in my children's lives, especially after their dad passed away. What was nice was that we still lived just four blocks from my parents, and my sister, Rachel, was still at home, so my kids would go to my parents' house after school every day and spend a lot of time with Rachel. It was funny because Rachel was about the same age as my oldest nephew, Mark, so my kids would call her "*Auntie* Rachel" just to tease her.

Rachel has always had a close relationship with my boys, even after they went off to college. Robert, who was Rachel's boyfriend at the time, though we knew they would eventually get married, needed a place to live, and so he moved into my home. We were roommates for a year and a half. When Josh was home during the summer, it was just like a college dorm, except I cooked and cleaned, but actually not that much. They took care of their own rooms quite well. Because of Robert's close connection to my two boys, he has a very special relationship with them. I think that his staying at my house was a really good way for him to begin his acquaintance and then relationship with the Anker family. Robert is such a nice guy.

How would you describe your family growing up?

For starters, I have a problem living alone. I always had a large family so now I don't like living alone. My family took in their first foster child when I was 4. I still remember her name. Her name was Kay. She was 2 at the time and, sadly, a very troubled little girl emotionally. She didn't want to go bye-bye anymore. You could just see that this poor little kid didn't want to be shuffled to more people. I was only 4 and could see that. She would dig her fingers into the buttons of the couch, and my mom would attempt to explain that we were just going to the store and she was going to buy her some new clothes. And Kay would say, "No more bye-bye, no more bye-bye." She kept repeating those words.

After that, my mom announced to the family that she would only take in babies. I must say that it was nice having a baby in the home. Kimmy was the baby we had the longest, and, as you know, we adopted her when she was 5. I remember her birth mom getting off the bus at the end of the block and walking to our home to visit her. She would visit her every month, and then every other month, and then we'd see her twice a year on Kimmy's birthday and on Christmas, and then Kimmy would just get a card. This was before the law took place … that if a child is placed into foster care, the birth parents only have a certain amount of time to decide to legally take the child back … well, this was before that law. So the birth mom could hang on to the baby forever and let the baby live with someone else and never sign the child over for adoption.

Out of frustration, probably, with Kimmy's birth mom, and that I was a little brat when I was a kid, I was the one who told Kimmy's birth mom that Kimmy was deaf. We found out that Kimmy was deaf one Sunday morning when we came home from church. My dad happened to stay home that Sunday. He asked us to watch as he rang a bell over Kimmy's head as she lay in her bassinet. She did not respond to the sound of the bell! My dad kept ringing this bell over Kimmy's head, saying, "This baby is deaf." Perhaps Kimmy's deafness was one of the reasons why the birth mother gave her up permanently.

How do you fit into the time line when Rachel came to live with your family?

Rachel was only two days old … tiny, tiny, tiny. One Sunday I stayed home from church with her and when I went to change her diaper, she wouldn't let me put her leg down. She kept her leg buried into her chest, wouldn't let me stretch it out. I couldn't even put the diaper on her. So I just wrapped her in a diaper and a towel and held her because she was crying. When my parents got home, I told them, "She won't put her leg down, she's really hurting." So my parents called our doctor, and Dr. Noble, bless his heart, made a house call on a Sunday afternoon. What a wonderful man, a great doctor. He said that he wasn't a hundred percent sure of her condition but that he thought it was serious and that she needed a specific shot to save her leg. He recommended that she be transported to the University of Chicago as soon as possible for further diagnosis and treatment. It turned out that Rachel had osteomyelitis, which was the doctor's initial, and correct, diagnosis.

Osteomyelitis, as I understand it, is an infection that happened to be in the growth center of Rachel's leg. So my parents took Rachel to Chicago to Wyler's Children's Hospital. She was so very sick. The doctors operated to remove the infection and they put her in a concrete cast, from her toes to her armpits, with just a hole for the diaper. We called her the "concrete kid." She was in that for about six weeks. My mom put out a lawn chair right by the front window in the kitchenette so she could lay there and see the outside.

Growing up with so many foster children in our home, I learned that you enable the children's senses when they are encouraged to see or feel things. We've had babies that were mostly blind and deaf, and one had a heart problem, and you would just have to touch her, enable all the senses she had. So my mom was good at propping Rachel up in this lawn chair in the kitchenette, and then we would go outside and make faces at her through the window.

How did you feel when your parents decided to adopt Rachel?

Rachel was transferred to a state agency, just like Kimmy was, because they both had a medical condition that was considered to make them "unadoptable" until at least a decision could be made about what medical care they would need growing up. Rachel was 4 then, and a major newspaper informed our family that they had put her in "Wednesday's Child," which is a newspaper article and a TV section where they highlight children who needed homes.

My mom was horrified. She thought that the media advertised Rachel like a used car! But they, the media and children and family services, found an adoptive home for her, and I remember my dad asking "Is it a Christian family?" We always adopted or got foster children through a private Christian adoption agency, but this one said that's irrelevant for the adoption. And my dad said, "No it's not …" Well, yeah, it's a state agency so it's irrelevant to the adoption. My dad said, "I did not raise this child for four years in a Christian house for you to tell me it is irrelevant on whether or not I find out if she is being adopted by a Christian family."

The other issue was that Rachel had a lasting physical handicap because the osteomyelitis in her one leg caused that leg to become two centimeters shorter than the other one. Therefore, my mom wanted to hold her back one year in school, also because her birthday was in November, just to give her a little edge scholastically, because she would not have an edge physically. The potential adoptive family was in the army … they were going from army base to army base, and she would be placed in the grade level for her age, so there was potential not to get that extra consideration. So, my parents, after great consideration, agreed that it would be best if we adopted her. I don't remember my mom ever debating or questioning the idea of adopting Rachel. But I remember saying to my dad, "You can't let her go!" He reminded me that deciding on adoption is not the same as making a decision about keeping a puppy. I think he was also concerned about his age. By now he was a grandfather. His was thinking … I'll be 72 when she does this, or I'm going to be 60 whatever when she does that. But when they told him that it was irrelevant whether this adoptive family was a Christian family or not, my dad forgot all that and we adopted her.

Then my parents were told by this agency, "That doesn't happen. We don't place children in mixed racial homes." My dad said, "Yes, we'll see what happens." I remember when my parents went to court to finalize the adoption. I don't know the ethnicity of the judge, but I remember the judge who was going to be sitting on that bench was sick that day and a different judge sat in, a much more liberal judge, and listened to my parents and *granted* the adoption. So right there that was a God thing to me … totally a God thing, because I remember the case worker saying in effect, "It's going to be tough with this judge … he is real traditional." That judge was sick and some other judge sat in, and we got Rachel. Thank God we did.

What was your relationship with Rachel growing up?

It was more "aunt"-like, I would say. We had thirty-five foster babies. Through high school my oldest sister was married and out of the house. My other sister, Mary Ann, was away at college. All through my high school years we seemed to have this surge of foster babies … this was just before abortion was legalized, and there was a surge of babies who needed homes. We had twins sometimes, and we always had Rachel and we had adopted Kimmy, so I went through half of high school taking care of kids. My mom would give me the baby that slept the most, and I would wake up with a baby at night and then go to school. I learned to sleep in shifts. You wake up, you feed a baby, you put him or her back to sleep, you go back to sleep yourself, and then you wake up and you get ready for school. And after school I had a job. So my schedule now compared to back then is not a big deal.

I've been taking care of children since I was 14 years old. I remember that there were activities like my volleyball games that my mom couldn't attend because we had a baby in the house. My mom's not interested in coming to volleyball games anyway. I remember when I was pregnant with Eric, Rachel was just this little girl thrown into a family of siblings much older than her, sisters who were having babies, getting married, and buying houses.

One time she and her girlfriend, Jodi, were playing the piano. I was eight and a half months pregnant, and I said, "Oh! I have to go to the bathroom." And Rachel looked up and calmly asked me, "Did your water break?" I burst out laughing, because she was only like 6 or 7 years old. Oh, we laughed so hard. At 7 years old Rachel's world was with us.

What kind of conversations did you have with Rachel growing up?

I remember one conversation we had. This one family that lived down the block from us was mean to Rachel because she was black. This couple was the same age as my parents, and they had a son and daughter a couple of years older than me. The daughter, who was a teenager back then, had these twins, so they, too, lived in the house. And these little twins were Rachel's age. One time Rachel came out, and here was this one little twin "peeing" up against the wheel of my dad's truck. They were just, you know, one of those families on the block. And Rachel yelled at him, and he turned around and called her the "N" word and she yelled at him again and he ran home. I came outside and asked Rachel, "What's going on?" "He called me the 'N' word," she said. I asked her what she thought about him saying that word to her. She said that he was ignorant. I agreed but then asked her if she knew what that word meant. And she said, "Yes." And then continued by saying, "He's never been taught what's right or wrong, and he doesn't know any better."

How old was she?

I already had children, she was 7 or 8. But she got it right on the mark.

Yes, she did.

And then she turned around and said, "Besides he's just a dirty old hill-billy!" I remember desperately trying not to laugh and telling her that she was not to call him names either. Personally, I was called a "nigger lover" repeatedly, this was in the seventies, in high school, in a white community mostly, and this was right when this big high school was built at the end of our street in the white community, and blacks from neighboring towns were coming to the school. There definitely was racial tension then. At the corner from where I worked, there were a bunch of kids who hung out. When I took Rachel for a walk, I would walk by some of these kids and would have the buggy and the baby. Not just Rachel, but a lot of the babies that we had were black and we also cared for Hispanic babies, any baby who needed a home, it didn't matter if they were purple. So because of that I experienced the whole "nigger lover" thing by those who were watching me with these little ones. And when Rachel was in high school, she was called an "Oreo" several times by other kids. But she came home and it was like, ok, they're ignorant. And that's how it was brushed off in our home.

The biggest lesson I learned growing up with Rachel and from my relationship with her is that I don't see color. I would say the same thing for my children. We don't even see color. Oh, by the way, Rachel does not say she's African American. She says she's Dutch. She'll say, "I'm not African American, I'm black, I've always been black, I've always been Dutch. I suppose I'm a black Dutchman."

Here's one story I can tell you to explain how I don't see color. One of my employees, an [African] American employee, had a car accident and didn't want to take another vacation day but needed the car towed. So I told her that I would come and get her. I drove out and picked her up, and I had to stop at the Burger King and use the restroom before we went back to work. She was in the car and I ran into the Burger King and there was this weird man sitting by a table in the dining area. He gave me the creeps, talking to himself, yelling at people. And there were a few other people sitting in that area having morning coffee or whatever, but he wasn't the only person there. I got back in the car and I tell this employee that there was this man in there giving me the creeps. I told her he was talking to himself, and yelling at people. She said, "Where?" And I said, "Right there by the window." And she said, "Where?" And I said, "Sitting right *there* with the red shirt on." She asked, "The black guy?" "Yeah," I said. That's when she said to me, "You know what, Lynn? I knew you weren't prejudiced but I just realized I must be." I asked her what she meant by that. She said, "You're a white person and you said 'the man sitting by the window.' I was sure that because it was a black man you would have said 'the *black* man sitting by the window,' because, honest to goodness, as I sit here thinking about it, I would have simply said 'the man' because he's black and I'm black. Had it been a white man, I would have identified him as being white."

My son, Joshua, is dating a black girl right now, and she is just so wonderful. Joshua was my problem child. He was a bit on the wild side. And Kim came along, and he just thinks she is so neat and he actually listens to her. She started in on him early on in the relationship: "Don't do that, Josh, grow up!" He listens to her and stops. He's totally grown up and turned around. Joshua has had more black girlfriends than white girlfriends. It partly may be because of where he lives down in Chicago; it is predominantly black. He meets more black women than white women there, but he is generally just more attracted to black women.

How did it happen that Rachel's boyfriend, Robert, came to live with you?

Rachel and Robert stopped in one night and we were watching a movie. Rachel started with "his stepfather did this" and "his stepfather did that" and "his mom didn't even stand up for him" and "they're just doing this to him" and "they're just …" and Robert's, like, Rachel, that's the way life is, no use complaining about it. I looked at him and said, "Well it sounds to me like you've reached that age when it's time to get out on your own." I asked him, "How much do you give your stepfather to live there?" And he told me. That is when I said, "Well, move in here for the same amount. It's more than enough to cover what you eat and extra utilities that you might use." I expressed to him that I could sure use the company, because both my boys were in college at that time, and he could probably use the independence. Both Rachel and Robert just kind of looked at me, and they left and obviously they talked about it because Rachel called me up and said Robert wants to know if you're serious. I'm like, heck yeah. So that's how it happened that he moved in here, because we were hanging out together one night when the two of them came over.

How did that work out, rooming with Robert for a year and a half?

Oh, perfect. It's so nice because I don't do "alone." When Robert moved here I quit waking up to all those little noises. Even when he came in late at night, I was glad that he was living here. I'd be half-asleep and say, "Robert, is that you?" And he'd say, "Nooooo." Smart aleck. He'd go to his room. He very much kept to himself. He worked an awful lot.

There were times when Robert first moved in when his aunts and his mom would call him frequently telling him that he needed to move back home and they missed him, especially his mom. She would try to change his mind about moving out. One night Robert was sitting alone in the dark when I came home. I asked him what was going on. He asked me, "Don't I have a right to a life, a right to be on my own, a right to make money, a right to buy a ring, a right to get married, and a right to buy a house?" I said, absolutely, yes, you do. It's still hard as a mom. I'd love it if Eric and Josh still lived with me. Anyway, that's when I knew Rachel would be getting a ring. He makes a really great brother-in-law; except for the time he pointed out that I'm the same age as his mother. Brat!

Clearly, as you've established in this interview, as an adult you have a very close relationship with Rachel and with Robert.

Absolutely. I'd come home, and Rachel would be cooking in my kitchen, which is great as long as she makes enough for me. We grew up the same. So she cleans the stove the same way as I would. It's when Robert cooked that we had the problem.

Rachel and Robert recently got married. Tell me what their wedding celebration was like for you.

It was a very nice wedding. I was the photographer. Since I worked for a photographer professionally years ago, I agreed to do the photography for their wedding.

Here is a long version of the story: Robert has an 11-year-old half-brother, Andrew, who he did so much with. After he moved out of the house, he would go and get his brother and take him to a ball game or other activities. He made sure he kept very close in touch that year and a half with his younger brother, even though he was not living at home. As the story goes, Robert's younger brother was going to be the junior groomsman. The rehearsal dinner was Thursday because the hall was busy Friday and then the wedding was going to be on Saturday. So we had the rehearsal dinner Thursday.

The other part of the story that complicated things was that Robert's family are Jehovah's Witnesses, but Robert had joined our Christian church which caused tension within his family. Because of that, Rachel and Robert decided to have the ceremony at the banquet hall, in a separate room, and then moved to the next room to the reception because his family was against going to a Christian church for a wedding. In my opinion, Rachel and Robert very much accommodated the religious differences between the two families.

Then on Thursday, before the rehearsal dinner, Robert's mom calls up and says she's not coming to the wedding or to the rehearsal dinner because there will be evil spirits there. Robert said to her, "We purposely did not have it in a church because I knew you would not want that, I really would like you to be there." She would not change her mind.

As if that wasn't enough, Robert's mom informs him that his younger brother may not come either. That hurt him a lot. So here it is Thursday night. Robert calls up my son, Eric, and says, "Dude, I need you to be a groomsman, not an usher. I need you to get a tux." Eric was in Wisconsin, so I called him up and asked him what his measurements were and then I went to the tux place to order a tux to be ready by Saturday morning.

The people at the tux place asked me who the tux was for. I said Rachel Anker, my sister. So when I said my sister, Rachel Anker, they're like, "Who? What?" So I had to explain, OK, my parents had a foster house, there were 40 siblings, and 5 of us were either born there or adopted. Rachel and I are sisters. And everybody is like, oh, but they are shaking their heads in confusion the entire time. Then the manager, so I thought, said, "Rachel is so nice. Here, take the tuxes in three different sizes. Bring them back on Saturday." Everybody and their brother and sister loved Rachel. It turns out that this was the president of the company, saying "Here, take these three tuxes in three different sizes. Bring them back on Saturday."

At the wedding itself, what was it like having white people and black people from different religious and cultural backgrounds coming together for the first time?

The wedding was like a United Nations event. It was very nice. Rachel's birth mom was at the wedding. I'll tell you about that later. My son was there with his black girlfriend, and, of course, Rachel and Robert are black. My sister Kimmy is married to an Algerian, so her kids are beautiful olive-skinned children. So Rachel was, like, here's my UN wedding picture, because it is.

How did Rachel locate her birth mother?

Rachel, largely because of her medical conditions, went through an organization to locate information about her birth mother. That organization also will write a letter to the identified party, in this case Rachel's birth mother, and ask that individual if she (or he) wants to be contacted. If that party says yes, then identifying information can be exchanged by the persons involved, the adopted child and the birth mother.

Rachel was able to read information about her life as an infant before her actual contact with her birth mother. She found out that she has two older siblings and one younger. And that bothered her. "Why give up me in the middle?" It was weird to her and possibly made her more interested to find her birth mother to find out why.

As it turned out, Rachel's birth mother had two kids by age 20 and was living with her mother in the projects. She then got pregnant with Rachel. Apparently she realized that she was not going to be able to support all three kids, so she decided to give Rachel up for adoption, go back to school, and support her two older children. Later she met another man, got married, and had another child. So Rachel has two older siblings—a half-brother and a half-sister, and one younger half-brother. So that answered the question of why she, in the middle, was given up for adoption.

Shortly after Rachel contacted her birth mother, she was invited to a family reunion in Chicago. Rachel's birth mother wanted her to meet the rest of the family. My mom was nervous about Rachel going. Rachel went. When she came back home, she walked through the door and said, "Mom, Dad, thank you!" She told us that there was no one there who reached the age of 20 who didn't have at least two kids. Also, she said, "Essentially they led totally different lives without the values that our family has."

What are your family's values?

We are a family that tries to lead a Christ-like life. None of us are perfect, of course, but we try.

How do you view the importance of an African American child who is adopted in a white family learning about her heritage?

I may have mentioned that Rachel and I are going to Weight Watchers together, and you know you start talking when you're in those group meetings. Rachel said something about my mom, and I said, yeah, our mom … and the people in the group looked at us funny. That's when we gave them the typical spiel: We were a foster family, forty siblings; five of us were either born to them or adopted.

One woman came up to us after the meeting and said, "My son recently married a woman who has a biracial child from a previous marriage, obviously to a black man, and now they have a new baby and so they have this three-year-old biracial child and now a one-and-a-half-year-old white baby themselves." And her son's job got moved to a little town in Indiana, and she was worried about whether that community would accept this half-black child.

The woman wondered what it was like for Rachel growing up in a small white town. Rachel essentially said that being black was not the paramount issue for her. According to Rachel, not everybody is going to accept everybody, and as long as she was loved she knew she could get through anything. Love is what mattered most to Rachel. The woman then said that she wanted to make sure that her son and daughter-in-law taught this child about his heritage, his African American traditions.

Rachel and I just looked at each other, and I could tell her brain was going a mile a minute. Rachel said, "You know what? I was taught all about my heritage. I'm Dutch." The point Rachel was making was that if they teach that little black child about the African American heritage, make sure that their white child is taught about it, too.

That's a very good point.

Rachel asked the woman what her son's nationality was. It turned out he was German. So Rachel recommended to this woman that she help teach her grandchildren about their German background. I also said to her that the biracial child shouldn't be singled out because of his skin color within the home because that would alienate him regardless of what the people in the town thought of the little boy. That is why I say you have to learn how not to see color. Maybe it's because I started when I was 4. But I told this woman that, as a grandmother to both these little boys, she would have to learn that lesson fast.

For someone who strives not to see the racial differences in people, does it bother you that others may see it differently?

Yes. There are African American people where I work who didn't give me the time of day until they saw that I had a *black* sister. You know what? They are too prejudiced for me! There's another thing I've always kept in mind: as I told you, Joshua tends to be attracted to black women. I would always ask him how the parents of the girl he was dating felt about their daughter dating a white guy. It's usually the other way around; the black girl's parents are concerned about how their daughter's white boyfriend's parents are going to feel about them dating. I'm more concerned about how her parents feel about my son. I have no issues. *I want to make sure her parents have no issues with him.* There are two sides of the story here.

What type of attitude does it take for someone to look beyond color?

It is a real definite point—it's a make or break kind of attitude that you have to have. In the case of my boys, for them to have a healthy relationship with the young women they date, they have to have this kind of attitude. The likelihood of my kids meeting a black girl, whose sibling is white in the household, reverse scenario, is next to none. But they still have an attitude that is non-prejudiced where they don't see color. Sadly, I haven't met very many people like that. I wish we had more in this world. I like the mind-set of Tiger Woods. There is a wonderful quote from him. Somebody asked him, "Do you expect to be the best black golfer in the nation?" Tiger Woods said: "What's this black thing? I expect to be the best golfer." I love that quote! And that perspective is not just the absence of prejudice; it goes beyond it. My parents introduced that very mind-set into our family, and it is definitely what I pass along to my children—"Don't see color."

When you talk about not seeing color, do you mean that the black child—let's just say Rachel—should then not identify with her African American heritage or recognize that her skin is different? Or does it mean that you do not put a higher value on white versus black?

I don't put a higher value on it, white versus black. My thinking is that if Rachel wanted to seek out the African American heritage and see what that was all about, that's great. Personally, I never sought out what Dutch traditions there were; I tend to think of myself more as an American than a Dutchman. I say I was born Dutch, and I outgrew it when I was 12. My point, though, is if Rachel wants to do that, she should knock herself out. Yet, you cannot, like the woman at Weight Watchers thought, make this biracial child identify with his African American heritage, particularly within a white family. But you don't stop them from finding their own identity. My mother, and especially my father, taught us kids that we could be whoever we wanted to be but that they would not push us in any direction.

After we adopted Rachel, some of my parents' friends asked really dumb questions. Granted, for people born in the 1920s there's some inherent respect that goes along and you cut them some slack. Here's an example. Soon after we adopted Rachel, one of my dad's friends said to him, "You know this little black girl in your white family, who is she going to date when she grows up, blacks or whites?" My dad said, "Well, maybe we should wait until she's 16 and ask her." I was like, that's my dad. He doesn't say a lot, but what he says you can hang your hat on. That was a wonderful answer.

What are your views now that you are well immersed in this transracial adoption experience? Is this something you would promote to other families?

Oh, yes. I definitely support transracial adoption. Not just black and white but also the adoption of Asian babies and refugee babies from overseas ... and I would have no problem at all promoting adoption to other people. Every child deserves the love of a family.

RHONDA'S SIBLINGS

WE BEGIN this chapter with Rhonda's own words from *In Their Own Voices*: I was born into this world as a medium-brown child with kinky hair and a winsome smile. I don't know, and have never met, my biological parents. What I do know from court records is that my birth mother had a son when she was sixteen. Similar to other African American homes, my biological brother was informally adopted by his maternal grandmother. Ten years later, in 1969, I was born. My birth mother, then 26, decided that what was best for her daughter was to grow up in a stable home and environment. She believed that through formal adoption I would have a better opportunity to make something of my life. And my birth father, what did he think? I am not certain. He was pretty much out of the picture from day one.

Not all things happen at a synchronized speed or with much logic. Shortly after my birth, I was placed into an African American foster care home. A match made in heaven, right? No. On the surface it looked almost perfect. I was African American and so was my foster care family. They had the financial resources to provide for me and even another child that I could play with. Perhaps my case history painted a picture that would have made the National Association of Black Social Workers proud ... and then, abruptly, my life with my foster family ended. Two years after I had been living there, I was adopted by a white, young couple with a son one year older than me. With my new life, the memories of my foster family were fleeting except the remembrances of bright toys, a play pen, and a feeling of isolation.

How could this happen ... being placed in a white family? Could this have been what my birth mother wanted for me? Or was this a trick God was playing on me? From two extremes, black and white, I faced an uphill battle, one that I didn't think I could win.

I was raised in a Christian home. My parents emphasized the importance of building good character. They recognized the relevance of culture and ethnicity as a part of that. In 1972 we left East Palmyra, New York, and moved to the Washington, D.C., area. There I attended Christian schools from nursery school to eighth grade. In my classes I was only one of very few black students. But race did not become an issue for me until I was 13. Or maybe I should say, until then I could push the subject to the periphery of my mind. As I've often heard it said in my life, "Nothing worth achieving is easy." And, I would add, especially if you are trying to hide from something, including yourself. After living in predominantly white neighborhoods, my parents, namely, my father, decided that he was going to build a geodesic dome in what was a predominantly black and working-class neighborhood located on the outskirts of Washington, D.C. In addition, as a way to confront a hidden fear that was surfacing, I pushed myself and my parents to allow me to enroll in a large ethnically and economically diverse public high school. I learned that race and culture were extremely important to people. And somehow, particularly to black students, their perception of me was that I did not match up to their definition of what being "black" meant. Fast forwarding to this point, even amid race issues and societal tensions, I believe that God has not played a trick on me. To say that being black in a white family is not complex would not be a true statement. It has been difficult. I think that I have gone through every emotion in the spectrum. I have been determined to answer the question, "Who am I?" That question has taken me to urban centers throughout the country, overseas to Central America and Africa, through books about and by black Americans, through the academic doors of higher education, and to the Constitution of the United States. I've come to realize that the crux of who I am is based on my belief in God, the strength of family and friends, and the commitment and viable presence of my godfamily, godfather, and mentors guiding me through my journey. Through the formation of my life, I have seen individuals in black and white America working together for the sake of a child.

Rhonda has two siblings, a brother and a sister, who were born to her adoptive parents.

The following interviews were conducted by Rita Simon.

CHRISTOPHER "DUFFY" ROORDA

LARGO, MARYLAND
2006

Christopher "Duffy" Roorda is one year older than Rhonda and is the oldest child of the Roorda family. At 37, he is a teacher/administrator of a predominately African

American middle school. He holds a B.A. in education from the University of Maryland, College Park, and is pursuing a master's degree at McDaniel College in Westminster, Maryland. He describes his economic status as middle class. He is Protestant. Regarding his relationship with Rhonda as children, Christopher says, "Growing up, Rhonda and I were very close. We did everything together except for sports." Even today Christopher feels that he is closer to his sister, Rhonda, than to his sister, Jean, who is his birth sibling. Jean is nine years younger than Christopher. Christopher says, "I feel I can share more with Rhonda because she and I are a lot alike. Emotionally, I think we are very similar." Yet, Christopher describes his relationship with Rhonda as "neither close nor distant," and regarding his views on having a transracially adopted sibling: "I feel blessed to have Rhonda as a sister, and I think it made my life a whole lot more interesting."

Christopher, tell me briefly about yourself—your age, where you live, your immediate family, and so on.

I am 37 years old, and I live in Largo, Maryland. I've lived there for about nine years and have lived in Maryland for over thirty years ... most of my life. I happen to be single and do not have any children.

What is your education background?

I earned my bachelor's degree in education with a specialty in English and drama at the University of Maryland, College Park. Currently I am working on a master's degree in Curriculum and Instruction through McDaniel College, which is located in Westminster, Maryland.

What sort of work are you doing?

Right now, I am a pseudo administrator in the Prince George's County school system. I work in a predominately African American middle school. As far as my duties, I schedule all the kids' classes. I handle a lot of data, and help with counseling, cafeteria duty, hall duty, monitoring instruction, and school improvement, that sort of thing.

How old were you when your parents adopted Rhonda?

That was back in the early 1970s. I think I was 3 and Rhonda was 2.

Did your parents talk with you about their decision to adopt Rhonda? Understandably you were quite young.

No, I don't think they discussed it with me.

So she simply arrived on the scene?

Right.

Do you remember your first reaction when Rhonda showed up?

My mom tells me this story—I'm sure you've heard it, I think it's in the first book—my first reaction when Rhonda got in the car was that she took my blanket, either that or my parents gave it to her. And the first thing I noticed was that she looked different from me. And I said that she was red and I was blue. My mom says that this is the first thing I said to them or to her. Other than that … that was my initial reaction and I let her have the blanket; I didn't protest or ask for it back.

Do you remember whether you were happy to see her or puzzled?

I don't remember. I just go on what my mother tells me about how I behaved.

How would you describe your relationship with Rhonda as the two of you were growing up?

I would say that we were very close. We did everything together except for sports. Rhonda wasn't very much into sports, and I was into sports a lot. I played on a lot of soccer teams. She didn't really do that. I had friends who were boys, and her friends were girls, so while we were close, we didn't really hang out with the same kids. That changed a little when we got older, like in sixth grade when we left Hyattsville, Maryland, and moved to Burke, Virginia. There we did have some of the same friends. In high school, we hung out with the same friends at church. Our church was great because it was (and still is) multiracial, and we had a vibrant youth group that put on plays and had lots of fun together.

Were your friends black or white?

Mostly white. I think that there were maybe one or two black kids that we played with. And then in high school, when we lived in Takoma Park, Maryland, we went to different high schools, so we really didn't hang out very much at all. We lived in different worlds, because I was in private school and she was in public school. I did have friends in high school of several different races and backgrounds though.

Which private school did you go to?

I went to Takoma Academy, which is Seventh Day Adventist.

Why did you go to a private school?

My parents wanted me to go to a Christian school and to be geographically close to our home. Takoma Academy was a mile away, so I could walk or bike to school.

You said you were interested in sports. Did you have any of the same interests as Rhonda?

Yes. I think that we both liked music and recreation. Rhonda liked to play with kids in the neighborhood and I liked to do that too, although she was much shyer with the kids in our neighborhood. Once we were in high school, we liked watching TV together, and that was a bonding experience. As a family we had dinner together. And Rhonda and I liked the youth group at our church.

Was there anything that you resented or struggled with having an adopted, black sibling?

When we were younger, I was kind of like the protective older brother. I very much disliked that role at times. But because our parents said I should do that, I did. I felt like I should protect her, if nothing else because I had an advantage—I was taller than her. She was kind of shy and she seemed to sense that she was very different from us, the rest of the family, in terms of appearance. Also, there were times when people in our community in Takoma Park and generally in the Washington, D.C., area directly questioned her about that. So I would feel like I would have to step in and defend her and explain why she was different. Sometimes I would tell people that she was my adopted sister, and not some vagabond off the street. Back then, especially in the early 1980s, people were very inquisitive when they saw the two of us together, a white boy and a black girl. Even nowadays when Rhonda is back in Washington, D.C., and we are riding in the car together, people sometimes take a second look at us. I think that they assume we are boyfriend and girlfriend, which is also interesting. I go along with it, but when people ask, I tell them we are brother and sister.

What did the two of you usually talk about as you were growing up?

You know, typical kid stuff. Like in high school, we would talk a little about our peers, or such and such person did this or such and such a person did that, talk about TV shows.

Did Rhonda talk to you about being adopted?

We used to talk a lot about that actually. Because when I was about 15 or 16 I would ask her, are you going to try to find out who your natural parents are? I think I asked her earlier, like when I was 12 or 13, and I was just starting to get curious. And she said that she had to wait until she was 18. So I was like, OK, are you going to do it then? And she was like, "I'm not sure, I'm not sure. Probably." So then, when she became 18, I was really curious about it. I know that she did take steps to locate her natural mom but I am not sure how far she went.

Do you think that having Rhonda as your sister, having a sister of a different race, affected how you saw yourself? Did it change your own perceptions of who you were?

Definitely, I think it did. I think after I read *In Their Own Voices* I thought about that a lot more. Actually I thought about that a long time ago, but I read the book and I thought about it deeper. I think her being adopted into our family influenced how I acted in high school a bit. My peers who I interacted with weren't all Caucasian, plus it helped that the school I went to was pretty racially and ethnically diverse, there were Indians, there were Latinos, there were blacks and Caucasians, and people from many different races, so I had friends of many different races.

And you think having a sister of a different race made you seek out some of these people?

I think so. I felt closer to some of my black friends as a result. I reached out to them a little more, and to this day one of my best friends is a couple of years older than me, he's a black guy who is a pastor of a church in Akron, Ohio. He is also Rhonda's godbrother and his family were members of the same church that we were for many years. Anyway, he's somebody I reached out to in middle school and high school. I think that he reached out to me, too, because of Rhonda. We are good friends still to this day.

What about your and Rhonda's relationship with grandparents and uncles and aunts? Was it the same? Did they treat Rhonda and you the same? Do you feel that you both had the same degree of closeness or distance to them?

I thought it was the same, but then in high school I sort of noticed little things to the contrary. Rhonda, too, would kind of bring things up where it seemed to her that, for example, the grandparents treated her differently.

How did she explain the different behavior?

She felt like they weren't treating her the same or they were treating her special, in a negative way.

Were these your father's or your mother's parents?

These were my mom's parents. Sometimes I could sort of see what she was talking about, but most of the time I couldn't.

But she would talk about it.

She would talk about it with me, just kind of express her frustration. And more so after she became an adult, and then I would see it a little clearer. Yet, I think for the most part my grandparents were fair and treated us equal. Granted she was a girl so they would treat her a little different than me because of gender. For example, they didn't put me up on their knee and bounce me around like they did with Rhonda when she was a little girl. But, for the most part ... like all the aunts and uncles ... I felt like everybody treated us the same.

But did she and the aunts and uncles get along well?

She got along well with our aunts and uncles. I think her issues early on were just with my mom's parents. I think she felt some animosity, particularly with my mom's dad, who has since passed away.

There was one time I remember distinctly, I think it was when she was in high school, maybe when she was like 19 or 20, we went to the Poconos in Pennsylvania and we had a family reunion and my grandfather apparently called her a derogatory word. I don't know if he said it directly to her, because I wasn't there when it happened. But I caught it later on; because I was wondering why all these people were going off to their separate places and not talking with one another ... we had the reunion in two houses that were adjacent to each other. I was off reading a book or something ... I was kind of clueless, Rhonda knows this. I didn't really notice a lot of family tension at that age, because I was in my own world. So Rhonda was very upset about what went on there, and I was, too, and unfortunately it ended up with people taking sides. Not to make any excuses, but I think my grandpa was upset because my mom was going to get a divorce, this is prior to that happening. So one of the things he said, apparently, I heard all this through Rhonda, of course, was that he didn't want my mom to adopt her in the first place, and so I think in that context he used the derogatory word. I am sure that both my grandpa and Rhonda wished that incident never happened. Later, I know they came together and reconciled. He passed away in February. His wife, my grandmother, is still alive and living in Virginia.

Does Rhonda have a good relationship with her?

I think so. She recently visited Rhonda, and she stayed with Rhonda and her husband for a couple of days.

What about your father's parents, were they around?

Well, my dad's dad passed away before I was even born. He died when my dad was 21. My dad's mother lived in Western Michigan so we didn't have a lot of physical contact with her growing up. Later Rhonda became very close to her, closer than me, because she went to college in Western Michigan. My grandmother has since passed away, but Rhonda was very close to her. She showered a lot of love on Rhonda. I think geography made a difference, too, simply because Rhonda was living in Michigan. I know that my grandmother was very supportive of Rhonda and really supportive of *In Their Own Voices* being published. Unfortunately, I didn't really maintain a close relationship with her, even though I wanted to. I would see her maybe every other Christmas, or once every other summer. When Rhonda and I were little, our family would go to Michigan every summer, but then when we got older we didn't go to Michigan much.

How is your relationship with your birth sibling, Jean? Is it different than it is with Rhonda?

It is really different because Jean is nine years younger than me, so it's like she is in a totally different generation ... although it helps now that I'm dating someone who's nine years younger than me, so I get her perspective and I get Jean's perspective and they are very similar. With Jean, growing up, I played a lot more with her. She was very tom-boyish, and we played a lot of sports together like kickball. I'd teach her some other sports. I remember those times as really fun times because I was the big brother. But then when I got out of high school there was that separation. She was going to school, and I was going to college. So I had my own life. I did go to a few of her volleyball games. After high school Jean went off to college in Michigan, so there was that disconnect. I stayed in the Washington, D.C., metropolitan area. During that time I didn't keep in touch with her, especially when a year or so later she was pregnant and had her baby, I was like, wow, stuff is going on in her life. Then I was busy pursuing my career and college studies, and so there was even a bigger gap between me and Jean. I feel closer to Rhonda to this day than I do with Jean.

What do you attribute that to?

I feel like I can share more with Rhonda, because sometimes she and I think a lot alike, especially on an emotional level. I know how she is going to react for the most part. I am not sure when it comes to my sister, Jean, how she is going to react. I didn't really experience a lot with her.

In my sister Jean's preadolescence I didn't know any of her friends ... well, maybe one or two of her high school friends that she would invite to the house and who I would happen to see. With Rhonda, I knew most of her circle of friends. I knew all of her circle of friends at church.

What type of school did Jean attend?

She went to a Baptist school ... a very strict Baptist school.

So Jean went to a Baptist school, you went to a Seventh Day Adventist school, but Rhonda went to a public high school? Is there a reason for the three separate schools?

According to my parents, they wanted Rhonda to be in a "diverse environment" with more African American kids, and Northwestern, where Rhonda went to high school, had that. And they wanted me to be in a Christian school, not necessarily that they didn't want me to be around African American kids; because my school had those too ... granted they weren't in the majority like they were at Northwestern. I don't know why Jean went to this Baptist school. To give you more perspective, Jean went to high school after my parents had divorced and she was living with my mom in a suburb of Washington, D.C., so the school she attended was largely my mom's decision.

Did you leave home to attend college?

Well, I went to Montgomery College first, and I lived at home until I was 21, and then I moved out.

Was Rhonda at home while you were at college?

No. She had gone to college by that point.

Did you and Rhonda write or phone each other?

No, not very much.

Were you ever jealous of Rhonda?

Maybe there was a little resentment toward Rhonda when it came to her college education. Rhonda was going to a private college and received grants and maybe a few loans, and my dad was also helping to pay her tuition, though I didn't know that at the time. On the flip side, I was living at home and paying my own way through school, so maybe there was a little resentment there because my dad was helping Rhonda but he wasn't helping me financially. Although, my perk was living at home and not having to pay rent. That was my advantage. I had my own car, so I was paying bills on that but I wasn't paying any rent. And then I quit college for a while, too, because I didn't know what I wanted to study.

What did you do when you quit college?

I worked different jobs. I worked for the *Washington Post* where my dad was also working. I worked at U-Haul for about two and a half years and almost became a manager there.

When you started dating, did you date any black women?

Yes, I dated black women in high school.

Do you think you dated black women partly because you had a black sister?

I think so. I don't think that I intentionally set out to date African American girls. In high school, I just found this one particular black girl attractive. It was mutual. She liked me, and we hit it off really well as far as things to talk about and things to do.

And did Rhonda date any white boys?

I don't think so. Not in high school. I mean she had boys who were friends from church who she hung out with, but she didn't really date white boys. She didn't have a car for one thing early on in high school, but she did have her own phone line so maybe she talked with boys that I was not aware of. Just an aside: my parents set up her own phone line, and I think she had to pay for that, because we both had to work to pay for things that we wanted.

How would you characterize your relationship with Rhonda today? Do you think it is close, intimate, or distant?

It's neither close nor distant.

How often do you talk on the phone?

Rhonda and I talk maybe once every week or two. I tend to e-mail her more frequently. I send her stuff that I like. You know ... check this latest news out, or inspirational things. Rhonda does tend to call me more than I call her. I'm trying to get better at that.

Do you know Rhonda's husband?

Yes. I don't really call him out of the blue, or anything. I mostly call Rhonda on her cell, because I know I can get her on her cell. I make it a point that when we talk that I ask her to give my regards to her husband, Floyd. Her husband is a good guy, and I think he's perfect for her.

How do you think the adoption affected your overall family life?

Shortly after my parents adopted Rhonda in the early 1970s we moved from a rural area in upstate New York, to Hyattsville, Maryland, which was a more racially and ethnically diverse area.

Did your parents seek out a black church once they arrived in Maryland?

They sought out a church in Washington, D.C., a Christian Reformed Church, largely because there were other families there that had adopted children of color, specifically African American kids. In fact, the pastor and his wife had adopted an African American child, who also had two biological kids. This was in the mid-seventies. So I think my parents felt like, wow, this is a perfect fit. There were other African American kids there; there were other kids of other races there, too. The church was close to where we lived. It was only a fifteen-minute car ride to church.

Did your family do other things that they would not have done had they not adopted a black daughter?

It is hard to say. Obviously the move to Maryland … was one step. I don't know if that would have ever happened had they not adopted Rhonda. But my parents were culturally aware people. My mom, in particular, was an art teacher, so she exposed us to a lot of creativity. She (and my dad) took us to the museums all the time and to Folk Life Festivals in the city. There were a lot of free events in Washington, D.C., that you could participate in. Rhonda and I were even on the cover of the Style section of the *Washington Post* eating watermelon sitting under a tree down by the Lincoln Memorial.

During one of these events?

Yes, the picture was taken of us during a Folk Life Festival, and I saved a copy of that from the 1970s. So our parents exposed us to a lot. We went to plays and different cultural events in the area as much as we could. I don't know if my mom would have gone out of her way to do those types of activities had Rhonda not been adopted into our family. However, our mother is very creative, so perhaps she would have done these things anyway.

Did your parents seek out black friends, or did they already have black friends?

They did seek out black friends. There was an older African American woman in our church in the 1970s that my parents made a point of visiting on a frequent basis. They also made sure that Rhonda spent quality time with her, too. This woman became a grandmother figure for Rhonda. And then there was also another African American family in our church. The mother became Rhonda's godmother. We made sure we visited with them a lot and that Rhonda got a lot of time to hang out with them. That family had a son; their son is my best friend, the one I was telling you about who is a couple of years older than me. In our church there were a few other black families, not many, but a handful. It's a small church to begin with, less than a hundred people. But I would say there is a core group of five or six black families that our family joined a Bible study group with in the early 1970s, and they are all still friends today. As a family growing up we went on camping trips with our church friends. Those times were a lot of fun, and Rhonda and the rest of our family got to interact and bond with people.

You mentioned that, when Rhonda was in college, you were somewhat jealous that she received financial help from your father for tuition. Did Jean also get money from your father?

Jean went to the same college as Rhonda but only for two years. I am not sure whether she got financial help from our father. I think Jean received more grants than Rhonda because Jean had stellar grades in high school. Rhonda and I had mediocre grades, like B's, but Jean had A's straight through, so I think she got money through scholarships, and maybe both our parents helped out financially. I am not sure.

Where would you have liked to have gone to school?

Looking back, ten years later, I can say that maybe it would have been nice to go to Calvin College in Michigan, where Rhonda went. At the same time I also think I wouldn't fit in there, because I grew up in a more multicultural community here in the Washington, D.C., area compared to the diversity I saw in Western Michigan. So, I mean, part of me says, yeah, it would have been nice, but part of me says no, I don't regret my decision to stay in Maryland for school. I just made different choices than Rhonda. I love Rhonda. She is blessed and a blessing to all.

Were there any other times during childhood that you were jealous of Rhonda?

I don't really think so. If anything, I feel like I got better treatment from our parents. Even Rhonda says that sometimes, too. She thinks that they gave me preferential treatment, but at times I think the same thing of her. But it's nothing that we butt heads over, because it doesn't really matter much anymore.

Is there anything else you would like to say about Rhonda or Jean?

I think that, to this day, Rhonda is trying to understand how she fits into our family. Also, when my parents divorced, that was really hard on my sisters especially. It was easier for me, because I stayed in this area so I could see my mom and dad with a short car ride. I saw my dad every day until I was 21, pretty much. But my mom was just a short car ride away. But I think it was harder on Rhonda because she was away at college.

And she had been very close ...

She was very close to my dad. Now as an adult she's not as close to him. I think that there are still some disagreements or a rift there between my dad and Rhonda, through some things that have happened. For example, I know she invited him to her wedding in 2000, but he didn't go because he said his wife couldn't make it so he didn't want to go. The rift is that Rhonda doesn't see eye to eye with my step mom which I find so interesting, because I think they're very much alike. They're really hard workers and are the kind of people that pay meticulous attention to detail. So it's interesting. There were times a while back where Rhonda tried to get my dad's perspective from me, because I'm a lot like my dad. That may be why in part she wants to hear what I'm feeling. I don't like seeing that the two of them have this rift. But I take it day by day. It's stuff I didn't notice as a child, didn't really notice how close my dad and Rhonda were until after she became an adult and she told me these things, and then I look back and think, oh yeah, he did this, and he did this, and started to see how similar they were emotionally when she was younger.

Did Rhonda tell her father what happened to her in high school when she was sexually molested by a teacher?

Yes, as far as I know.

Did she tell you?

No, I didn't know about it at that time. My parents kept that from me.

Did she not tell her mother either?

My mom and Rhonda, they butted heads a lot when Rhonda was in her preadolescent and adolescent years, and my dad was the one to give more emotional support. My mom was a disciplinarian to Rhonda, which is usually the case with mothers and their daughters, at least up to a certain age. I had no idea about all of that.

Would you encourage white families to adopt black children? Do you think it is a good policy?

In my opinion, the government shouldn't legislate transracial adoption one way or the other, but I think it definitely works for some people. I don't think that white families should be prevented from adopting a child of another race. The National Association of Black Social Workers came out early on with that statement against it ... I heard that and I couldn't believe it. I think that racial genocide goes on among African Americans more so than it does across races. I work in the local school system, and I see a lot of dysfunctional families there and sometimes I think if there are families waiting to adopt why hold back because of race? It also sends the wrong message to people when you just look at race. I think it is close-minded to say, no, this group of people shouldn't adopt this group of people. We are all God's children.

Assuming you get married at some point, would you ever consider adopting a child of a different race?

Yes, I would. I think it would be very challenging, though. I admire my parents for doing what they did. I think it is very difficult, and I didn't realize all of this, of course, until I became an adult and you look back and you say, wow. Especially now, working in the school system, I work with parents a lot and I see all the hardships they have, especially single moms, and I wonder how my parents did what they did, especially in the area that we are, where racial tension and politics is ever present. I especially think about what my parents went through in the early 1970s which was pretty impressive. There was a lot of racial tension when they came to the Washington, D.C., area in the early 1970s, and when we were kids my mom told me that a lot of people would be almost abusive to them because of their adopting Rhonda. Just the attitude and how some of these people carried themselves, like they would say, "What is she doing with you?" that kind of thing. From the voice to the body language, were some things that I think my parents weren't culturally used to. So they had to be educated with almost trial by fire. People probably told them a few things, but that was in upstate New York, which was kind of lily white at that time, versus the Washington, D.C., metropolitan area.

All things considered, are you glad that your parents adopted Rhonda?

Yes. I feel blessed to have Rhonda as a sister, and I think it made my life a whole lot more interesting. I don't think I would be as successful in my job if I didn't have Rhonda as a sister. How I treat African American people is because of her influence. Also I learned a lot about racial and cultural understanding partly through my church roots, but we probably wouldn't have gone to that church if it hadn't been for Rhonda. And it's opened my perspective up a lot more. It still does. I don't know much about African American culture, but I know a little bit through living for thirty years in the D.C. metro area. I am learning to appreciate differences of opinion and different ways of looking at the world. It is ongoing, everyday, and lifelong.

JEAN ROORDA

ASHLAND, OREGON

JUNE 2006

Jean Roorda, who is 28, is Rhonda's younger sister, by eight years. About her relationship with Rhonda, Jean says, "Growing up, I think our relationship was awkward and sometimes conflicted, as lots of sisterhoods. The age difference was such that we did not have the same group of friends. She was more like a parental figure." Once Jean was in college she reports that she had a similar type of relationship with Rhonda as when they were growing up in the same house. As Jean describes it, it was "not necessarily close but closer than we had been when she first left for college and I was at home." (Both Rhonda and Jean went to Calvin College in Grand Rapids, Michigan.) Today, Jean and Rhonda are not especially close but they maintain a cordial relationship. According to Jean, they talk about every other month on the phone and e-mail each other sometimes. Jean received her B.A. from the University of Maryland, College Park, and is a minister/entrepreneur. She reports no religious denomination. Jean has an eight 8-year-old son, Judah, who is multiracial.

How much schooling have you had, and what are you doing now professionally?

I have a bachelor's degree in cultural anthropology and women's studies from the University of Maryland, College Park. Since then I have been doing a lot of spiritual work, as in clairvoyant healing. I am a pastor but not in a traditional church.

How did you study to become a spiritual healer?

I studied at a training center for people who are sensitive/aware.

And how do you meet your congregation or the people that you work with?

I just make myself known in the community, and people come to me if they are drawn to that kind of work. I also attend a church where I live in Boulder, Colorado, the Church of Inner Light, which supports what I am doing. The spiritual work that I do does not fit into any religious philosophy ... but rather it is based on an ancient spiritual tradition. Within this spiritual context, I do hands-on healing.

Do you earn a living with this work?

Yes, I do.

Are you married?

No.

I take it you don't have any children?

I do have a child. I have an 8-year-old son, Judah.

And he lives with you?

Currently he stays with me during his school breaks. I raised him until he was 7, and then he moved in with his dad.

Where does his dad live?

His dad lives in Eureka, California, where he's been living for a year and a half minus the summer break from school.

Will he come back and live with you at any point?

That is actually being determined right now by sort of a group consensus, between me and Judah, and his father. We're going to sit with it all summer and see how we all feel about it. If he wants to move in with me, he will.

Going back to your own childhood, how old was Rhonda when you were born?

She would have been 8, I guess.

Do you remember when you first realized that Rhonda was black?

No. There might have been a specific occasion where it dawned on me, but I don't remember that specific occasion if there was one. I think it was more of a gradual thing, people explaining it to me at some point, but I don't have a specific memory of me going, "Oh, she's black." We grew up in a very, well in my memory, a predominantly black neighborhood. I had white and black friends, but at many times I was the only white kid among my friends.

How would you describe your relationship with Rhonda as the two of you were growing up? Was it close? Was it distant?

I think our relationship with each other was awkward and sometimes conflicted, as lots of sisterhoods. I think there was a little bit of pressure on Rhonda's part and a lot of competitive energy, but it was unconscious, I think. Yet, I don't think that that was necessarily because she was a black child adopted into a white family, but more so because of chronology; I came much later in our family.

Did you share the same group of friends?

No. The age difference was such that we didn't play together or have the same interests. Rhonda and my older brother, who was just a year older than her, they were more like my babysitters. So, my relationship with Rhonda was also probably a little conflicted because she was more like a parental figure at times, you know about that older sibling dynamic.

Did you share any of the same interests in music or sports, or anything?

I always really enjoyed knowing about the things Rhonda was interested in. I looked up to her because she was my older sister, and so if she was into music, I thought that was cool and I wanted to participate, or just me being curious about what she was getting into. When I was in elementary school, she was entering high school, so she was the cool high school girl and I felt I needed to check out what she was getting into. So I definitely looked up to her in that way, as a cool, older woman, and whatever she liked must be really cool.

Did you spend a lot of time together in any capacity?

I remember there being times after school, but it was sometimes us fighting over the TV ... we had one TV ... and she wanted to watch soap operas and I wanted to watch cartoons; that was again the age factor. So there would be sort of these battles over the one TV and who got to watch what. Sometimes, if she let me, I would just kind of hang out in her room.

Do you remember anything more about what you might talk about?

I remember when she was in high school she was on the pom-pom team and I was just curious about what that was all about. But I think there was also the thing where she really didn't want her little sister to know what was going on in her life—the privacy thing. I was just the curious little sister.

Do you think having a sister of a different race affected how you saw yourself?

I think I considered myself different from my other white girlfriends that didn't grow up having a black sister. I think I felt like I was comfortable being with other black kids.

Did it affect how you perceived your own family?

Not until I was older. We had a family vacation when I was 8 or 9, this RV trip around the country; and I remember parts of that experience being difficult for Rhonda, especially when we were clear out in parts of the Midwest and West, where there were no black folks anywhere to be found, and no ethnic hair products.

How did Rhonda manifest her feelings?

She would talk about it. I could sympathize with how she was feeling, but I didn't think that we were this abnormal family.

Did you and Rhonda have the same quality of relationship with grandparents?

I don't think so. I think I was completely oblivious to the fact that Rhonda's relationship with them was very different until I was older, and heard her stories. Either I wasn't present when she would have certain uncomfortable if not ugly situations with them and sometimes other relatives, or I was completely oblivious. And looking back on it, I think I was favored by my family. They were able to accept me, not only accept me more, but really nurture me a lot and feel like I was their prize that they needed to make something out of; Rhonda was accepted, but I don't think she was treated the same at all. But that is only looking back. I think I was completely oblivious to what she was experiencing at the time.

Has Rhonda since talked about some of those childhood experiences?

She has talked about things that were said to her or ways that she was treated by others in our family, and I know that I didn't experience what she experienced. That was not how I was treated. Some of it was the way our family is, and part of it comes from the traditional Christian perspective which nurtures a lot of judgment, and was evident primarily on my mom's side of the family.

While I was raised in that kind of environment, I, too, was treated based on the values of our home, but still much differently than Rhonda.

Did Rhonda go off to college when you were still home?

Yes.

How old were you when she went off to college?

I think I was 10 years old.

And did you have any relationship with her while she was off at school?

Not that I recall. Rhonda went to Calvin College in Grand Rapids, Michigan. It was also right around the time that my mom split up with my dad, so I don't have much memory of that time period, much less what my relationship with Rhonda was. We didn't write letters. I think if we talked on the phone, it was when she was calling our mom. There was very little correspondence until she came back to the Washington, D.C., area after graduating from college to begin a job on Capitol Hill. She moved into the same house with my mom and me, and rented her own space in the lower level of the house. At that time our relationship did become closer.

Did you leave home to attend college?

Yes. I went to Calvin College as well, just for the first two years.

Did you have contact with Rhonda while you were in college?

Yes, we talked on the phone a little bit, and she visited me a few times on campus because then she was living back in Michigan attending graduate school and working.

Did you become closer to her during this period?

I think we had about the same type of relationship as when she was living at home; not necessarily closer, but closer than we had been when she first left for college and I was at home.

What about dating? Did each of you date people of different races? Did you date black men?

Yes, I dated black men. My son's father is very light-skinned black.

Do you know whether Rhonda dated white and black men?

I can't remember. I don't think I was ever aware of her dating much, until later. But yeah, she did now that I think of it.

Today, how would you characterize your relationship with Rhonda?

We're not especially close. We don't, like, talk every week, but when we do talk it doesn't feel like there has been a large gap. It's kind of like that old friend … it can be years, and then … hey … and you kind of talk as if there hasn't been a lot of time apart. Still, we are not so entwined in each other's lives that we call each other frequently.

Roughly, how often do you talk on the phone?

We talk probably every other month … sometimes more, sometimes less.

Do you write letters to each other or e-mails?

I e-mail her sometimes; it is usually short and sweet.

Have you met Rhonda's husband?

Yes, I met him several times in Michigan, but unfortunately I don't go to Michigan often and they don't come to Colorado, so we don't see each other often.

Did Rhonda know your husband?

I was never married, but she does know Judah's father.

How do you think adoption affected your family life?

I think adoption was positive for my family. I think it can only be positive to have any kind of relationship where you are encouraged to nurture someone and to love someone different, and you learn to love yourself more, and to know what love is. I think that is positive. I think people should be encouraged to adopt, including transracially. I think definitely learning to love and nurture someone, whether it is a birth child or not, challenges you. There are issues that are going to come up, and I saw that happen in my family, yet it still was a positive experience.

Do you think that your parents acted in ways that they would not have had Rhonda not been in your family?

It is difficult to say if they would have picked the same neighborhood or not because of Rhonda. I get the impression that they chose to move to that community, the Washington, D.C., area, because of her, but it's still hard to say. The neighborhood we lived in was certainly mixed, and the majority was black. However, my parents could have made that choice because of Rhonda, or because there the land they wanted to build a house on was more affordable than in other areas in the Washington, D.C., area.

Did they join a black church?

The church we went to was diverse, black and white.

Did they have black friends who came to the house?

My parents had church friends who came to our home, some of them were black. That was part of the community of friends that they interacted with.

Were there times during your childhood when you were jealous of Rhonda, perhaps for attention she received?

I am sure there was jealousy that came up, but I don't recall any specific time when she got something that I really wanted. By the time I got to high school, my parents had split up and I was living with my mom and that was way out in the suburbs and because of that I chose to go to a Christian high school in that area, which happened to be small. Then I thought Rhonda's high school was cool; it was different and it was large. Yet I was scared to go to a school like the one she was going to.

Did Rhonda talk to you about her experiences in high school?

She talked to me about her experiences a little bit at the time, more so after. Again, I think because of the age factor we did not discuss things in a lot of detail or intimately. We talked about more personal things when we were both adults. I heard about her experiences in high school when I was much older … some of them not so pleasant.

Your mother apparently did not know about the struggles Rhonda had in high school.

That may be true. I remember that my mom wasn't happy a lot during Rhonda's high school years. She kept to herself.

Would you consider adopting a child of a different race? Of course, you already have a son.

My son doesn't necessarily look like he is racially mixed, but yes, I would adopt a child of a different race. If I was to adopt, I wouldn't consider that I would need to adopt within a certain race. I would adopt the child that came to me, whatever he or she looked like. Again, because of my work, working with people on the spirit level, that's what's more important to me.

I also think that transracial adoption is a wonderful benefit in general to families. It was good that Rhonda was raised by the family she was, that she's doing this book, that she is passionate about letting people speak up about their experiences. To me she pointed out that people are people, and we need to be sensitive to society's portrayal of people of different races and that is an important thing to be sensitive to. You don't want to completely ignore racial and ethnic differences among people, especially children, but it is very important to acknowledge that love is essential as well.

KEITH'S SIBLING

AS WE learned in *In Their Own Voices*, **Keith J. Bigelow** was placed directly into foster care from the hospital in Prince Georges County, Maryland. The social worker stressed that his birth father had finished high school and was a hard worker. His birth mother had two older children and did not feel able to care for another child. His birth grandmother was said to be a strong, caring woman. Keith did not live with any of his biological family.

After being in several foster homes, including one where there was abuse, he was listed for adoption. Keith was nearly 3 years old and celebrated his third birthday in Vermont, November 27, 1971, one week after arriving in his adoptive home. The fifth of ultimately six children, he was raised in an American Baptist home in Essex Junction, Vermont. His sister, Susan, had been adopted in February 1968, at one week of age. She is part Hawaiian. In 1973 Khai completed the family, arriving from Vietnam at two and a half years of age.

According to Keith, his adoptive parents handled issues relating to adoption and ethnicity discreetly. When Keith needed special products for his hair and skin that could not be purchased in Vermont, Keith's father would go across the lake to Plattsburgh, New York, to the air force base to get the products without bringing unnecessary attention to Keith. Actually, the trip was a great reason to take the ferry across Lake Champlain and have dinner at the Officers' Club!

"Room For One More" is a support group for adoptive families. The Bigelows attended this group regularly and found families who adopted black children. The group helped the Bigelows to become more sensitive to issues affecting African American children living in transracial settings. Keith remembers interacting with many of these kids, reinforcing his "normalcy" in his family.

From Washington, D.C., to Vermont, to Lansing, Michigan, Keith has learned how to adapt to extreme circumstances. He has retained the values his parents instilled in him and strives to do what is right. His appreciation for his own ethnic heritage and the plight of others was actually nurtured by his wife, who is Haitian American. In his understanding of himself and African American communities, Keith has dedicated himself to minister to people living in urban neighborhoods. From *In Their Parents' Voices*, we learned that Keith serves as senior pastor of Antioch Full Gospel Ministries of Lansing, Michigan, which he proudly formed, and he has been promoted to master sergeant in the Air National Guard. Both he and his wife, Francoise (Magda) are raising their two children: Taryn, 12, and Keith II, who is 5. Keith continues to "keep the faith" in his journey.

The following interview is with Keith's sister, Hilary Tomasson.

HILARY TOMASSON

OLNEY, MARYLAND
SEPTEMBER 2006

Hilary Tomasson, 40, is the third oldest child out of a total of six siblings in the Bigelow family. The Bigelow's first three children, including Hilary, were born to them and the latter three were all transracially adopted. Hilary is three years older than Keith. She describes her religious affiliation as Protestant. Currently Hilary works for a marketing software company, where she is able to use her master's degree in telecommunications management. In 2003 she was divorced, but she continues to raise her two sons—Stefan, 13, and Koby, 10—in Olney. Regarding her relationship with her brother, Keith, she says, "There is not much about the relationship ... it is not close because of logistics." She adds, however, that she has very positive feelings toward Keith. She admires and respects him.

Tell me briefly what's going on in your life and where you are currently living.

I have lived in the Maryland area since college, almost twenty years now. This part of Maryland—Olney—is a relatively small town located near Washington, D.C., and Baltimore. Olney is a great place to live and a great place to raise a family. I have two boys, Stefan who is 13 and Koby who is 10. They are both very active in school and church activities. In my life there is a lot of activity on a regular basis juggling work and home life, like handling the logistics of what to make for dinner and managing my kids' hectic schedules. Yet I would describe my life as your average kind of life, but it is nice.

Living in the Washington, D.C., metropolitan area, I would think the traffic congestion does not help your life become less hectic.

Yes, it is quite congested here, but I am actually fortunate that I have some flexibility with my job making the commute less stressful. Currently I am doing marketing for a software company in the telecommunications industry. Thankfully, I am only about thirty to thirty-five minutes away from my job on a regular traffic day, and I do have the ability to work from home if necessary. Some afternoons I come home when my older son comes home from school so that he is not completely by himself for hours at a time.

Would you say, demographically, that Olney is ethnically and racially diverse?

It is becoming more so. I would not say that it is super diverse at this point. I live in a town home community which, interestingly, is more diverse in that way than when I lived in a single family home in the community.

So what made you decide to move to a metropolitan area from a place like Essex, Vermont, which is a rural community?

I love this story. My parents moved into the house in Essex, Vermont, on the day that I was born, which was in 1965, and stayed there through my high school years. Obviously my mother wasn't involved in the moving. I lived in the same exact place for so long that I wanted to go off to school a little bit farther away. So I went to school in upstate New York, Clarkson University. Actually, that is where I met the man who became my husband. When we graduated in the late 1980s, it was not a great time to get jobs in the New England area so we went to an area where I knew it would be easier to find work. His family lived down here in Maryland. A lot of our friends actually went over to Boston, but because his family lived here it seemed like a nice place to get started.

Describe Essex.

Essex was always what I had known, so it was home. It felt safe. You didn't know everybody, but you knew a lot of people. Going back to your earlier question, the community of Essex was not diverse when I was there growing up. I knew one girl who was Jewish in school, and I think that was the extent of the religious diversity there, as far as I knew. Racial diversity … definitely more within my own family than in anybody else's probably. There was an African American family up the road from us, a boy who was in my grade. That's about it.

Your family was quite blended ethnically and racially. What was it like having siblings who were African American, Vietnamese and Hawaiian, along with having biological siblings?

It was all that I had ever known. It seemed that was the way it was supposed to be for me. One thing that was nice, and you may have heard this from speaking with other members of my family, was that we belonged to this group called "Room For One More." I always loved the name. It was an adoption group. We got together with other families who all had adopted. Most of the adoptions were racially diverse. We would have Christmas parties and summer picnics together. Over time, we became very close to these families and would see them on a regular basis. I really looked forward to those gatherings.

What was your relationship like with your brother, Keith, who is African American?

Keith is my little brother and I have two older brothers and two younger sisters. The way I remember it, Keith was just always fun to have around. He was just a sweetheart. I remember when we were younger that sometimes I would cut his hair. (This would happen quite often actually, as my mom would ask me to cut his hair.) I really did not know what I was doing but I was trying to do my best to cut his hair evenly. He probably put up with quite a few bad haircuts from me, but I meant well.

Describe your family life back then.

There were always kids around. We would fight with one and not the other. Sometimes it was five against one and you are the one, and sometimes you are part of the five. There was always somebody to do something with, and if you wanted space by yourself, you would have to find a corner to get a little privacy.

Were you close with your extended family, that is, uncles, aunts, and cousins?

Yes, we were. Actually my mom's brother and his family lived only twenty minutes away in Burlington, Vermont. We went to the same church, so we would see them regularly on Sunday mornings. We would often get together those afternoons. But then we would visit with more relatives during Holiday gatherings. My mom's parents were also living in Burlington, so we spent a lot of time with them as well. My dad's parents were about an hour away, so we would take little trips up to see them, too.

Do you remember times growing up when race might have been an issue within your own family or in the community where you lived?

I never thought it was an issue within my family. I certainly saw indications where other people in the community thought it might be an issue, generally speaking. People have come up to me when I am with my family, and they ask, "OK, which one is your *real* sister?" They are all real, what are you talking about?! I still struggle with how to differentiate, because I don't differentiate. There are obvious physical differences, but Keith is my brother as much as Brian is, and Brian is biologically related to me.

What did your parents teach you that nurtured that view?

For me, that's just the way it was. I remember when my parents adopted Keith and we went to pick him up in Maryland. That same day I recall walking around the reflecting pool in front of the Lincoln Memorial with him and realizing that we're going home with a new brother. I thought that was cool. I don't remember when my sister, Suzy, was adopted, because she was a baby and that would make me two at the time. I was a couple of years older when we got Keith. Only later do I remember a time when my mom said something about adopting another child, an older child. I think I was in high school then. That is the only time I remember even talking about adoption.

Do you remember what was discussed in that conversation?

Yes, it was my mom talking with me as opposed to the group of us. She was saying that there was a boy in a bad situation. I am not sure if he was in the school district that my mom was working in at the time, but I do know that she and my dad were considering if it was something that they could do. My mom was interested in knowing what I thought. I was quick to say O.K. In the end, my parents did not go through with this adoption. I am not sure why it didn't happen. Even later, after they already had six kids, they were thinking about having another one.

Is your nuclear family the only one that you are aware of that chose to adopt transracially compared to those in your extended family?

Yes. I mentioned my uncle that lived near my parents. He often had foster children. I don't recall if any were of different races or not. I do remember thinking that fostering children must have been harder than adopting because the kids would be there for a while and then they would be gone.

While you indicated that, in general, your community was racially and ethnically homogeneous, you mentioned that an African American family lived up the street from your family. Did you take the opportunity to get to know this family and their experiences?

I did not personally. I am sure that was just because of the "self-centered" kid point of view. I did not think about how I could help Keith understand where he came from; nor did I think about what he should know about the African American culture.

Did your parents establish any kind of relationship with this family?

I don't recall if my parents and those parents were especially friendly or not. As I said, I remember one boy from that family who was in my grade. We hung out in similar circles. I would not say we were best buddies, but he was someone I could hang out with. He was another kid in the neighborhood.

Because you are close to Keith in age, do you recall any acts toward Keith that occurred in school or in the community because of race or adoption?

There was a neighbor in the other direction who I thought was a friend of Keith's. But at one point he made a derogatory comment about Keith's race. I remember being so surprised by that, especially because I thought this was somebody who was his friend. Outside of that, I don't remember this happening often. It is possible that Keith may not have been open to sharing any of these kinds of situations with me. When we had our family council meetings together, I don't remember conversations about this topic coming up that often. But I may have just been oblivious.

Did any of your other siblings bring up issues about race or adoption at your family council meetings?

No. I don't recall any discussions like that. Certainly not having gone through that myself and not being in Keith's or Khai's, who is Vietnamese, situation, I don't know exactly what they went through. I have wondered actually if things were more difficult for my sister, Suzy. Although Suzy does have this Hawaiian background, she kind of looks similar to me. She does not stand out as different. Not having been in any of those siblings' situations I really cannot say for sure how they felt. But that was one thing I have thought about. Keith and Khai were obviously adopted. Suzy was, but she did not look like she was.

What were your interests growing up, and how did they compare to the interests of your other siblings?

I had a friend I went horseback riding with. I liked boys. Suzy was on the basketball team, she was a little star. I tried ballet, but we won't talk about that. I wouldn't say that I had specific interests that I shared with anybody. Obviously I had these two older brothers as well and then the younger siblings also, so I often wanted to do what the older siblings were doing. So I did gravitate to what my older brother, Brian, was doing. It is awkward to say that now. We had this pond out in our back yard. We would shovel that off and go skating on it. That was a whole family kind of activity. We did a lot of stuff together. Yet Keith and I didn't go to, let's say, an art class together, and so on.

Looking back on your experience growing up in a blended family, would you say that having both biological and transracially adopted siblings has helped you as an adult, a mother, and a career woman?

Absolutely! When I first came to Maryland I was working in a government office, which was one of my earlier jobs here, with some African American women. I had been at this job for a couple of months, and one of these women asked me about my family. I told her and the rest of the women about my older brothers, and siblings of different races, etcetera, and one of the women looked at me and said, "Oh, that's why you are OK." There was an article at that time—I believe in *Ebony* magazine—that cited Vermont as being the

whitest state in the union and this woman had read that article. She was saying, well, you are from Vermont … and you are OK! But I would totally say
that I hope I am much more open to all people of different ethnic and racial
backgrounds because of the situation I was raised in.

**Has your upbringing helped you in addressing potentially racial or eth-
nic situations?**

Yes. Relatively recently after my divorce, I had been seeing someone who
had this prejudice against African American people … and this became quite
clear in our relationship. That's when I knew that this was somebody I was not
going to spend any more time with. I did not see any actions on his part related to that prejudice though. There were just comments and his perceptions
about race … still I knew that this relationship was not for me.

**What is your relationship with Keith now that you are an adult and he is
a family man and a pastor?**

I would like to say that we talk every week. Unfortunately, we don't. Frankly I have not seen Keith in far too long. I think the challenge is that the time
I get off from work, often I will head up to Vermont because that is where a
few of the siblings still live and my parents are often there, so I like to "kill two
birds with one stone." And Keith will get back there sometimes, but it is very
rare that we will line up. So growing up and into adulthood: Keith sang at my
wedding, which was great! He and a cousin of mine got together to sing a song
at my wedding, and surprisingly Keith actually took the lead part in the song,
whereas I thought he would choose to sing the harmony part. He was great.
It was so good. They gave us such a nice present by doing that. The fact that
Keith was willing to do that for me, I really appreciated that.

My boys have actually seen Keith and his family more recently than I have,
mostly because my parents take them on these trips that they do. I think it has
been the past couple of summers that they have spent some time with Keith,
his wife, and his kids.

**Describe the relationship with your kids and their cousins, Keith's
children.**

It's funny, because Keith's younger child, Keith II, was not quite putting
the names together, so he was calling my boys "cousins." It's easier that way;
you don't have to remember names, right? This was just a few weeks ago. We
still exchange the basic gifts at Christmas and school pictures of our children.
I see his kids growing up that way. I am very happy that my boys have seen
Keith and his family fairly recently and more regularly than I have because
I do want them to recognize that these people are part of their family, too.
Even though they look different, they are still as much a part of their family as
everyone else. I think that for them it is a given. Keith is Mommy's brother;

therefore, to them, he is their uncle and his children are their cousins, so they just get that. Going back to your question, my relationship is not as close as I would like it to be with Keith, and I think that it is attributed to the day-to-day life and that we are geographically distant.

There was actually a time a few years ago when he came here to interview for a job, and I was very excited thinking that he may live near me. I was really looking forward to that, but it didn't quite work out. But we got together when he was here. I hate to say it this way, but when it is convenient, it is very welcome.

I myself have often wondered that if my sense of identity was growing at a different pace or direction than my brother's or sister's, would that ultimately affect my relationship with them. Have you ever asked yourself, "Wow, I can see Keith and me going in different directions; how do I feel about that?"

That was obvious a few years ago when my mom's mom died. It was a horrible time, my parents were out of the country, they could not get back for the service, but Keith was there. Both of us participated in the service. For me, I was barely able to do even this: basically I read a poem that I had written ages ago about her, so I did not have to speak extemporaneously. I was so impressed with Keith, because he just got up there and was doing a little preaching. I was looking at him in a new light and seeing the talent that he has. I am happy to see that growth with him; and I hope to see more evidence of that growth, not that it is not happening, just that I am geographically far away.

If your children wanted to date someone outside their race or culture, would you be open to that?

Yes!

Would you be amenable to your children adopting when they are ready to build a family?

Yes.

What are your views on transracial adoption?

Because my experience has been a good one, I am all for it. I understand that there is a school of thought about keeping kids within their same race-adoptive families. But if that is not a possibility, I would not want to have these children not be adopted. I do understand about having a cultural tie or, for lack of a better word, "fit," but to me it is more important that these children are given families. A cousin of mine wanted to adopt transracially a few years ago and was told that she couldn't, so she ended up adopting Caucasian children.

What state was she living in at the time?

New Mexico. She wanted to adopt children of Mexican descent, knowing that there were plenty of children from that background needing homes. She was also willing to adopt older children. Still, she was told no. There were these other children who were in need as well so I think things worked out, but I just think that there were children of Mexican descent who lost out.

Do you recommend that parents who adopt transracially instill racial and cultural sensitivities in their family's blueprint for their children?

Yes. I definitely would. I feel that I don't have a good understanding necessarily of what my parents may or may not have done to help Keith, Khai, and Suzy as kids, but I have certainly read stories about kids who were adopted from South Korea, for example, and their parents find a way to take the child back to Korea at some point. They educate these children about their history and make sure they convey an understanding about the Korean culture. So I think that that kind of exposure is definitely a great way to help the children understand their identities from a genetic point of view. Also, the culture in which you are raised is such an important component as well. I think that if you put those two elements together, you can really help to build the personality and character of the person.

DANIEL'S SIBLINGS

THROUGHOUT HIS life Daniel Mennega fought against the confines of being labeled "black" or "white." In *In Their Own Voices*, he said that he wants to be identified by how he thinks and what he likes to do. To him, his identity includes more than his ethnicity and skin color.

Raised in Sioux Center, Iowa, Daniel was adopted into a Dutch family as an infant. Both his parents emigrated to America from the Netherlands and were in their thirties when they adopted Daniel. They wanted to provide a home for a child who would otherwise not have one. Though as a young boy Daniel was not exposed to the African American community or heritage, he believes that the love and consistency his parents showed him gave him the confidence to explore his own ethnic identity and interests later in life.

In the early 1970s Sioux Center, Iowa, where Daniel grew up, had a population of about five thousand. At that time the community was predominantly white and Protestant. Family and community were cherished. To Daniel, Sioux Center symbolized the value of a small college-town atmosphere, a place where many of his childhood friends attended the same church and went to the same schools. He felt comfortable there.

Daniel mentions that he was always aware of his skin color, particularly during his adolescent years when race issues were introduced in conversations. He refers to a book by William Faulkner, *Go Down Moses*, where a character who is biracial comes to terms with his two different races. In Daniel's own journey, he has come to appreciate that he is mixed, black and white. Paradoxically, he finds that the definition others use to determine the validity of one's "black identity" does not recognize him or his experiences.

Daniel has four sisters, one of whom is adopted and biracial. Born in Grand Rapids, Michigan, in 1969, Daniel earned a bachelor's degree from Dordt College in Iowa and went on to pursue additional course work in graduate school. He earned a master's degree in English. Currently he works as a technical writer for a company in Texas and plans to travel overseas. Daniel maintains close relationships with his father, a retired biology professor, and his mother, who was a bookstore assistant. According to *In Their Parents' Voices*, Daniel continues to live in Austin, Texas. He is supportive of transracial adoption and values his individuality.

The following interviews are with Daniel's three birth sisters: Yvonne, Annette, and Michelle; two of them are older and one is younger than Daniel.

YVONNE THORNTON

SIOUX FALLS, SOUTH DAKOTA
AUGUST 2006

Yvonne Thornton, 46, is the oldest child of five in the Mennega family and is nine years older than Daniel. She is married and has four children: Emily, 18; Bryce, 16; Ian, 12; and Caleb, 7. Yvonne, who has a B.A. in nursing, has a career in the medical field. She is Baptist. Her economic status is middle class. Regarding her contact with Daniel, she says that she sees him once every year or two and shares occasional e-mails and phone calls.

Yvonne, where do you live, and what do you do?
I live in Sioux Falls, South Dakota, with my husband and children. Sioux Falls is a town of 140,000. I work at the local hospital part-time; I job-share with somebody, so I only work half-time.

How many children do you have?
I have four children.

Are they your biological children?
Yes.

Is the community where you live ethnically diverse?
It is becoming more diverse. It still looks pretty white, although there is a fair number of African Americans, Hispanics, Native Americans, and an increasing number of refugees—from places all over the world—who are living in the community.

What brought you to South Dakota from Iowa?
Sioux Falls, South Dakota, is only about an hour's drive from Sioux Center, Iowa, where I grew up. I came to Sioux Falls to go to Augustana College to get my nursing degree. And I had always wanted to work at Sioux Valley Hospital, because everybody had raved about Sioux Valley. I worked there as a

nurses aide before going to school. Once I graduated I got a job at Sioux Valley Hospital, and I have worked there ever since.

Tell me about the town of Sioux Center where you were raised.

Unlike other small towns, Sioux Center is a college town and so people there had lots of opportunities that probably other people in towns that size never had. When I was growing up we had the opportunity to have great music programs in the Christian schools. I was part of a community orchestra when I was in middle school and high school. We performed operas and operettas with the college community and also had other opportunities to participate in a variety of musical activities. What was nice was that I didn't live that far from the school, so I could easily get to practices and back without much hassle for my parents.

Since you are the oldest sibling in your family, do you remember your parents mentioning to you their interest in adopting children?

Yes, I knew that they were planning to adopt, but I have no recollections at all of the exact conversation.

How old were you when your two adopted siblings came into the family?

I believe I was about 9, right around the same time my parents mentioned that they were going to adopt. I have four siblings: Annette is about seven years younger than me; Rene, who is adopted, is eight years younger than me; Daniel, who is adopted, is nine years younger than me; and then Michelle, who is my youngest sibling, is 10, almost eleven years younger than me.

Do you remember how you first felt when Rene and Daniel came into your home?

I remember when we adopted Rene. That was a big deal, because our family took a trip to Grand Rapids, Michigan, from Illinois where we were living at the time to get her. I remember it being so much fun ... picking her up and having a new baby sister and then traveling back home with her. About a year and a half later Dan was adopted and came to live with us. Unfortunately I had to go stay at somebody else's house that time, and I wasn't particularly happy about that! But when he did come home, it was fun to have another baby in the house and be able to play with him, too.

What did you do as a family for fun?

My parents were really interesting people. They loved to play games, and so Friday night was always game night, and that was really fun. You got to spend some fun-family time together. Also, my grandparents lived in Michigan and Ontario, Canada, so every summer we took a trip to see them and many of our other relatives. We did quite a bit of traveling as a family in the summer, going on vacation and seeing everybody we could.

As a teenager did you have a good relationship with Daniel?

Yes, I had a very good relationship with Dan.

Would he discuss personal things with you?

I was so much older than he was. It was me, and then seven years until Annette, the second oldest child was born and then the rest of the kids came. So it was me, a seven-year break, and then the four little kids. Growing up, I was more like a second mother to the four of them. They played together all the time, and I had a great time watching them. I was more the oldest sister that they enjoyed being around. But because I was so much older, we did not have the closeness where I was like a confidant, in this case to Dan.

In the community of Sioux Center where you were raised, did anyone mention the race of your adopted brother and sister?

I don't ever remember race being an issue, I really don't. The way I looked at it, I was biologically related to my parents and white, but I had a pretty noticeable birthmark on my face, and so I always felt like I was pretty different, that I was kind of odd, if that makes any sense.

Were there any African American families in the community or at the college who your parents befriended?

Dordt College, which is in Sioux Center, is pretty white. There are very few minorities on campus. My parents tended to befriend people who were from far away and who didn't have family nearby, and would invite them to our home especially for certain holidays. It seemed that we always had a great big group of people that my parents would sort of pull in.

You mentioned that you were a close family growing up; do you recall if Daniel or Rene were accepted equally by your extended family members, such as your grandparents and aunts and uncles, compared to the rest of the kids in your family?

Absolutely. We were all one. Everybody was friends, and we all stuck together as a family. As far as I could tell, there was no difference in how any of our relatives treated Dan or Rene.

Has the experience of having a blended family, with Dutch influences, American influences, and biracial siblings, shaped your perception today about people?

My dad used to always say it doesn't matter what color people are, it's what is on the inside. And so that was very much how I looked at people, always. It didn't really matter what was on the outside. That was something I had to come to terms with myself … because I was a little odd on the outside and people needed to look at the inside of me. And it was very much in that same spirit that we accepted Rene and Dan. They came to us as small kids, and, as far as I was concerned, they were just like the rest of us; skin color never meant anything to me really.

While recognizing that the color of one's skin was not a priority in your family, do you know if Rene or Dan recognized their own physical differences? For example, did Rene have hair issues?

Rene ended up with really straight hair for being an African American and Dan's hair was curlier, but in the 1970s it was cool to have an Afro. So a lot of Dutch kids looked just like he did but they had to perm their hair.

As adults, has Rene or Dan talked with you about some of the things they have encountered now that they have left Dordt College and Sioux Center?

The only thing I remember is that when Rene started working at a local grocery store here in Sioux Falls, somebody made an ignorant comment to her because of the color of her skin. Rene looked at the person funny, because when she was in Sioux Center everybody knew who she was, and it wasn't a big deal what her skin color was. But when she got to Sioux Falls, I think it seemed to matter a little bit more, because it wasn't a community where everybody knew her and accepted her for who she was as a person. I don't remember Daniel ever saying anything to me about any racial issues he may have dealt with. I don't know if that is just because I am the older sister and still more like a second mother to him and therefore he wouldn't confide that information to me. Still, I don't have any recollection of race really being an issue for him.

When Rene and Dan were growing up, do you know if either one struggled with dating, trying to find someone who was African American?

I don't know. I got married and had a baby by the time either of them graduated from high school, so I was just in a whole different world. I don't remember them saying anything to me about dating matters.

How do they interact with your children?

My kids just love them. They don't think twice about what color they are. When we were in Michigan last summer, my kids thought that their Uncle Dan was the coolest because he went with them boating and fishing.

How often do you see Dan?

We see him once every year or two. Dan doesn't come home very much; he keeps more to himself. We get e-mails from him off and on, and once in a while we'll talk on the phone, but he is pretty much a guy that does his own thing. He doesn't call home often either.

When you reflect on your experiences growing up with your family, what would you say to other families who are looking to adopt transracially? Is it something you would promote?

Yes. I have the perspective that everybody is the same on the inside, and the outside of a person really doesn't matter. I think if you raise your kids with that kind of mentality, then I would think that race would not really be an issue. There are a lot of families in my church that have adopted from Guatemala, China, or other different places. It is just really fun for me to see that and to have my kids raised with families that have transracially adopted. I think it is wonderful.

How has the adoption experience shaped your life? Has it made you more open to and aware of different issues?

I think so, because I don't usually look on the outside of people, you look at their eyes and they are transparent as far as I am concerned. Sometimes it just takes me back because I don't think about it as color. I think sometimes the culture is more of an issue for me than the color issue, mostly because I don't understand the black culture, and because my African American siblings were raised to be Dutch on the inside, I didn't experience the African American part of it. So the culture for me has been something that I have had to learn, because that is a whole new experience for me.

Has Rene adopted any of the "African American culture"?

I think so. Rene loves to cook like her African American mother-in-law, and loves to have them over to her house. She definitely loves to dive into the whole black family tradition. In my opinion, Rene has done an awesome job of becoming a part of the world that her husband Derrick, who is African American, relates to.

So Rene identifies mostly with the African American culture now in her adulthood years?

Yes.

Tell me about Rene's wedding. I imagine that it was very ethnically and culturally diverse.

Derrick and Rene got married by the Justice of the Peace, so the wedding itself was pretty quiet. But afterward they had a nice reception where family members could eat together and hang out.

What was that like?

It was fun. It was great to meet some of the relatives from the other side and to eat all kinds of different cooking.

Looking back, are you happy that your parents adopted? Were there any jealous feelings that you may have had toward your adopted siblings?

Again, I was so much older by the time my siblings all came that it was more of a dethroning of the queen. It wasn't a race issue. I used to be the one who had all the attention, and now there were all these kids, and so yes, there was some jealousy I am sure, because there they were, all these little ones. Looking back, I was really spoiled to begin with and so it was kind of a royal dethronement. Well, when you're spoiled you have issues to deal with. I had to learn to be a servant and I had to learn to put others before me and I had to learn to be part of our family and that it wasn't all about me, and that was a big thing. I think that was something God had to work on my heart for a long time—it's not about you, you are just part of the group, and you need to be doing what you need to do for the best interest of the entire family.

One last thing ... I am eternally grateful that Rene and Daniel came to be part of our family. It is such a blessing because it has broadened my view. I wouldn't trade that for anything. I just can't imagine how our lives would have been without them. Yes, I am thankful that they are part of our family.

ANNETTE VANVOORST

MAURICE, IOWA
NOVEMBER 2006

Annette VanVoorst, 39, is the second-oldest child in the Mennega family and yet she is closer in age to her younger siblings. She is only about a year and a half older than Daniel. Annette is married with four children: Kodie, 17; Kelsie, 14; Kassidy, 12; and Kolten, 9. Annette and her husband are raising their children in the Christian Reformed (Protestant) faith. After spending one year in college, Annette pursued entrepreneurial opportunities, including starting her own hair bow business called Bows 'N Stuff and purchasing two separate Curves franchises. According to Annette, she sees Dan once a year for Christmas when he comes home, and she talks with him on the phone perhaps two times a year.

Annette, tell me about your family and where you live now.
We live in the town of Maurice, Iowa. Maurice has a population of 254. I am married to Tom, and we have four kids: Kodie, who is 17; Kelsie who is 14; Kassidy who is 12; and Kolten who is 9. Currently my husband is working at Hy-Vee, which is a grocery store, and I am working at a furniture store. I have also obtained my real estate license and stage homes for sellers so their home sells faster.

How did you and your husband meet?
We actually met at a Hy-Vee Food store. I had just turned 17 and I was a checker—or better known as a cashier—and he was a "carry-out boy."

I've always said that it's great to find somebody in the vegetable aisle of a grocery store. Were you anywhere near the vegetable aisle?
No, I was just a cashier.

Why did you move from Sioux Center, Iowa, to Maurice?

We still lived in Sioux Center for about twelve years after we married. It's been about seven years now since we moved to Maurice, which is only seven miles south of Sioux Center. We decided to move because housing was more affordable in Maurice.

Are you raising your children in similar or different ways compared to how you were raised?

Definitely, similar. My kids go to the Sioux Center Christian School and to Unity Christian High School, just like I did. We also go to Bethel Christian Reformed Church, just like I did. We are pretty much raising the kids like how I grew up.

When you were growing up in Sioux Center, almost thirty-five or thirty-seven years ago, how did you view that community? What were your experiences within your family of having a biracial brother and sister?

We lived in Sioux Center in a house on Second Street.

Was the community diverse ethnically?

Not really. There was only David Adams who was adopted and biracial — you mean people of a different race?

Yes.

Well, there was David Adams and then there was another one of my brother Dan's friends, John De Mol, who I think was half-black, half-white. Other than that, there were not very many at all.

Describe Sioux Center.

Sioux Center probably has about six thousand people now. It might have been about 5,000-plus back then, when I was raised there.

There are five children in your family?

Yes, there are five of us. Yvonne is seven years older than me; Rene is a year and a half younger than me; Dan is about a year and four months younger than Rene; and Michelle is a year younger than Dan.

Were you close with your neighbors?

No. In fact, we really didn't do anything with them at all. Even up to like four or five years ago when my folks lived there, not much was done with the neighbors, and then my parents moved to a different house where they still live, and their new neighbors are wonderful.

What was it about the neighbors back then that caused conflict?

I'm not even sure. I would have to ask my parents what the problem was, but I know they did not like us.

Who did your parents socialize with?

My dad was a professor at Dordt College in Sioux Center, and both he and my mom made friends with other professors and their wives. They were also really good friends with a doctor and his wife who had a Dutch background and had similar beliefs and interests as my parents. My mom, especially, was really good friends with the doctor's wife.

Do you recall if any faculty and their families at Dordt College came to your home, particularly those from different racial and ethnic backgrounds?

Yes, Dan's friend, John De Mol, his mother was faculty at Dordt: his family came to our home. Also the Adams family who adopted Dan's friend, David, they were friends of my parents and would come to our home. Mostly they would all come to our home for Sunday dinners. If there was a student from Nigeria going to Dordt, my parents would have that student over, too.

When you were growing up, what types of activities did you enjoy as a family?

We did lots of things like go on walks, and go to Oak Grove which is a park with a river and hiking trails, and we'd take roasting sticks along and have hot dogs and marshmallows. We hiked a lot. My dad would do fun things like crack some peppermints and act like they came off a tree. We played a lot of games. Friday nights were usually our family night and we'd play the button game and other fun games. I also remember mom would make homemade pizza every Saturday night, while we'd have piano lessons in another town about nine miles away.

You were already born before Rene and Dan were adopted into your family.

Yes.

Do you have any memories of when they came into your family?

No, I don't.

Do you remember if your parents ever discussed with you why they chose to adopt?

They always dreamed of having a dozen children, but my mom had miscarriages and had a hard time with pregnancies, so they chose to adopt.

Growing up, what was your relationship like with your siblings, and specifically with Rene and Dan?

For the most part my relationship with them was pretty good. Of course, all brothers and sisters fight and have squabbles and stuff. Looking back now, I hope they didn't think that I was mean to them because they were adopted. I would feel bad. But I would still say my relationship with Dan and Rene was pretty good.

Did you have similar interests?

No, not necessarily. I enjoyed reading magazines. My siblings all loved to do things like play Trivial Pursuit, and figure out crossword puzzles, and that just wasn't my cup of tea at that time. I thought that was weird. Yvonne and Michelle liked to be creative. Dan liked to read, which is probably why he is good at English now. I remember that when Dan and I were little we'd play outside a lot. We could entertain ourselves very well. We just needed a wagon and we'd push each other around and make up games.

Were you ever jealous of Dan or Rene?

The one thing that crosses my mind is that Dan was my mom's "favorite," so if there was a fight between Dan and me she would always side with him. My dad had Rene as his favorite. Sometimes it was like, "Hey, wait a minute, how come they're your favorite?!" "How come you're siding with them when I'm right?" I remember that that's just how it went. My mom kind of gave Dan that little bit of extra love, and then my dad did that with Rene, but they gave us all love.

Do you recall wondering why Rene's hair was a little different than yours or why Daniel's skin was different than yours?

No, not really. There was Dan and there was Rene. I would notice that Dan's hair was curly and mine wasn't, and that his skin was maybe a little different color. I can remember that I had white dolls, and Rene had a little black doll. I am not sure where she got it. There was a little bit of a difference, yes.

Living in your community, did you ever have to rationalize that difference?

That is a hard question to answer. I would say it was a big thing in our community because not very many people had adopted kids, and if they did they had adopted white ones. And we had two interracial kids in our family. That's why I felt like our family was a little bit different. We just weren't the "normal" family in Sioux Center. But then again we were Dordt professors' kids, and we grew up with very strict rules and had no TV.

Because of that difference, did you feel that you needed to stick up for Rene or Dan?

Yes, especially because some kids were not nice to them. Nowadays a lot of people in Sioux Center adopt kids from places like Guatemala, China, and Haiti, and it is very well accepted. Kids don't ridicule them for their color, but I can remember Rene coming home and saying that this boy made a snide remark as she was walking down the hallway at school. Both Dan and Rene got ostracized by other kids in school because of their racial differences. They both worked at a diner, and one of the owners would make racial jabs.

When they were ridiculed, did they ever come to you directly?

I don't remember. I think they approached my mom or dad about issues like that. I didn't know a lot of what was going on.

What were your interests in elementary school and high school?

I was into volleyball and was on the drill team. I loved hanging out with my friends. I did schoolwork; I helped my mom a lot with housework. And then I started working at Hy-Vee when I was 17.

Did you consider dating someone outside your race or ethnicity?

I believe I would have no problem doing so. Interracial dating would have been more of a normal thing for me because of how I grew up. Because I knew Dan and Rene were just as normal as anyone else, I think that if the right person had come along I would have dated him regardless of race.

What was it about your experience that made you recognize that option … that you could cross the racial line and feel comfortable dating somebody that didn't look like you, versus other families in that community who perhaps thought differently?

Again, I would say it would have been more normal if Dan or Rene dated interracially, or if I would have brought somebody home from a different racial background because it would have been well accepted within our family. Many people in Sioux Center talked highly of Dan and everybody remembers Dan, and I think it would have been fine for him, or any of us kids, to date someone from a different racial background.

Let me restate this. What if you flip that scenario and you looked at a white family in that community who had not adopted transracially. Would the parents in that family in your opinion be receptive of their white Dutch son or daughter dating a black person?

I understand. I think the white son or daughter would probably have a lot more grief from their families just because that wouldn't be normal for the typical family. There are people in Sioux Center who didn't, and still won't, let their kids date outside their race, just because of what others might say.

What do you think allowed you to be able to move beyond your comfort zone racially?

Well, growing up in my family there wasn't a choice of who my adopted brother or adopted sister was going to be. It wasn't like, well do I want adopted brothers and sisters or don't I … it wasn't a choice. Ever since I was very little, that's how it was, and that was great. That was fine. That's all I knew. It wasn't like I was ten and mom and dad asked, "Should we adopt a child?" And then we all decided. It wasn't like that. I don't even remember when Rene or Dan weren't part of our family.

Did you ever feel sometimes that, wow, if they hadn't adopted them, my life would be easier?

Sometimes back then I thought that if my adopted brother or sister weren't there we'd have more money. Going to Christian schools and doing other family things were expensive. Saying that, I don't think I ever thought that I wanted to trade them. We as kids were still able to do some fun things. My parents had us kids on the swim team and we took violin and piano lessons. I don't think I realize how lucky I was as a child and a teenager.

What, if anything, pops into your mind as you recall your first memory of your adopted brother and sister being racially different than you?

When I was probably 5 our family was in Grand Rapids, Michigan, on vacation visiting relatives. We were driving through the downtown area where there were a lot of black people around. I remember looking at them through the car window, and then looking at Dan and Rene sitting in the seat next to me, and that was my very first realization that they were different from me, that they were "black." Before that moment, I don't think I had a clue.

Reflecting on your experiences as an adult, do you think that transracial adoption affected your life in a positive or a negative way?

I would say in a positive way.

Can you elaborate?

I think that having experienced something that a lot of people haven't experienced—having a transracially adopted brother and sister—only enriched my life and helped me to become a better person versus someone who's never experienced transracial adoption and just lived their sheltered lives.

How has the experience been a positive one, and how has it been a challenge?

It was positive because if we didn't have Dan and Rene there'd only be three of us sisters; and how boring would that be? My adopted siblings enriched our lives just from there being more of us and having more to laugh about together. Sure we had fights and we didn't get along sometimes too, but when it was family night, game night, there were just more people around the table to play games.

What were some of the challenges?

One was hurting for them when people were unkind to them. For example, they worked at a restaurant in town and one of the owners would make racial jokes about them which were very hurtful. I felt bad when they'd come home and I'd hear what someone had said to them or done to them. You don't want people to say derogatory stuff like that ... because it's your family member that they are talking about. I used to think quite often that my adopted brother and sister were really not so different than me, but when stuff like that would come up it would remind me that they are different. To me that difference, though, was not a bad thing.

Given your experiences, and what you just said, if you chose to adopt today what things would you hold on to that your parents taught you and what things would you do differently?

I just wouldn't care what anyone thought. If I would adopt someone today, because of what we went through, I just wouldn't care. If someone walked up to me and said "Oh, why did you do this?" I'd be like, "Whatever!" and probably walk away, whereas maybe ten or fifteen years ago I might have been much more concerned about what everyone thought. Now it would be … this is how it is and if you don't like it … whatever …

What things would you keep the same?

Sioux Center is a good place to live and now would be much more accepting of transracial adoption versus thirty or so years ago when I was growing up.

What changed?

Well, more people in Sioux Center are adopting from China and Guatemala so that kind of adoption is a bit more acceptable, it is a little bit more of a normal thing to do right now. Back when I was growing up I know my parents got a lot of grief from people in the community because they had adopted interracially, black and white. Nowadays it would be more accepted, because we have a lot more Mexicans in Sioux Center and basically a lot of all different races.

Are you saying that the community of Sioux Center was not supportive of an integrated family back when your siblings were being raised?

Correct, I would say the community as a whole was not supportive. I would say we were almost always treated differently because our family was not the same as many in the community. We were looked upon in a different way … or maybe that is just how I perceived it. In that community, everyone, for the most part, is related to each other, and so therefore some people there didn't necessarily make time for people who didn't have a lot of family around or those who did not look the same. But, again, maybe I perceived it as if they thought we were weird instead of them just not wanting to pay attention to us.

What was your relationship like, in your adolescent years, with your extended family—grandparents, aunts, and uncles?

My last grandpa died in 1978. We would visit our grandparents maybe once a year. My mom's parents lived in Canada, and my dad's parents lived in Grand Rapids, so we would go up to Michigan about once a year and then try to make a trip up to Canada, but that was not always possible. So I didn't see my mom's parents as often as we saw my dad's parents just because of distance. Most of my aunts or uncles lived in either Michigan or Canada.

Were they open to your parents adopting transracially?

I think so. They treated everyone as normal and equal family members.

Now, as an adult, what is your relationship like with Dan?

Dan comes home once a year for Christmas, and I probably talk to him maybe twice a year. I call him for his birthday and he calls me for mine. We also e-mail each other more regularly. E-mail is a big communicator for us as adults.

Has Dan in his adulthood years talked to you about his experiences growing up in a white family and in Sioux Center?

No.

Have you raised the subject with him?

No. If I would have read what he said in *In Their Own Voices*, I might have asked him some questions. But I have not read the book, yet.

What is your relationship like with your other siblings?

Good. Michelle comes home every Christmas, and we e-mail in the meantime.

Yvonne lives about an hour away; she has four kids. We don't do a whole lot together, because she's busy and involved with her family and I'm busy here with my family. Rene, I haven't seen for a while. It has been maybe three years since I've seen her, but we talk on the phone and e-mail.

Has Rene raised the issue with you about race and adoption or her biological family?

Yes. From what I know Rene did find her biological father. His name is Ned. From my understanding, Rene's biological father then called Rene's biological mother to tell her about Rene. Apparently she, the biological mother, didn't want anything to do with the situation at all. She told Rene's biological father that she didn't want him to ever call again and hung up.

As you know, Rene is interracial and is married to Derrick who is black. When they come home to Sioux Center, you can tell they are not very comfortable being here, especially Derrick. According to Derick, everyone is looking at him because he is black. I don't see that. When we go out I introduce him as my brother-in-law. I don't see the difference in the color of skin, whereas he is very clearly bothered by it. Even Rene will make comments about the racial differences. She has mentioned that Dan relates more to his white side, like he has had white girl friends, etcetera, and she associates herself with being black, even though she is half-white and half-black.

Rene identifies more with the black community than with the white community?

Yes, but what is interesting is that she's not really accepted in the black community either because she's not totally black. She has pretty creamy, light-brown skin with dark hair that, if it is short, is kind of straight. Black women don't always like her because black guys are apparently attracted to her looks. So I know she doesn't feel totally accepted there either because a lot of the women are jealous of her for being half-white and having those qualities. If you know Rene she is the most fun person and can make you laugh.

How do you see Rene?

When I see Rene, I do not see someone who is half-black. She's just my sister. And she talks like a white person. She doesn't make herself different. She's just my sister, and I don't really care what color her skin is because …

Would you go into a black community to see her?

Yes.

And that wouldn't bother you?

No.

When she was married, were you at the wedding?

Yes, my husband and my son, Kodie, who was 2 then, also went. Rene and her husband have been married for about fifteen years now. Her wedding reception was fun. I thought it was so interesting because I hadn't seen or interacted with a lot of black people before that. Both Rene and Derrick are hilarious. They are bubbly people. They laugh a lot and they're just a lot more laid back than what I am used to around here in Sioux Center. I definitely enjoy talking with them.

Have your families gotten together?

No, only at their wedding reception.

Has what you gained in this experience matriculated in your own home?

Definitely. My family is open-minded. When my kids see people of a different race, it is normal for them.

Would you recommend transracial adoption to other white families?

Yes, definitely. I would transracially adopt myself, but we already have four kids. I would recommend it because there is no difference. Maybe there's a little bit of difference in skin color but everybody's a person. I think it made me a better person because of having an adopted brother and sister. It didn't matter what color they were. They could have been white kids and adopted and we might have had the same fights and some of the same qualities.

MICHELLE MENNEGA

VISALIA, CALIFORNIA

JULY 2006

Michelle Mennega, 35, is the youngest child of the Mennega family and is a year younger than her brother, Daniel. She says, "Dan and I were the closest in age so we did everything together when we were little. When we got to school we developed our own friends. Today, as a family, we are pretty close. We all live far apart now but we are still close, and when we get together we have a great time." Michelle received a B.A. in biology and is a laboratory technician. She identifies with the Christian Reformed tradition. Her economic status is middle class. Michelle is single with no children, but she plans to marry in the near future.

Michelle, you are the youngest in your family, correct?
Yes, I have three sisters and one brother, and they are all older than me. Two of them are adopted, my sister, Rene, and my brother, Daniel.
How old were you when your parents adopted Daniel and Rene?
I did not exist! I was the surprise.
How old were Rene and Daniel when you were born?
Rene was 2 and Dan was 1.
So you pretty much grew up with them.
Very much so.
Did you ever see Rene or Daniel as different as far as their skin or their hair?
I don't remember thinking that. I think that eventually I figured it out that they were different. It was never something that I really noticed.
Tell me what it was like growing up in a small town in a Dutch Christian Reformed family. What were your traditions?
Our family went to church twice on Sunday; we went to the local Christian school all through grade school and high school.
Within your home, did you practice the Dutch tradition or was it more American?
We were raised very Dutch. My parents were about 18 and 19 when they emigrated from Holland, and so they maintained their Dutch customs. The food my mom would make was very typically Dutch, like meat and potatoes.
Did you have Oliebolen, which is similar to a donut but with raisins?
Yes, and it was fantastic.
That's my favorite, too.
We grew up more Dutch than American.
Did your parents introduce the family to any aspect of the African American tradition?
No. My parents had no concept of what the African American tradition was.
When you were living in Sioux Center did you interact with any other African American or biracial children?

Yes, because there were a couple of professors who taught at the local college, Dordt College, who had also adopted biracial children. The kids were all in similar grades as us.

Do you recall whether the topic of race ever came up at the dinner table or in your classroom?

No, not really. By the time we were in school, it was normal for people to accept Rene and Daniel; they saw them as part of the community. True, when they went to a new school, from grade school to high school, where kids did not know them initially, I think their racial difference was always more of a big deal, especially when they interacted with students from outside towns that came to the school. Eventually, though, people would just stop noticing that they were different.

Did Rene or Daniel ever mention anything to you about race?

Yes, I think Rene really felt that guys did not ask her out on dates because she had a different color skin.

How did you or other family members respond?

I think we always just tried to encourage her. I know that my dad really, really encouraged her and would say, you know, you are a beautiful girl, you're a wonderful person, and you need to find somebody who can appreciate you for who you are.

Did you think of race differently once you made the transition from high school to college, because you grew up with biracial and adopted siblings?

Yes, definitely. I think that in Sioux Center many people were afraid to talk to other people that had different color skin or that were from a different background than them. I think that our family was very exposed to people from different cultures and nationalities. When students came to Dordt College from, let's say, Nicaragua, my parents would invite them into the home. And they also had friends in the Laotian community. My parents were very welcoming and had them over. It was fun.

When you consider how Daniel and Rene developed their identity, how do you think they tried to deal with some of the unique struggles they had because of their racial difference? Did they address their feelings within the family, or did they keep their feelings inside?

I think they dealt with them more internally. I don't think that they were afraid to talk to me about it, but I don't think that I would have necessarily been able to understand as well either, even though I was very close to both of them.

What was that relationship like ... your closeness to them?

Dan and I were the closest in age, so we did everything together when we were little, and then when we got to school we developed our own friends in our own classes.

What about your relationship with Rene?

Rene was a little closer in age to my sister, Annette. But we still did a lot of stuff together. We were on the swim team together, we played together, and we played with all the neighborhood kids together.

When you were with Rene and you were swimming and playing together, did you see any differences between her hair and your hair, for example?

Yes. Rene had naturally curly hair, and so her hair would frizz up more than my hair would. I think she noticed the differences more than I noticed them. I was a little bit oblivious.

So it didn't matter to you growing up that she was biracial?

Not at all. I was very proud of them.

What was it that you admired about Daniel and Rene?

They were both just very fun people.

Would you say that all your siblings grew to be close?

Yes.

Are you a close family?

Yes, we are pretty close. Now we all live kind of far apart, but we are still close, and when we get together we have a great time.

How old were you when Daniel and Rene went off to college?

Dan and I ended up being in the same grade, but we were juniors in high school when Rene went to college, and a couple of years later Daniel and I went to Dordt College together.

Did the two of you interact in college?

We had a different circle of friends, but we would see each other on campus and we would always talk.

When you were at college, did you tend to communicate with all your siblings by phone?

I called more of the ones that were closer in age. I was very social in college, and it was a time in my life when I kind of detached from my siblings. I did my own thing for those four years.

Did you date people from different races, nationalities, or religion, or were you pretty much focused on dating white Dutch men?

That was pretty much all that was available at Dordt ... white Dutch people.

Did you ever think, as a white person, how potentially challenging it might be for your black siblings to live in such a white world?

Yes. I think that I considered it fairly often, because I think that I knew it was hard for Rene especially; at times it was also hard for Dan.

How did you know it was hard for Rene?

Because she would talk about it sometimes, and you could tell that she struggled a little bit with who she was, just because she felt like she was not as attractive because she was not white.

Did Dan and Rene take in the Dutch heritage that your family promoted?

Very much.

Did they ever ask you or your siblings about where their blackness would fit in?

Not that I remember.

You mentioned that you dated primarily white Dutch men. Would you have thought about marrying outside that demographic group?

Yes. I have always been fairly open-minded about it. I think that I found that I just tended to be more attracted to people who were the most like me. But if somebody had grown up similar to me, the skin color wouldn't really matter. I looked more at the personality and the baggage of the person, not the skin color as much.

If Daniel married an African American or an Asian woman or Rene married a person of color, how would you respond to that?

Well, Rene did. She married an African American man. They got married by the Justice of the Peace and had a reception afterward. At the reception there was basically his, the groom's, family and friends and our family. He has a very nice family.

So it was culturally and racially diverse?

Yes.

How did she meet her husband?

She met him working at a grocery store.

Was that in Sioux Center?

No, she met him in Grand Rapids, Michigan.

So Rene left Iowa?

Yes, she did not like living in a small town. She wanted to live somewhere that was bigger and more diverse culturally and ethnically.

Did you feel awkward or was it natural for you to interact with your brother-in-law's family?

There were some awkward moments, but I think ... most of the people in our family are pretty outgoing, and most of the people in his family are pretty outgoing, too.

What were the awkward moments?

Just the feeling it was different than I was used to.

When you look at race and adoption and the fact that you were raised in a transracial adoptive family, do you think that experience has affected

your life in any way? Do you think your life would have been different had you not had siblings that were adopted and biracial?

Yes. I think that my life has been affected for the better. First of all, I can't imagine our family without either Rene or Daniel. I think having the two of them in our family made us all less narrow-minded. When you grow up in a family like ours, you realize that people are people no matter what color their skin is.

You mentioned that in your family you didn't talk a lot about race. Yet do you think that your parents did things differently because they had children from different ethnic backgrounds?

No, I don't think so.

Were there times in your childhood, adolescence, and adulthood years when you were jealous of your adopted siblings?

I think when I was little I might have been jealous of the attention that they got, because I was just a normal, boring white kid.

So they got a lot of attention?

Yes ... they were pretty darn cute, so they deserved it.

Would you encourage other families to adopt black children transracially?

Absolutely.

What would you say are the benefits of transracial adoption in general and what would you say are some of the challenges?

The challenges probably would be more so with the transracial adopted child and their finding their identity, in our case in a white family; although I think all kids go through identity crises, especially when they are in junior high school. I think sometimes that some kids who are adopted kind of blame their issues completely on adoption. To me, I don't think that the color of a child's skin should prevent that child from becoming adopted by a family with a different background. If a child needs a home, he or she needs a home regardless of race. I hope people can become open-minded enough to see that.

Would you consider adopting a child of a different race?

Yes, definitely.

Would you talk to either one of your adopted siblings about that? For instance, if you adopted a black child, would you be open to what Rene had to say about the importance of the development of the black identity for the child?

Yes, I would definitely be open to her thoughts. I think, back when my parents adopted, they innocently really didn't know anything about the black culture or identity so they had nothing to tell her because they didn't know anything.

Do you know whether your parents had any African American friends or worked with African American professors at the local college?

No, I don't think they had any contacts like that. The only contact they had originally was with the adoption agency, where they adopted Rene and Daniel. Other than that, I don't think that they were even given any resources.

Looking back at your upbringing, are there things you would do differently now that you have seen some of the issues Rene and Daniel have had to deal with?

I just don't have a quick answer on that.

Now that you are an adult and are engineering your own life, tell me where you live and what your future looks like.

I moved to California eleven years ago, and I live in a town of a hundred thousand. I work in a veterinary diagnostic lab, which I enjoy. In April I went to Europe for a month, and I met someone special. We are planning on getting married soon and then in December moving overseas to Holland. My brother, Daniel, actually got to meet my fiancé.

Is your fiancé's family O.K. with the fact that your family is racially diverse?

That is a good question. I know that sometimes I feel bad for Rene, because when she and I were in Holland, it amazed me the stupid questions people asked her because she did not look like me physically or racially. That kind of prejudice actually exists in the states too. We have experienced it when our family has traveled around. Rene and I will say we're sisters, and people will look at us, like, you certainly don't look alike! I think it irritates Rene, sometimes, that people are so rude. Obviously we are not going to lie and tell them that we're not sisters. So then they always ask questions about why we look different and are sisters. I think it bothers Rene, because she doesn't like to be singled out.

Do you think racial issues are more pronounced in the Netherlands compared to the United States?

I don't know enough to answer that question.

In the Netherlands, do you see black people?

Yes, there are actually a lot of people from different countries that live in the Netherlands.

Do you think it should be important for African American/biracial and transracial adoptees to find value in their racial and ethnic identities, or do you think it is better for them to overlook that part of their identity when living in white families?

I think not mentioning it is kind of like the elephant in the middle of the room that nobody is talking about. Race, adoption, and identity need to be addressed. It is part of their identity; it is part of my brother's and sister's identity. When Rene and Daniel were growing up, they were willing not to talk about it just because they wanted to protect the family. But I think it would have been better had it been openly talked about.

Do you think it would have been helpful for them and for your entire family to have more African American influences and the influence of other people of color in your life?

We just never had the influence that you are talking about, so I don't have a good answer. I am sure I would have loved it, because we were always interested in different cultures and countries; our family was a little bit unique like that. We always found that people who were different were more fascinating.

You mentioned that Daniel moved to Austin, Texas. Isn't that a diverse community?

Yes. I think he is very comfortable there. I also think Rene is more comfortable in Grand Rapids, because she (or her husband) doesn't feel like she is conspicuous. They just blend in with everybody, and I think that was probably the hardest part of growing up in a small town like ours. It wasn't necessarily that they totally stood out but they were more visible; and I think they didn't necessarily want to be.

What do you think was something that worked well for your family in raising transracially adopted children, or just being a family? What were the main foundational values that you would carry forward in your own life?

We were a very close family. We grew up going to church, that was a big part of our lives.

What words of wisdom do you have for families who are raising black and biracial children in a place like Sioux Center, Iowa?

Try to expose them to a wide range of people and experiences. You have to put forth the effort to do that, especially if you are living in a small town. I don't think that is impossible. Maybe get your kids involved in a camp where there are lots of different people from lots of different backgrounds. Go to a summer camp where there are not just all Dutch white kids.

TAGE'S SIBLING

FROM *In Their Own Voices*, we learned that **Tage Larsen** is a classical musician and plays trumpet in the prestigious President's Own Marine Band based in Washington, D.C. His dream is to play principal trumpet in the Boston Symphony. Tage's professional course and passion for classical music developed early in his life, when he was exposed to the compositions of Beethoven and Bach. In 1995 Tage earned his bachelor of music degree from Michigan State University and completed a master's degree at the Eastman School of Music. His dream and unwavering discipline to contribute to the arts through his endeavors in classical music were inspired by the love and support of his family and friends.

Tage was born in 1970 in Hartford, Connecticut. An African American male infant, Tage needed a permanent home. Separated by race and circumstance, there was no reason why the life of this child should be united with a prospering young white couple who had the American dream in their grasp. As their history shows, the Larsens redefined that dream. They began building their family, first by taking in one of society's children and raising him as their own. And, one by one, the Larsen family expanded, adding nine more children. Four of them were the Larsen's biological children; the rest were chosen from some of the most economically and politically turbulent communities in the world. Truly a mosaic, the Larsens learned how to appreciate different cultures and ethnicities while each family member learned how to become an individual.

Raised in Cambridge, Massachusetts, Tage lived in a culturally diverse community. He played with both African American and white kids from different economic backgrounds. Many of his parents' friends in the African American community were lawyers, doctors, artists, or musicians and became Tage's mentors, opening his eyes and mind to a life of excellence and unlimited possibilities. Clearly Tage's upbringing gave him the foun-

dation to determine his professional path and social perspective, and ultimately his own identity.

Ten years later, *In Their Parents' Voices* reported that Tage expanded his
classical music career where he is in his fifth season as a trumpet player with
the Chicago Symphony Orchestra—the first full-time African American
member. His career has brought him to places all over the world. In addition,
he teaches at Chicago's Roosevelt University and gives private trumpet lessons. With his musical gift, he makes it a personal conviction to reach out to
children and young people who have little exposure to classical music. Tage
is committed to his family and especially cherishes his two children Zachary,
5, and Ethan, 4.

The following interview is with one of Tage's sisters, Anika, who is biologically related to the Larsen family.

ANIKA LARSEN

NEW YORK CITY
JUNE 2007

Anika Larsen, 33, is one of ten children, totaling four biological and six adopted,
in the Larsen family and is a younger sister to Tage but the oldest biological
child. She received a B.A. degree in theater from Yale University. Anika is a
Broadway actress who has performed in *Rent*. She claims that the cast "looks
like my family." She has also performed in a one-woman show, *Shafrika, the
White Girl*, which addresses her journey living in a transracial adoptive family.

**Anika, professionally you are an actress and co-founder of a theater com-
pany based in New York City. It sounds like your career is moving in an
exciting direction!**

I am in my third Broadway show which is fantastically exciting, but at this
point for me it is mostly a means to an end; it is instrumental for helping me
get the resources and attention that I want for the theater company that I
have helped to start called Unbounded Theater [now called Jaradoa Theater].
[Jaradoa] Theater is a company whose mission it is to promote mercy, beauty,
and truth through performance and service. Our mission, our purpose, is
twofold: we want to create a great theater and we also want to serve the community through theater outreach and partnerships with charities. Everybody
who wants to be a member of this theater company has to commit to work on
every show, since we all know that it is truly democratic and collaborative to

do so. We all have ownership of every show, and therefore our responsibilities are cyclical. If one time we're acting, the next time we're painting the sets, the next time we're doing props. Then every single month we all commit to doing community outreach.

How did you become interested in acting?

I started singing because it got me attention. Being one of ten kids I quickly realized how much I like individual attention and singing loud was a great way to get that attention. One thing that certainly contributed to my interest in singing was that my mom had the idea that for every year at their Christmas party all of us would perform, especially because we were all so cute. My mom thought we were the von Trapp family. So we sang at the Christmas party. That was when I really caught the bug. That's when I knew that I loved performing. Out of everybody in our family, I was the one real performer. Everybody else would get into duets and trios but I always got a big fat solo. I couldn't wait for it every year because that was part of the Christmas tradition for me. Singing did eventually turn into theater and musical theater and has now become my life's work, but it certainly started because of my family.

Tell me about your family, where you grew up.

There are ten of us, four by birth, six by adoption, and we lived in Cambridge, Massachusetts. My parents moved there because my father was going to Harvard Business School, and then they stayed there because the public school system was so diverse and so good, and both my parents were firm believers in public schools. They also wanted to be in a city that was diverse if they were going to raise a diverse family.

How did the fact that you had siblings from all over the world shape your life and shape your childhood?

I have found throughout my life that when I go out into the world and perform that I find myself in shows or in groups that look like my family. *Rent* is one of the Broadway shows that I've done, and that cast certainly looks like my family. Another show that has done nice things for my career is an off-Broadway musical called *Zanna, Don't!* and that cast looks like my family. I am in *Xanadu* right now, and it's just a bizarre coincidence that the cast is diverse. Also, when I was in college, I was in an a capella singing group which is a big deal at Yale University, and there's like thirteen of them. I was in the one called Shades, which is a multicultural group. I have often found that I don't think I am consciously drawn to groups and shows like these, but I sort of end up in those that look like my family.

In growing up in a transracial adoptive family and in a diverse community, what do consider was a huge plus and what do you recall was a struggle?

I discuss this in my one woman show, *Shafrika, The White Girl*. I think that there is a paradox to be found. I think growing up in my family the way that I did and in Cambridge, we were so exposed to so many cultures and such open-mindedness that it is ... actually so much more open-minded than the rest of the world, that it is in a strange way sheltered. The world isn't actually like that. And so as I went off into the real world I found that I was in many ways prepared to fit in anywhere with any kind of group and then also in this strange way, prepared to really fit in nowhere.

I had an interesting experience singing with Shades. Our group always sang at *Black Solidarity Day* at Yale. They would have all the African American groups on campus come and perform on this day. Often Shades would sing the gospel song in our repertoire, and I was the soloist on that—the white girl in the group singing the solo at *Black Solidarity Day*! I think because everybody on campus knew who I was, it was cool.

When we sat down and watched the other performances I was sort of struck by the realization that I could relate to many of the references the singers were making. What they were singing about I experienced or knew about because of my family background and the fact that I attended an elementary school that was also completely diverse. I then thought if you took 750 white students and put them in this room and they started making references to stuff, I don't know that I would fit in as well as I fit into this room, and yet I don't belong here at all. Essentially I have been raised to fit in anywhere, and yet I fit in specifically nowhere. There isn't a group that I specifically adhere to or where I believe I fit in. At Yale they have a Nordic Society, which is a group that generates knowledge about Nordic countries and puts on fun events for that purpose. At one of their events during my sophomore year I met a cute guy who was going to go to the Nordic Society at Yale party. I thought, well, I'll go with him to this party and I'll get in touch with my people, with a capital P. I walked into the room and I couldn't have felt less comfortable. I felt like I absolutely didn't fit in. It really was a strange sense of, well, then where is my group? Where is the group that I can relate to? Where is the culture that can be mine, one that I can embrace?

I believe my place is sort of in the future but that it's coming. When I discuss this in my one-woman show, people come up to me afterward with completely different stories than mine, but saying they know exactly how I feel. They, too, have had the sense that we live in the global ... that it is more and more the norm that our group is becoming the cultural corroboration, our group is the cornucopia of ethnicities. I believe that is an irreversible trend as countries blend, and people keep mixing races and mixing cultures; it is going to be the way we are all moving. We're equipped to handle that, I think, but for right now, people really do like to define and categorize other people. Perhaps it is the nature of the way the human brain works. In my opinion, we're going to have to start adjusting soon. It is not so simple anymore to categorize other people in a superficial way as the human race continues in the vein that it is going.

How do you explain that kind of existence that you talk about?

It's like when you ask me about religion. I don't think that it is possible to define that in anything but a paragraph, so I don't generally do it, unless I am with somebody who is truly interested and we have the time. It's enough to basically tell them about my family, basically saying that I have nine brothers and sisters, and six of them are adopted from all over the world. I have found that it helps. I keep baby pictures in my log and in my day runner, so people can take a look at them and it is so much easier to understand when you can see pictures. I think that helps people a lot to understand who I am.

Often it comes from ... the woman who I share my dressing room with in the show *Xanadu*. She's African American ... I think ... we have known each other six weeks or maybe eight weeks now, and throughout this time there have been a lot of references to music, especially cultural stuff that I have understood or laughed at or appreciated with her. She has been surprised that I can relate to what she is saying. Once I showed her the pictures of my family, I could tell she understood where I was coming from. That happens to me a lot, that people initially don't understand why this white girl understands the nuances in different cultures.

In *Shafrika, The White Girl* it often comes down to the idea of assumptions that we make about each other. In looking at me, I couldn't be paler and I couldn't be blonder and you wouldn't think that I possess the sort of cultural knowledge and tastes that I do. I'm reading an article that was in the *New York Times* magazine about Native American cultures and how they are sadly being more and more diluted and how the new generations don't want to learn the language. In the article, the author highlighted a woman who is as much Native American as a lot of people are these days. She might be an eighth or a sixteenth but doesn't actually look Native American. (I think she is part German, and appears pale with blonde hair.) But she has the gift to speak the language of a particular tribe, and so she goes around teaching it to other Native Americans who lost their language. The elders hire her to teach it especially to the young people. It is always a bit of a struggle for her to prove her Native Americanness to the young ones who look Native American but don't want to embrace the culture; and here she is not only embracing the culture but perpetuating it for them.

Your experience has given you a sense of rhythm within many different cultures outside your native culture, which leads me to ask if you have had room to take an interest in your Norwegian roots?

Yes. There is something so quaint and old worldly about the European connection. My father and my mother, though she wasn't Norwegian, embraced that side of my father, and so we did often celebrate Norwegian traditions. We went to Norway a few times when I was little. I think because especially my mom made a very concerted effort to celebrate all the different cultures that came into the family that was one of the many cultures that we celebrated. She bought flags of every country that everybody was from, and Norway was one of the flags ... we had a little row of flags in our home. So, yes, I certainly love Norway, but I don't feel like I connect with it anymore than I connect when I see stuff on TV or hear about a Norwegian movie or a Norwegian celebration that's coming around. I find myself interested in it to the same degree that I find myself interested in hearing about a Vietnamese movie or a Cambodian festival or a soul food restaurant because these were all the different cultures that I was interested in growing up. So even knowing that Norway is the country that is mine particularly, specifically, by birth, I don't know if I really feel a connection to it to any greater degree than I feel a connection to countries of my brothers' and sisters' birth.

Here is an interesting story. I went back to Norway last summer with a group of friends because we had an invitation from a Norwegian friend of ours who we had been working with. I had an extraordinary time, and in so many ways I had similar feelings as I did when I was in Norway during my childhood. I remembered the food and the traditions. What I wanted to do mostly on this visit was to go dancing. On the last night we were in Norway, some friends of mine threw us a going-away party, and it was supposed to be followed by going out to clubs and dancing but everybody was too tired and nobody wanted to go dancing. I was belligerent, so I went by myself. I was told that it was safe in Oslo, and, besides, it was midsummer when the sun never really sets so even though it was midnight it really appeared only to be dusk outside. My friends told me of three places to check out for fun dancing. I went to each one, and I didn't like the music they were playing. I'm pretty particular about the kind of music that I'll dance to. So I kept wandering, because I didn't want to admit defeat.

I finally passed a club and I loved the music ... the music was hot, kind of a combination of hip hop, reggae, and a little bit of a Latin feel. So I went in, and there was nobody on the dance floor. The place was empty, so I went up to the bar and had another glass of liquid courage, because I don't mind dancing by myself but I need a little good wine in me before I do that. So I had a glass of wine, and they were playing *Crazy* by Gnarls Barkley, which was hot at that time and was one of my favorite songs at that moment. I squealed, and I jumped onto the dance floor and I just started dancing by myself, and I danced a good forty-five minutes to an hour before the dance floor slowly got more and more filled.

I'm a performer. We don't care what people think about us ... especially strangers in a foreign land. I got over that right around graduating from high school. So I danced and danced and I realized suddenly that the dance floor was crowded because I had been in my own little world. Then, I looked around me and I realized I was the only white person in the room. There are maybe a handful of people of color in the whole country; there were more people of color in that room than I had seen in the country in the two weeks I had been there. I sort of laughed out loud and thought, leave it to me ... to find the one place in the whole country where I am the only white person in the room. But I had the best time that night dancing and dancing within a rainbow colored room. I walked back that night after I closed down the club, it was 3:30 in the morning, and the sun had been rising, it was midsummer and it was that far north, and I just was thinking how extraordinary the night was and how much fun it was, and how it was going to have to be the conclusion of my one-woman show.

What in your opinion put you in that rainbow-filled room that night?

It was not that I had grown up in the family I grew up in that had put me in that room, because that wasn't what made me choose the club that I did and that wasn't what made the people who were dancing in the club with me come dance with me. It wasn't that ... it wasn't a conscious choice. It was culture, it was music, and it was the environment.

In the elementary school that my parents sent us to, I was surrounded by kids who liked R&B and hip hop. That was when my taste in music was defined and that was when I learned to sing the way that I did. I sing with a little bit of an R&B, pop flavor, so in the groups and in the shows that I have been cast in, I bring that flavor. So it was not a direct path, but an indirect path. Because I love the music that I do and because I love to dance the way that I do to the music that I do, that's what sent me into that club that night. The great hope is that you don't have to come from a family like mine to be able to breach that cultural gap. There are lots of people out there who love music and culture that is not the culture they were born into. There's hope for all of us to find quite literally racial harmony. You can't go back and change whether or not you were raised in a family like mine, but you can use the cultural piece that you have to meet people you wouldn't ordinarily, necessarily be put in a room with. *But you can put yourself into those rooms.*

What has made you so open minded? Is it because you are an actor? Or is it that you are courageous to be in touch with your feelings?

No, I think that coming from our family you absolutely have to be racially and ethnically open-minded, and then that tends to extend itself to other kinds of open-mindedness.

Was it a struggle for you to define your identity as a white female given that you were the minority among your siblings?

With me, the struggle wasn't so much my racial identity. I think that it was when I sort of left the shelter of my family and Cambridge and was at college that I began to reckon with identity issues. That's when I realized that there would be assumptions made about me because of the way I looked. I think for me as a child it wasn't so much my racial identity or my ethnic identity as much as it was about my *individual* identity, especially being one of ten children.

I found more consistently that I wanted my own personal identity, particularly because I have a biological sister who is only three years younger than me and who looks generally about the same age as me. People could never tell us apart. So my sister, Britta, and I often got confused for each other, because we were the white kids. It didn't help that we didn't have stories as interesting as our adopted siblings had. For me it wasn't necessarily that I was white, it was that I wasn't adopted and didn't have an interesting war orphan story. I was born out of my mother's womb, and nobody wants to hear that story. The adopted kids got lots more attention, not because of their race but because they were adopted and because that was much more interesting story-wise. I just wanted to be thought of as my own person, not someone that was continually misidentified with Britta, in any kind of way. That was why, for me, I was determined that I'm going to sing, and I'm going to sing loud, and you're going to hear that I can sing, and I'm going to perform for you, and that's how you'll know that I am different, and that's how I'll stand out, and that's how people will know my name.

In the theater world I am very particular about people spelling my name right, and in general they are very careful because of our union rules about spelling our names right in the program and in pictures that are in the front of the theater, but backstage often wardrobe will get our names wrong and they have to put our names into all of our costumes and our shoes and on our socks and if my name gets spelled wrong because people often spell "Larsen" as L–a–r–s–o–n and if it is not spelled with an "e–n" I get very irate. And I will get my own sharpie and I will change it. I will fix it in everything, because that little girl in me needs people to know her name right. And so I make sure Anika Larsen is spelled right in all my costumes.

And we'll make sure it's spelled right in the book!

Oh, you better!

Would you endorse transracial adoption?

Oh yes, absolutely, for obvious reasons. They are the kids that need homes, and I think that supersedes everything. That is the most important thing to provide these children with homes. I can think of so many reasons to adopt transracially, and no really valid reasons not to do it. I suppose the objections would be that because the world doesn't understand, and that it will be easier for kids to be raised by people who look like them. I just don't think that the problems are large enough to outweigh the benefits. I think that certainly in so many ways children like me and my brothers and sisters have a greater awareness and understanding of cultural and ethnic and racial differences. In terms of other people's views, I think that it helps even those who are not raised in families like ours to see how easily this kind of harmony can be achieved. I think that not only through adoption but through people of different races getting together and having babies that it's the way the world is moving and it's irreversible. In my opinion, any of the issues that people think they might have in raising an interracial family, I think they are going to become less and less important … less divisive, less critical.

In the adoption world, I so often hear the term "color-blind" used when addressing how to view the transracially adopted child. What is your view on that term?

Yes, that is for sure. I don't think there is any reason not to adopt interracially, but I do think there are considerations that have to be thought of before you do. I don't think it is probably a great idea to do it if you are a white family adopting a kid of any other color and you are going to raise them in an all-white area. I think that that means you've got to think it through a little bit more because it is important for these kids if people look like them in their immediate family; and then to not have others that look like them in their immediate neighborhood and city would probably make it harder for these kids.

Clearly people would never make this decision lightly, but if you're going to do the interracial adoption thing then you have to think hard about where you live and about the resources that you'll have in terms of helping your kids. Adoption comes with so many issues layered on top. In terms of being "color-blind," I don't think "color-blind" is the goal and I don't think that it's realistic either. I don't think it is true that you don't see their color. Certainly you get beyond the point where their color is their most salient characteristic and you see just simply who they are and the person who you love, but race is always there. It isn't something we should pretend isn't there. There seems to be sort of an element of shame, if it is something that we're trying to ignore. I don't think that that's it at all. I think we should see it as one of the many things we love about a person, and that we embrace that they are different, we embrace that they have a different color. Often growing up in Cambridge they loved to say that this country isn't a melting pot, we don't want everybody to be poured into one big pot together and all end up looking like the same stew. It's that we're a salad, and we want all the different ingredients of the salad to come together and they maintain their own identity but they each help make the salad a better salad than it would be without all the different ingredients.

Society hasn't figured out yet as well as it could the importance of making the salad better. We're having a hard time integrating. You're white in your family, and you were willing to struggle for your individuality and at the same time extend yourself to your siblings from places all over the world. That is remarkable to me.

I don't know if it is. Because when you are born into something, you don't question it. It was the norm for me growing up to be surrounded by people who looked different from me, so I wasn't able to cultivate that xenophobia that people who live in isolation do. For me, almost all hatred comes from a lack of exposure. I really think it is hard to actually meet people and know people who are different from you, and still hate them. The more we remain isolated, the easier it is for people to perpetuate racism and prejudice. Again, I do think that as the world gets smaller it is more and more inevitable that races and cultures are going to mix more and more and it's going to be harder to judge people or to dislike people based on their race.

It is sort of sad, but I think there is an instinct in humans, something like "survival of the fittest," where whatever way people need to find their footing above other people, so if it's not going to be race they are going to find some other characteristic. We have so many problems in the world right now based on religious intolerance, it seems like there's this need for intolerance in order to … I don't know what it is. But it all comes from an anger, so I don't think that race really is it … I think that is what it is for now, and I think that if there's a day when everybody is comfortable and happy and has enough food and enough shelter in their life, that is when it is going to be a lot easier to confront any of these issues.

As long as you are suffering you are going to want to blame it on somebody and it is easy to blame it on people who don't look like you or people you have never met. There is a lot more that we need to deal with … socioeconomic inequality, the devastating poverty that people live in. They say in the Middle East the unemployment rate is sky-high, 50 percent or something. If you don't have any hope, if you don't have any future, you're not on any track to anywhere, you don't have a nice house to protect, and it is a whole lot easier to strap bombs onto your body and go and kill yourself for nothing. It's just a whole lot easier to fight, to hate, to pick up a gun if you don't have anything ...

How is your relationship with your siblings today?

Well, I have nine of them so it would be hard to generalize about nine people. It is certainly different with each one. On the whole in our family, I'm not sure why, the girls have always tended to be tighter than the boys, and they have been a little bit more scattered. But for the most part there's a core eight of us at this point who are really pretty tight and show up at every family event. It doesn't actually seem too hard for us to stay in touch. When it comes to e-mail ... hitting that "reply all" button certainly makes it easier to stay in people's lives. It is a lot of people to keep up with. It doesn't feel like much of an effort. It is a good group of people. For instance, today I'm going to do my matinee, and my mom and two of my sisters are coming to see the show. It really helps that we are mostly still in the Northeast ... either in Boston or New York and then in Chicago. I love my family.

DAVID'S SIBLINGS

WE LEARNED from *In Their Own Voices* that **David T. Adams** was a screenwriter, educator, husband, and father of four. David was born in June 1970 in Hartford, Connecticut. He spent his childhood and adolescent years in a predominantly white and close-knit community. From 1979 to 1992, David attended private Christian institutions in the Midwest. Thrust between the Dutch community, where he was raised, and the black community, to which he was ethnically linked, David grappled with finding harmony within himself.

After remaining in foster care for three months, David was adopted into the Adams family. The couple were in their early twenties and socially compassionate. Largely influenced by the civil rights movement, they believed it was their responsibility, as well as their personal desire, to adopt one of society's abandoned children. Initially they preferred to adopt a black child, but the social worker handling the case encouraged them to consider adopting a biracial child as a way to reduce the awkwardness the child may feel living in a white family. So they adopted a biracial son.

He was raised a middle child in Sioux Center, Iowa, along with his two brothers. The only African American in his family, David grew up protected from the harshness of racial prejudices. As a youth, his interests focused on spending time with friends and having fun. Though he knew that he was physically different, David saw his brown skin as a welcomed novelty among peers and family members. Not until he was in his late teens did he recognize that the color of his skin merely touched the surface of the African American heritage and experience.

In the span of time tracing more than twenty years between his rearing in Sioux Center and living as an adult in similar towns but across the country in northwestern Washington State, David has learned that there is value in learning and appreciating his ethnic heritage and teaching his children about their diverse heritages. Still, he reported that, ultimately, what matters most, and what people judge him on, is not race but his work and his personality. In addition to making his family a priority, David continues to nurture the Indie Film Group which he founded in 1998 to educate young filmmakers about the trade and offer networking opportunities to them with more experienced and well-known professionals in the field.

The following interviews are with David's siblings, Chuck Adams and Mike Adams.

CHUCK ADAMS

SHEBOYGAN, WISCONSIN
AUGUST 2006

Chuck Adams, who is 37, is the oldest sibling of three in the Adams family. He is two years older than David. Chuck received his B.A. in English from Dordt College in Sioux Center, Iowa, and later his J.D. He is a lawyer, married to Kimberly, and they have three children; Jesse, 12; Micah, 9; and Hannah, 6. Chuck and his wife are raising their family in the Christian Reformed denomination. He describes their economic status as upper middle class. Today Chuck has a good relationship with both brothers, but he says that because they all live relatively far away from one another and are also very busy, they do not see one another very often. When they do, they get along very well.

Chuck, tell me about the town of Sheboygan, where you live. How big is it, and what is another major city located nearby?

Sheboygan, Wisconsin, is a town of about fifty thousand people and is located approximately an hour north of Milwaukee, right on Lake Michigan.

Do you also work in Sheboygan?

Yes, I am an assistant attorney for the city of Sheboygan.

What are your responsibilities?

We joke in our office about how we divide the work load: I do all the things that involve going to court and my boss does all the things that involve going to meetings. Granted, that is not quite true, but I focus a lot of my time on the prosecution end of things. I do a lot of the work as it relates to the police and the fire department, building inspections, zoning, and administration matters within Sheboygan.

Tell me about your family.

My wife, Kim, is a teacher, although she is a stay-at-home mom right now. She taught for six years. We have three kids, all in grade school now. Jesse is going into seventh grade, Micah is going into fourth, and Hannah will be in the first grade. We attend a Christian Reformed Church, and the kids all go to Christian schools. My wife and I have not strayed too far from how we were raised. Kim is Dutch. She, too, was raised in a traditional Dutch community, even though both of us have some traits that set us a little outside the Dutch community. For me, it is not being ethnically Dutch and having lived on the East Coast for a period of time. As for Kim, she grew up in a broken family. Still, we both consider ourselves part of that Dutch community. My dad says that he considers himself "adopted Dutch."

Where were you born?

Hartford, Connecticut. My parents had just moved there months before. My dad had recently graduated from college. The Vietnam War was going on, and yet it was early enough that if you were planning to have a child and working in the defense industry, you did not get drafted. My dad chose to work in the defense industry and start a family. And, as the story is told, shortly after their move to Connecticut, I was born.

My dad worked for Pratt & Whitney Aircraft Company. That is why they moved from New Jersey, where both my mom and dad originated, to Connecticut. That is also how they got connected with the Christian Reformed Church (CRC).

My dad's family had become Christians through attending Sunday school in the Orthodox Presbyterian Church (OPC). My mom grew up in a Roman Catholic tradition and attended a Roman Catholic Church. So when my mom and dad moved to Connecticut, they were referred by their former OPC pastor to the Christian Reformed Church because of its close ties with the Orthodox Presbyterian Church at the time.

A few years after my parents made the move to Connecticut, my dad decided to leave his career in the defense industry and go into teaching. His goal in life was to teach at Dordt College [Sioux Center, Iowa], which is a liberal arts institution affiliated with the Christian Reformed denomination. He was told that the best way to do that was to teach high school first. That's when our family went back to New Jersey, where my dad was about to teach high school for a few years and earn his master's degree. Eight years later, he took a position at Dordt College and we left New Jersey to go to Iowa.

What type of community is Dordt located in?

Dordt is in the middle of a cornfield in the middle of Iowa.

Do you recall the differences between the communities in Connecticut and New Jersey and in Sioux Center, Iowa, that you lived in?

The Christian school I attended in New Jersey was fairly diverse ethnically. We had a large number of African American and Hispanic kids who attended that school. Most of the non-white kids there lived in Patterson, New Jersey, which was the nearby big city. Those kids were bussed in. The white kids came from a variety of economically diverse communities. When you are little, like in kindergarten, first grade, or second grade, one doesn't tend to notice racial differences. It seems as though everybody mixed together. One of my good friends in elementary school was African American. His name was Mike. I remember that I liked to touch Mike's hair because it was different than my brother's hair; Mike's hair had even tighter curls than David's. Other than that, I didn't really notice racial differences, for example, until I got a little older like in fourth and fifth grade. All of a sudden it seemed that things began to change as people in my age group and grade merged with the older kids in higher grades. That's when I noticed that the white kids would hang out with the white kids, and the black kids would hang out with the black kids. Where you tried to break away from the mold, you would get flack from some people. Again, with my friend Mike, I would hang around with him in class but outside of class, when the older kids were around, he didn't really want to hang out with me, because his [black] friends would tell him he shouldn't be hanging out with "that [white] kid."

Then in the 1980s, when we moved to Sioux Center, Iowa, that community was as white and Dutch as it could be. There were people riding around with bumper stickers that said "If you ain't Dutch, you ain't much." My brother David and his friend Daniel were probably the only two black people that half the people in Sioux Center had ever seen in their lives, other than on television. Sioux Center was really more of a rural community. At that time there were maybe a few refugees that moved into the community, but that was pretty much the only diversity in that community.

Did you ever bring up to your parents the visible differences between both communities, or was it "go with the flow"?

I think in some ways it was "go with the flow." I don't think that I asked my parents questions like that. I was a big reader. My way of dealing with the differences was to read as much as I could. I was interested about knowing different places all over the world. I liked reading history books and geography books, etcetera. Growing up in my home there were certain books that were required reading. My parents were academic-type people. So you read off of the required reading list.

Being the oldest child in your family, do you remember your parents telling you their reasons for adopting?

Yes. My parents were very concerned about race relations. They discussed that regularly. One of the books on my parents' required reading list was called *Edgar Allen*. It's a book about a little black boy who was adopted by a family in the South. After reading the book, asking my parents if that's why they decided to adopt David? They indicated to me, "Not exactly, but that book probably had some impact on our thought process." I do think that, for them, a lot had to do with their wanting to adopt a child. They didn't need to. It was not like they could not have children on their own. I think that they thought that adoption would be a responsible thing for them to do, to provide a home for a child that was in need of a home. Going through that process, I think that my parents had an interest in adopting transracially.

In terms of age, you were close to both your brothers. Is it reasonable to say that you were also close to David on a personal level, where you could discuss race and other intimate issues with him?

David and I did talk. But my brother, Mike, was actually only nine months younger than Dave, so they were closer. I was the older one by a couple of years. Those two were at times thick as thieves because of their close ages. We used to joke that they would like to gang up on me because the two of them could get one of me. To some extent David and I did talk, especially after moving to Iowa. I don't remember talking about those intimate types of things in New Jersey with David. True, I thought about racial issues in New Jersey but mostly in relation to my friend, not my brother.

What triggered your thinking about race and adoption in Iowa?

I thought about race issues more in Iowa because, like I said, David and his friend Dan were the only black kids in the whole town. Also, I think because of certain events that happened to me, I thought about racial issues. I remember getting into fights with kids who would call David derogatory names because of how he looked. In high school I talked with David about a few sensitive issues. A lot of times he would not necessarily bring them up, but my mom would tell me about things that were going on with him. I remember when David was fired from a job at a grocery store. I don't know what happened exactly, but he had only been on the job for a fairly short time. It seemed to the rest of the family that he didn't really get a fair break, as we were trying to figure out what was going on. As my mom told it, the manager of the grocery store said to David: "Why don't you go back where you came from?" I remember wanting to go over to that store manager, incensed by what he had said, and telling him that David's ancestry was probably here hundreds of years before his Dutch ancestors came over. And then my mom told me to calm down, which I did. I asked Dave if the story was true, and he told me yes. Incidents like that involving David I remember.

Did you have similar or different interests compared to your brothers?

Even though David is the middle child, I felt in between him and my youngest brother Michael. David is very much into literature, art, and movies.

He is very much an English major kind of person. Michael is an engineer. He is a science type of person. I am in between those two in my interests.

As a family growing up, our attitudes towards things were visibly different. My parents were very strong and outspoken in their beliefs. They were interested in being different. They would say that being a Christian does not mean fitting in but rather being different than the world around you. For example, we celebrated Christmas very differently than everybody around us. We did not get presents or have a Christmas tree. Instead, we had a rock. This Christmas rock! As we got older we predicted that when David got married and had kids he would have a Christmas tree and have all the presents and trappings; Mike wouldn't do any of it; and I would be somewhere in between, which actually turned out to be somewhat true. My brothers and I had some similar interests—music, for instance. That was probably the most common interest that we talked about.

Did having a brother who was African American affect how you perceived your family?

I don't know if it affected the way I saw my family, because I generally did not think of our family other than as fairly normal, or as normal as anybody is. It was more when people outside my family would make comments about how David could possibly be my brother because of his race, or ask me about my "real" brother. That's when I realized that other people did not see my family or my brother the same way I did.

Did you ever wonder who your African American brother would date, especially given the mostly white community where you lived?

I never thought of it until … it must have been in eighth grade. In eighth grade, at the end of the school year, the thing to do was to have a skating party. We went to the skating rink and you know how you are in eighth grade, the boys would want to skate with the girls and the girls would want to skate with the boys. This was a big deal then. Well, Rene, who is biracial and is also adopted into the same family as David's friend Daniel, was in my class. I remember someone saying to me, in fact, that my brother David would have to come to the skating party. When I asked him why, he said, "Well, so that Rene would have somebody to skate with." It took me a second to understand what he was saying. Then I said to him that she should be able to skate with anybody she wanted to. At that point he backed away so as to not get into an argument with me.

What is your relationship like with your siblings today as an adult?

I have a good relationship with both my brothers, but it is probably not as close as I would like it to be with either one of them.

To what do you attribute the relationship with your brothers not being as close as you would like?

I attribute it to the geographical distances between us and our busy schedules. David lives in Washington State, so I very rarely get to see him. Mike is very busy.

When we do see one another, we get along great. Last summer we all got together in Minnesota. My parents rented a cabin and arranged for David to fly out, because he has to travel so far with a family. One night, I think we were up at three in the morning talking about stuff from our childhoods, etcetera. My wife, Kim, was not part of the discussion, but the other two wives were. It was an enjoyable time. We didn't always agree on how we saw certain things. Although we get along, we are not the traditional close family where you are calling each other every day to see how things are going.

Do you communicate regularly with your parents and extended relatives?

It is the same thing with my parents. Some people are sort of shocked. I talk with my parents maybe once every month or six weeks. People question why I don't get along with them. To the contrary, I do get along with my parents but it is just that we don't spend a lot of time "gabbing on the phone." We do e-mail each other and send pictures back and forth. As for my extended family, I have some that live around here in Sheboygan. My grandmother lives in a little town about ten to fifteen miles from here as well as a couple of my aunts and uncles. A cousin is on the police force in Sheboygan. I talk with him frequently and also work with him. I probably talk with my relatives more than I do my immediate family.

Do you know if your brother David is close with his extended family?

One of the people in the family that is sort of the one my brothers and all the cousins really look up to is my uncle "Bud." He is my dad's younger brother, so he is halfway in age between my brothers and me and my dad. He is just the kind of guy who is open to talk about a variety of things. I know that certainly it is true that David and his wife, Shari, talk with Bud (and Bud's wife, Angela) more than they talk with my parents, and I do, too. I would not be surprised if Mike and Kim did also. It is not so much that we are not close to our parents; rather it is really nice to have an uncle close to our age. In fact, I am finding that some of my younger cousins who are in about the same age range as me relate like I do with Uncle Bud; we seem to have that same kind of relationship.

Given your background, are you supportive of transracial adoption?

Yes. I would say that I am supportive of transracial adoption. But if I were to adopt transracially, I would do some things differently than my parents did.

What would you do differently?

I would not live in Sioux Center, Iowa. Although I can't really say it was a bad decision on my parents' part because living there and working at Dordt

College was a goal in their lives. So I don't want to state it negatively, but I would not want to live in Sioux Center because it is too small, it's too parochial. I would have a hard time bringing an African American child to a community like that.

I would probably try in a different way than they did to encourage connections with whatever ethnic community that the child was a part of. My parents did it but in a very academic way. The required reading given by my parents to us kids always included books on black history. But there was for the most part an absence in cultural activities.

If you and your wife adopted transracially, what are some of the things that your parents did that you would incorporate in your family structure?

One thing my parents encouraged that I was happy about was their interest in learning about other communities. Case in point: Dave and I, when we were in high school, took a mission trip to Rosalind, Chicago. The cool thing about it was that most groups when they do something like that simply live in the church or a center. When our group went, we actually lived with mostly African American families in the host church. I don't know why that decision was made … whether it was because David was in our group or if it was because it was good for all of us. Regardless, it was an excellent opportunity! I would encourage that sort of activity in my own family. In fact, if I had an African American child, I am not sure that I would stay in Sheboygan. It might be wiser to move to a place like Milwaukee, where it is even more racially and ethnically diverse.

Here is an interesting story that happened when we were in Chicago. One day we got on a city bus on 108th and Michigan. We were going downtown. It was sort of an unusual thing. Here we are, all these white kids boarding on the bus in the middle of Rosalind. A black man, who was already on the bus, was talking to himself and the people around him. "Look at all these white people. Where are they coming from?!" And then my brother was actually the last one in line to get up on the bus. This same fellow looks at him, and says, "Look they got a brown one with them!" I just remember laughing.

It sort of fit the scenario. To that guy on the bus, my brother didn't really fit in with us but he didn't fit in with him, either. I think that there was always a little bit of that with David. I think that the way David ended up defaulting is that he does better with a Dutch white community than he does with an African American community. I don't know if it is a bad thing or a good thing. It is just the way it is.

Did you ever feel that David, because he was adopted, received more attention from your parents than you did?

No, I don't think that he got more attention. He probably got away with some things that I didn't, but, then again, so did Mike. I don't know that it is based on his being adopted or race. I think it has more to do with my parents doing things a certain way when the oldest kid came along, and then when they got around to the second kid they maybe thought they didn't need to be quite so tough.

As far as David goes, as a kid, I sometimes thought that, outside of our family, the wrong kid seemed to always be the black kid, and that David didn't care about that perception. In my opinion, I thought my brother was too flippant about issues like that. I thought he was too willing to make himself into a stereotype. He would see certain stereotypes of black people on television and would act like them. I would tell him that he did not want to be a stereotype but to be himself, whatever that was. But he liked to get attention, and for him that was a good way to get attention.

Does the fact that you were raised with an African American brother give you an added advantage personally and professionally as an assistant attorney?

It gives me a different perspective, yes. I think that a lot of white folks, even if they were raised to understand that racism exists, have not always had the opportunity to experience it. Even though I didn't experience racism directly, I saw it and it was personal to me—from things as stupid as calling persons derogatory names because of race. I could see from the way that David was treated by people sometimes that race was clearly an issue, even from people who weren't what you would call "racist," people who didn't outwardly hate other people from other races but just were ignorant, not knowing what they were talking about.

I think I do have an understanding of that and try to deal with that within myself. As a prosecutor, I understand that there is such a thing as "driving while black." When African American people talk to me about their tickets, and say it is partly because they are black, I think I am better able and perhaps more willing than some white people would be to actually engage in a conversation about why they think that. If I disagree with their conclusion, I'm willing to talk to them about why I believe the way I do in that particular case. What I am told is that a lot of folks won't even talk about issues relating to race.

It sounds as though your experience of being part of a transracially adoptive family gave you more freedom to talk about issues of race.

Yes. That is probably true.

Where does David live now, and is the community ethnically diverse?

David lives in Lynden, Washington. It is anything but diverse. It is a white, Dutch town.

He seems to have leaned toward the type of community where his parents raised him.

Yes, it is. I joke sometimes that David may look part black, but in some ways he is as Dutch and as white as they come. Obviously he has been affected by the fact that he is part African American and has had some experiences relating to that. But in some ways he is more Dutch than I am.

As an adult, have you ever had a personal conversation with David about some of the issues he may be confronting behind the scenes because of his dual identities?

This past summer we had some discussions. It seems to me that a lot of his concerns are based more on his looking back to his childhood and adolescent years. I actually think that now, when he looks back at things that happened, he perhaps understands that he didn't always take those issues as seriously as he should have and maybe wishes that he had done so at the time. He realizes that he may have lost something significant because of his choices then. As a result of that, I think he is more negative now than when you interviewed him for *In Their Own Voices* about things that happened to him growing up. I think my brother recognizes that his issues weren't all attributed to the fact that we lived in Sioux Center and that my parents were more academic kind of people and that the way they dealt with issues was to hand you a book to read. I think that he recognizes that he himself played a role in fostering some of the issues that affect him today.

The good thing is that David has not lost all his personality. He still likes to trick people occasionally in a fun kind of way, and that is a good thing. I think it is even in the first book that you interviewed him in that his oldest son, Luke, likes to tell people that he is African American. He doesn't look it at all. He is a white, Dutch kid with blonde curls in his hair. I think that Dave likes to rebel in that. But, to some extent, that is about all there is.

I know that when David and his wife, Shari, first lived in Lynden and they moved away for awhile, there were some racial issues then. I don't think that Shari's family was all that thrilled about their daughter marrying a black guy. I know that Lynden, as he described it, was in some ways more difficult to navigate at that time than Sioux Center, because at least Sioux Center was a college town. I think that in a college town there seems to be somewhat broader thinking, and Lynden did not have that mind-set. I do think things have changed a little bit there for the better. Like in Sioux Center, I am thinking that Lynden is a little bit more racially and ethnically diverse, not so much with African Americans but with Hispanics moving in. That has changed the dynamics, and the locals are tending to understand that there are people from different cultures.

To go back to something you mentioned earlier, why do you think David felt the need to act in a stereotypical way?

One thing that made things difficult for David, I think, is that, even though he is very intelligent and did well in school by normal standards, he did not do as well by the Adams family standards. Mike and I were both straight A students. He was an A–/B+ student, which should be more than enough. But I think sometimes he felt like he was competing with us academically. And because my parents were very academic-minded people, I sometimes thought that he didn't think he measured up.

When I used to complain about his acting up stereotypically, it could have been partly a result of his thinking, well hey, I'm not as good as these guys because I don't get straight A's like they do. I don't know how we could have done anything differently to help him other than to encourage him in doing well at the things that he was good at. David is an excellent writer, the best one in the family (although everyone in our family writes well). He is probably the best teacher of the three of us. But I think that is something that impacted him. I don't know if it is a race issue or a family issue or whether all families deal with those types of things and race becomes an added dimension.

You have a beautiful wife and three children, a distinguished career, and you were impacted by transracial adoption. Where do you take that?

I guess that I try to instill in my kids that while race matters, they should see themselves first as humans, not as white or black, etcetera. I don't agree with people who say that we should become a "colorless" society, because a colorless society is simply all black and white and that is kind of boring. I want my kids to see that there are all sorts of races and ethnicities and that there are components that are really great about that. I want them to get the fact that God created all different cultures and all different races in the world. He wanted it to be that way; and it is a good thing. When people start believing that one group is better than the other group, I think that is taking what God created and destroying it. We should be saying that racial and ethnic diversity are all great things. There's nothing wrong with the fact that my kids are half Dutch; if they want to go "Clompen" dancing, fine. I probably won't go, but they can. My point is that my kids shouldn't think of themselves as being somehow better than someone else as a result of their race or heritage.

What would your recommendation be for white parents adopting children of color and living in such places as Sioux Center or a community that is predominately white to connect with the black community?

I think these parents have to try to find connections where they exist. Within the Christian Reformed Church and community, it can be quite difficult to make connections with people in the black community, but it is not impossible. The CRC denomination has a significant number of urban churches, especially in Chicago (Illinois) and Grand Rapids (Michigan). It would seem to me that you would build from connections there. You have to work at it. You try to find people you can be faithful with.

Like myself, I would not even live in a place like Sioux Center given my goals, but if that is what another family wants, then I think they have to work harder at finding those connections that are good for the family members and communicate the importance for their family to reach out to diverse groups of people. I think my parents did that to the best of their abilities. First of all things have changed, in that transracial adoptions (maybe not white and black transracial adoptions) are much more common. I think there are more opportunities for parents who have children from different racial and ethnic backgrounds than their own to do more creative things in making connections to their child's ethnic communities.

Would you be opposed to any one of your children dating or marrying a person of color?

No, I would have no opposition to that at all.

Is it fair to say that your mind-set has been fostered by your experience living in a transracial adoptive home?

Yes, that is very true.

MIKE ADAMS

SIOUX FALLS, SOUTH DAKOTA
AUGUST 2006

Mike Adams is the youngest sibling of the Adams family. He was born one year after his parents adopted David. At age 35 he is an engineer and business owner. He received a B.A. in mechanical engineering at Dordt College in Sioux Center, Iowa. Mike and his wife, Kim, are raising their five children—Kinsley, 8; Justus, 6; Mason and Malia, 4; and Josiah, one and a half in a Christian home in Sioux Falls, South Dakota. Though their five children are all biological, Mike and his wife are very interested in adopting. Regarding his relationship with his brothers, Mike says that all three of them were close growing up. He did note, however, that he and David had different interests: David was more interested in music, and he was interested in sports. Even though Mike and David did not do a lot together, especially in high school, they still protected each other. All three of the Adams brothers attended the same college.

Mike, where are you living now, and tell me a little about your family.

I live in Sioux Falls, South Dakota, which is an hour away from where I grew up in Sioux Center, Iowa, with my brother Dave and family. I went to Dordt College in Sioux Center for engineering, where I also met my wife, Kim, who was majoring in psychology. Actually, we met in high school; she was a junior and I was a senior. We were married in college, and after graduation we moved to Sioux Falls. It wasn't until seven years later that we had kids.

I was working as an engineer for a company close to where we lived. We had Kinsley, she's eight now, and then Justus followed twenty months later, and he's six, and then we had the twins, Mason and Malia, and then Josiah. Both my wife and I are family-oriented so it keeps us close to home; especially being near to Grandma and Grandpa who live in Sioux Center is a plus for our kids.

What is your lifestyle like within your immediate family?

Our lives are centered on church, family, and work for me. My wife home-schools; we started that a year ago. (That wasn't something that we were going to do initially, but yet I think it defines us as being a bit out there.) We really like the Christian school in town, but it was just something my wife felt led to do.

From the work side, I ended up buying a couple of manufacturing plants from my previous employer. They were getting out of the market, that's a transition for me that happened in 2004. That keeps us busy. One of the things my wife and I gained from our education at Dordt College is the understanding of our vocation and calling. Dordt, like Calvin College, which is also rooted in the Christian Reformed faith, gave us a good foundation to move forward. It taught us the value of integrating our Christian beliefs and worldview with work and family. That's one of the things that I value and try to do in terms of living that out every day. I told you we were going to the First Evangelical Free Church in Sioux Falls here. We are pretty involved.

Going back to when you were raised in Sioux Center, Iowa, tell me about what you remember life was like there. Is there a connection between the values your family encouraged growing up and those you hold today?

Oh, there is no doubt. I think it is very defining. My parents were very reformational thinkers. They challenged authority. They are professors, kind of scholarly. Everything that they did they really thought about and tried to apply the lens of scripture to it. That doesn't mean they were perfect, but they really made an attempt to try to discern and not just go with the flow. I would say that was very defining. I see that in Dave as well, in terms of not just accepting the status quo but challenging things and thinking for yourself.

Clearly Sioux Center was a community where there were a lot of Dordt professors, and so in that micro-community that fit very well; although we were probably not necessarily mainstream. We didn't always do things that all the other kids did, but, on the other hand, Sioux Center was also a very protective community. It was primarily people that were Christians and trying to live that out in their lives. Sioux Center was a very clean town to grow up in as a kid; we weren't exposed to a lot of junk. There was not a lot of diversity, either. There's more now.

You were born a year after Dave was adopted into your family?
Exactly.

At some point did you ever come to the realization where you thought, wow, I have an African American brother, and did you ever ask what that meant for you?
No. Dave was always my brother Dave. I never saw him as black, per se. That doesn't mean that I disrespected that he was a different color, but I think maybe because I was younger ... Dave was always there. In general, I never really thought about it a lot.

Do you remember whether your parents ever talked to you about adoption or race and about what that meant as a family?
My recollection is no ... those kind of details ... I am not always a detail-oriented person. But I will say that I don't think that it was very prevalent. Growing up, they had us read *Uncle Tom's Cabin*, and we read about the Underground Railroad and we read about Martin Luther King Jr. and the civil rights movement, but it was almost a little bit by osmosis. In other words, their shelves had a lot of those books on them, and I don't remember how those books ended up being in my reading material, but they did. I would say that I don't remember family meetings around the dinner table where we talked about that at all, but I do remember reading those books, so I think I was sensitive at least to some extent to what Dave may face, though at the same time I am not sure I put the connection of him being African American ... he was my brother Dave. I never processed that as necessarily applying to him.

Since you were so close in age, what were some of the things that you did together?
We played a lot together as little kids, and as we got older, like in grade school, high school, we maybe went to a few track meets or cross-country practices together. But Dave's interests were a lot different than mine. He was very talented in artistic things; he enjoyed music. Sports were not a big interest to Dave. He did do running and so on, but I would say that wasn't really a focus for him. So his group of friends tended to be a lot different than mine; therefore, we didn't do a lot together in high school.

There were definite advantages to having the typical older brother. I can remember we worked at a Hy-Vee grocery store together. I think Dave worked at Hy-Vee first, and he helped me get a job there and kind of showed me the ropes. It sounds insignificant, but when you're a kid it is very significant. Even though we had different friends, he looked out for me in those ways. I think in later years, I was probably the kind of brother that if somebody would have called him a "nigger" or some other derogatory word I would be the first to rush in at that person. It was clear that we protected each other. It wasn't a major theme; it's just part of being brothers.

Was Dave, in your recollection, close with your aunts and uncles?

I don't think there was any difference between Chuck, my older brother, and Dave and I in that we were a pretty good distance … we were out in Iowa … and most of our aunts and uncles were in New Jersey or Wisconsin. So we would go every Thanksgiving to see the Adams clan in Wisconsin. And then we would also go, but not as frequently, to New Jersey and see my mom's side of the family. But because of the distance there, it wasn't like we had an uncle within driving distance. I think with grandparents, aunts, and uncles, they were loving but distant because of geography.

Was your immediate family, growing up, open to having conversations not just about race or adoption but about political issues in general?

Oh yes. I am not sure growing up I was connected to that, but my older brother, Chuck, was more aware probably of political things and had more interest there. My parents would talk about anything. That doesn't mean that you talked about it a lot. Obviously you need some kind of catalyst to talk about it.

But they were open to it?

Oh sure.

Did you grow up in a Dutch traditional family?

No, I wouldn't say our family is a Dutch traditional family.

So you pretty much grew up with Santa Claus and not Saint Nicholas?

Well, we didn't grow up with Santa Claus at all. And that's where … my parents wanted to be different in the right way. Their perspective was: take the lens of scripture and apply it to how we should do things in life. So Santa Claus was out. That was something that was viewed as taking away from Christ and the meaning of Christmas. We didn't get presents at Christmas, and most people would go, "Oh, my goodness!" But it was a point of pride, at least for me, and I think for us, it was a point of pride. My parents felt that that was commercializing Christmas; it wasn't that we didn't respect someone who did have presents, but they felt strongly about what they believed. For Easter you wouldn't find us with Easter eggs, and you wouldn't find us out on Halloween, either.

When you look at the family that you were raised in, the close-knit community you lived in, and the friends you had, did you ever think about race? Did you notice, at church, for example, if any Africans or Hispanics or African Americans were present? Were you sensitive to noticing somebody who was different?

Oh sure. But I didn't think much about it... Something that was very important to my parents, though I don't know that we talked about it a lot, was to be color-blind. I know that living in Sioux Center, growing up in a white community, some people would laugh at that and say, "Well, you don't even know what it means. You don't have the frame of reference to even understand," and that might be true. For instance, I would say that if we did see someone of a different color, our reaction was probably to go out of our way to talk to that person and find out more about them. It was probably a reaction that said we certainly don't see any difference. Dordt would have some people from Nigeria or South Africa, for example, and I remember that. Yet, there still wasn't a lot of diversity. As I was getting older, toward high school, I think there was kind of an influx of kids from Asia being adopted and it was becoming a little more diverse. I don't remember that ever being a big issue.

Do you think that growing up in a racially blended family opened your eyes, for example, if your daughters or your sons were to marry, would it matter to you if they married outside their race and culture?

No, it wouldn't matter at all. The only thing that would really matter is if they are marrying someone who has the same commitment to Jesus Christ.

What was it like going to high school and college with your siblings? All three of you went to the same high school and college, right?

Yes, we did. I think about the teenage years, which were very interesting. Recently, about a year ago, we got together as an extended family. Dave and his family, my brother Chuck and his family, and my parents all went for a week in the summer to a cabin in Minnesota, and we talked a bit about those things that happened during our high school and college years. Back then I really saw Dave as more different than I was ... and this is not related to color. Dave was free-spirited, more apt to hang around with the group that was maybe going to goof off a little bit, whereas I was more driven. At that time I was focused on athletics and studying. Not that I was a goody two shoes, I just was a little more driven in those areas. Dave, because I think he wasn't driven that way, had a little more time on his hands to look around his surroundings and say, "What can I do today?" He used the word "novelty" to describe himself.

Dave was pretty cool; he was an attractive young man, from skin color to build to personality, and he was a fun person to be around. Dave was probably … I would say, a little more laid back, more into having fun and doing things with friends. He was also creative. He would take time to draw and do things that I wouldn't take the time to do. As a teenager, it seemed to me that Dave was very popular among his peers. But talking to him later, on vacation in Minnesota, Dave apparently didn't perceive of himself in that way. That didn't really come out in his interview for *In Their Own Voices*. I don't quite understand it, but he may not have perceived of himself as highly as I did and as I think other people did. So there was a disconnect between how others perceived him and how he saw himself. He may not have had the confidence that I thought he had and, quite frankly, should have had. But who knows? Is that because he was different from us in terms of color? I don't know.

Dave always appeared to me to be socially well-adapted. Matter of fact, I would watch him kind of closely as we started to date—Dave was the guy who had it all down pat. He was well liked. He wouldn't have any problem getting a date, those kinds of things. From the social standpoint, Dave stood out as being very well connected, but that was just my view, what I saw. It seemed like he had a lot of fun, good friends. Maybe he didn't wildly succeed in academics or athletics but he didn't fail, he did fine.

Was there ever a time when you were growing up that you looked at Dave's journey in life and felt that it would be "cool" to live his life for a moment because of his personality, his interests, and his ethnicity and uniqueness?

I would say probably not. I don't think I was jealous, but that doesn't mean I didn't value him.

Would you support transracial adoption, given the relationship that you have maintained with David?

You know that my wife and I have five kids, and children are a big part of our lives and they are such a blessing. We are really interested in adopting. My wife would like to adopt from Africa especially because of the need. One of the things we were also both clear on was that if we were going to adopt it was going to be because of a need … a child in need that didn't have a family. We weren't going to adopt because it was cool. We were only going to adopt because the Lord was calling us to a child somewhere in the world.

We are technically in the adoption process, but I've got my foot on the brake. I support transracial adoption and I think that it is a wonderful thing. But I also feel the burden of asking ourselves: can we raise this child and do a good job of connecting this child to his or her heritage, their culture, and can I do that in Sioux Falls, South Dakota? I am sure the answer is yes, but it is something I am thinking about before we take that jump. I want to make sure that we have a child that doesn't say one day, "That was nice, but here are some things that you missed, Mom and Dad." My wife has strongly felt the call to adopt transracially, and I have felt cautious. Am I cautious because of my brother? Some of his struggle with his identity and so on? I don't know.

Has Dave ever discussed that with you ... the struggles regarding his identity?

Yes.

What was the nature of the conversation?

I think now I would say that it bothered me quite a bit when he shared his struggles with me—the very fact that it was a struggle for him and I never saw it. I felt like, well, where was I? It was such a struggle for him, and I'm his brother, how come I didn't know about that, how come I didn't sense that at all? He seemed to be extremely popular, certainly much more popular than Chuck or me (at least that was what I believed to be true). David, as I said before, seemed very well connected, seemed to be enjoying himself and enjoying life. But in talking to him now, it seems that it was more of a struggle than I had thought. That has bothered me to the point where maybe that is making me pause a little bit. At times I think that maybe I wasn't very perceptive growing up. I was just focused on being a kid and he was my older brother. It was not something that I saw growing up, so that in terms of adopting transracially ourselves, while my wife is feeling the Lord's call there and we are praying about it, I think that is something that I need to work through to be comfortable with that.

How did you react when he came to you with that?

I don't know if he really came to me necessarily. We were having a discussion and he just shared it. I was probably a little shocked because seeing some of his pain was very painful for me. It made me sad to see that he had those struggles, and, well, where was I as a brother? I think I probably said, now Dave that isn't how it was ... and that's not how you were perceived, and boy you were really ... One of the things that I would say that was true was that to me growing up, and he being my older brother by a little bit, he seemed much more confident and in tune with himself than he obviously was. And I didn't perceive the gap.

Now looking at this as an adult, where you see this disconnect between what Dave is saying he felt in the past and what he currently feels, how would you bridge that gap?

I don't know. I am very interested in the work that you are doing. If I just think forward and not about Dave's situation or our immediate family adopting, I would say that the separation that someone who is adopted is going to feel and then the problem of identity is something I want to learn a lot more about, and also about the significance of honoring that person's culture. I would say that I am not very experienced in my understanding on transracial adoption, but I see the significant issues to address in terms of reading the book, *In Their Own Voices*, and talking to you.

PETE'S SIBLING

BORN IN Ithaca, New York, during the late 1960s, to a Nigerian father and a Scottish mother, **Pete** was placed for adoption because of racial pressures forced upon interracial couples and their offspring. In Nigeria, where Pete's biological father would return home as a physician, interracial relationships of this kind were not tolerated within his own family. Six weeks after being in foster care, Pete was adopted into a white Protestant family with three biological children, two daughters and one son several years older than him. They were raised in Brooktondale, a small town near Ithaca.

Pete attended predominantly white high schools in New York from 1982 to 1986. In his sophomore year of high school his adoptive parents divorced. Pete moved with his mother to Ithaca where he completed his junior year. With his grades dropping, Pete knew his opportunities were dwindling. In 1987, after graduating, he pursued what he thought was his only option and joined the army. It was there, in a segregated setting, that he was forced to decide with which group, white or black, he would associate. In 1990, after returning home from the army, he took the civil service test and ranked in the top 3 percent.

At the time of his interview for *In Their Own Voices*, Pete was working as a police officer in Ithaca and was a volunteer with the local fire department. He indicated that as a child and adolescent he appreciates his experience living not only with his adoptive family but briefly with an African American family who opened their home to him. Struck by the clear distinctions between the black and white cultures, Pete believed that his background has helped him to interact comfortably with both groups. Nevertheless, he stated that he deals with misperceptions from both communities because of the color of his skin. Race, Pete said, is always the baseline, whether he is dressed in plain clothes, just walking in a store, or doing his job as a police officer. In the summer of 1995, Pete was profiled in *American Demographics*. He is interracially married. Pete stays in contact with his adoptive father, who is a businessperson in the printing profession, and his adoptive mother who is a librarian at the University of Central Florida. Contact with his siblings is rare. Soon after the taping of his interview for *In Their Own Voices*, Pete was reunited with his birth father, who visited him in the U.S. Pete also has biological siblings living in the Washington, D.C., area.

In *In Their Parents' Voices*, Pete reported that he and his wife, Brenda, have two biological children, aged 5 and 7. They continue to live outside Ithaca, New York. Pete now is sergeant of the Ithaca Police Department, the first black officer to serve in that position. He still volunteers with the local fire department when time permits. He also remains in contact with both his biological parents as important links to his identity. But paramount in his life, he says, is his role as father and husband.

The following is an interview with one of Pete's siblings who is biologically related to his adoptive family.

CATHERINE TYLER

CHARLOTTESVILLE, VIRGINIA

SEPTEMBER 2006

Catherine Tyler, who is 40, is the second oldest of four children—three biological and one adopted. Catherine is three years older than her brother, Pete. She received a B.A. in French and has completed graduate courses. She reports no religious affiliation. Working in the medical billing field, Catherine describes her economic status as working class. She was divorced in 1990 and has no birth or adopted children. Catherine says that she does not have a relationship with Peter and has not had any relationship with him since early high school years. In her own words: "Today, in some ways, even though I do not talk much with Peter, I feel closer to him more than any of my other siblings because he talks about real things at the drop of a hat whereas with the rest of my family it is not that easy."

Before this book went to press, Catherine reported that she is engaged to be married in June 2009. Also, she visited her brother Pete in the summer of 2007 after this interview was conducted. About her visit, she said, "It was very healing to reestablish a connection [with Pete], and meet his children. His wife is wonderful, and they were all very gracious and accepting."

Catherine, please describe the community where you currently live.

I live in Charlottesville, Virginia, which was recently voted number one by the people who wrote the book about the top ten cities. It is really beautiful. The county where I live is one of the richest counties in the United States, so there is a lot of wealth which keeps the economy going in this area and provides a lot of culture. It has the University of Virginia, so there are a lot of intellectuals and a lot of people coming and going from interesting places. It is near the mountains, so you get mountain views, and the climate is just lovely. Lately, in the last couple of years, Charlottesville has become much more popular and real estate has pretty much quadrupled in price. It is a pretty easy place to live. I have lived here for thirteen years, with a break to go away for school for about a year. I really love it.

What led you to Charlottesville, Virginia, from Ithaca, New York?

When I was living in New York I was dating somebody who got accepted to the University of Virginia as a graduate student. At the time I had just finished my undergraduate degree after ten years and decided it was time to make a move. So I followed him here.

Going back to your childhood, where you lived many years in Ithaca, New York, what was it like for you?

I was born in Ithaca, and when I was about 3 years old my family moved to Hawaii for about three and a half years, because my father had a job at the University of Hawaii. I vaguely remember that. Then we moved back when I was almost 7 and lived in the same place until I graduated from high school — which was a farm about eight miles south of Ithaca, on 140 acres. A lot of it was wooded, only about 30 acres were cleared. It was beautiful. We lived in an old farm house. Country-style living.

As a family with two brothers and one sister, what did you do for fun?

It was a little different because my little sister had Down's syndrome and so she couldn't be left alone. Somebody always needed to pay attention to what was going on with her. I tended to be the responsible one, so a lot of what I remember … it's not like I had a deprived childhood, but I remember that we always had to keep half an ear out for her when we got home from school. Not too long after we came back from Hawaii my mom got her driver's license, and a full-time job, and my dad dropped down to part-time work so he was available in the afternoons to be there when we got home. I want to say that I was eight when this happened. My siblings and I basically came home on the bus. We went to school, not in Ithaca because we were just outside the Ithaca school limits, but to a small town called Candor, about a thirty-minute bus ride each way. We would come home and do our chores and have free time. My mom would come home and then we would have dinner. We did not have TV. We did not grow up with a TV until I was way into high school.

I guess you did a lot of reading?

We all tended to amuse ourselves with the exception of my adopted brother, Pete, who was much more social. We had friends a couple miles walking distance from us. Sometimes we would go over to their house. I liked animals. I had a horse at one point, so I used to go riding. There was no possibility of being driven anywhere; we lived too far out for that. We knew we had to exist within a country setting, so that is what we did.

Do you have any recollections about when Pete was adopted?

Not really. I have hardly any memory of when I was under 5. I know some people do. But I was about 3 or so at the time he was adopted. One of my earliest memories of him was when he was being pushed around in a stroller in Honolulu. He would be hanging out of the stroller and people would stop and say what a cute baby. If anybody knew that he was adopted ... they would have to have known. But that stuff never really crossed my mind.

When you were living in New York, did it cross your mind that your brother was of a different race, especially when your community was predominantly white?

Something occurred to me that I look back on and laugh. When I was eight, we were having a family discussion about what would happen hypothetically if we each got what we wanted. What one thing did we want the most? I must have had a discussion with Peter beforehand. But all I remember was thinking that I'm going to be really altruistic, though I didn't know that word at the time. I said to my parents, and I think that we had company at the time, too, that I know what I wish. I wish that Peter was a little white boy.

Your parents must have given you an interesting look!

And I remember being so proud of myself, thinking, "Wow, I'm not thinking of myself." And that I could identify with Peter. Peter looked shocked. I remember saying to him, don't you remember that we had a talk about this and that you wanted to be the same? I got such a terrible reaction from my parents. I realized ... that I had dropped a bomb!

Don't we all do that once or twice in our families?

There were a lot of things going on in our family, looking back, that you would think we would have talked about. I mean a family who is open-minded enough to raise a child at home with Down's syndrome and adopt someone of a different race ... you'd think that the logic would follow that my parents would be politically aware, politically active, and openly discuss things at home, but that was not part of our family life. We just sort of lived as though nothing was different from anybody else.

How did you feel about that?

A part of me recognized that Peter might always need to be protected; that's the role I assumed with Peter and with my sister. Peter was always very popular and very good looking. He never had problems making friends or having friends. After a while I realized that this was not going to be an issue, but earlier on I totally felt really protective of him. I always had half an ear and eye open to make sure that he was going to be O.K.

There is a three-year difference between you and Peter. Did that small age difference make you close or distant?

We used to fight a lot. I used to be able to wrap my older brother around my finger, but not with Peter. He would show his emotions. If I hit him, he would hit me back. But then later on, it was like that stuff was fine. We were not antagonistic. I don't know how he survived in high school. He just had such a rough time. There was a point where Peter was fighting with my mom all the time ... this was halfway through high school. My dad could not do anything with him. He would be defying my dad. Finally, he just went and lived with a neighbor down the road, for like the last two years in high school. I think that it was good for him. We had all these problems in our family, and Peter was just dealing with them the best way he could. He was not getting what he needed at home. And then he dropped out of high school and kind of drifted until he went into the army. Then everything seemed to come together for him. I remember hearing about this—because at that time I was having my own problems—that he was getting his act together.

What kind of relationship did you have with your older brother, Stephen, who was white and your biological brother?

We were really close until he turned about 14 and I was about 13. We had a different set of friends and drifted apart. In high school he also was gone a lot. In his case, he got in trouble with the law.

So you and your brothers were going in different directions in high school. Your parents also divorced shortly thereafter when you were in college. How did that affect you?

I was actually relieved at the news, because they had been separated off and on for a couple of years. I was relieved to have everything out in the open.

So you are out of the house attending college. Were you able to get back in contact with Peter?

That is a difficult question to answer. My method of surviving was to stay away from the family as much as possible. I saw Peter at my uncle's funeral about a year ago. That was the first time I had seen him in a long time. Even though I feel like we have good feelings toward each other, I am sad to say that we don't have a relationship and we haven't had any kind of mutual relationship since early high school, which is entirely my fault. I am the one who has not maintained the connection.

As difficult as that is, can you look back and see any positive efforts that your parents or you as children put forth as far as learning about adoption or helping one another in your unique circumstances?

It was always clear that my parents wanted to do the right thing whenever possible, and that included doing the right thing by their children. I think they treated us all as though we had been born to them. One of the things that my parents have given me is that total lack of prejudice. That was their attitude. They would bend over backward not to fall into any kind of traditional prejudice. It was so much a given that it was never even talked about, ever.

I once initiated a conversation with my mother about why Peter was adopted. She said something about a miscarriage and sort of the way things fell into place. There was no question that Peter was always part of our family, so much so that I think none of us ever gave it a second thought.

As an adult, have you reflected on your experience of being raised in a diverse family with a sibling who was physically challenged and another who was racially different in terms of whether that had a positive or negative impact on you?

Yes, definitely, I think that experience had a positive impact on me. Do you know the movie *Guess Who's Coming to Dinner?*

Yes!

I remember seeing it once and thinking how could there be any questions where love exists. That's got to be the trump card; because I knew from the depths of my heart that we are all basically the same. Also, I dated a guy in college for a while who was black. I remember thinking: if I fell in love with someone from a different race, would that stop me from pursuing a relationship? And my answer was no, it wouldn't stop me. Some of my closest friends have been foreign students; and in law school one time there was a woman there who was black and we became really close friends. I have always felt lucky that way, and the same because of my sister. I think that because of my family I had a greater understanding about a lot of issues—how to communicate with people, how to be more patient.

What do you struggle with the most?

I know that nobody is perfect. My responsibility is to accept the past and go on with the present. Yet, I think it is also possible to have all that and talk openly about the issues. Why is it apparently taboo to discuss certain subjects? If we are obviously in this same situation, why can't we talk about it as a family?

What would you change from your childhood for the better?

It's funny not having children, and I am almost 41. However, I am now in a relationship so I should think about this. I think that communication is really important. There is one thing about most people in my family; I never saw physical affection expressed. That is one good thing about Peter. He is a physical person. I will always appreciate that about him. He was real. If he felt something, he knew it! It was not like the rest of us, born with the ability to wear a mask. I think that a lot of that is why he is the only one in our family who has children and a family and a career that is quite stable. He has done a lot of really good work on himself. I think we have done so, too. Actually, Peter has set a good example for us. He allowed us to adapt in ways that we were not used to adapting. He is an example of someone who is struggling with the real issues instead of putting them off and burying them. That is the kind of thing I try to do now, just to be real with people. I try to say what I think and address a problem proactively. I try not to be fake. The whole idea of staying together for the sake of the kids or for the sake of any other reason other than real love is not worth it.

Peter has done well with his life both personally and professionally. What, if anything, would you attribute that to in the years you all were growing up in your family?

My parents provided a lot of stability. I think that where we were raised was a great setting to grow up in. Peter participated in many sports as a child and an adolescent, and my parents did a lot to make that happen. I don't think there was any doubt that there was a home.

Based on your experiences being raised in a transracial home, would you encourage other parents to pursue transracial adoption?

Oh yes, but I think so much depends on the person adopting. I actually think that when adoptions happen, society as a whole matures. We move toward a greater understanding of one another and greater maturity through the process.

I have had friends who think very differently than I do about this topic. I just think that they are "out to lunch." Adoption, specifically transracial adoption, could be the wave of the future. You can see that occurring in other countries even much more than in America. Having said that, I also have to say that in some cases transracial adoption could be the worst thing for the poor kid, especially if someone thought they were doing this kid a favor. I can think of a number of poor reasons for adopting, let alone transracially. Yes, just like interracial marriage, I am totally for it. However, I don't think it is an easy road. Some people may perhaps think, oh, it will be OK if we just do it. But I think that, as in any other obvious challenge, it requires all the extra tools we have ... like extra communication, and extra time and love. Also, not just within the family unit, but I have come to believe much more in the community coming together in raising a child. For example, maybe find parents and families in similar situations where they can come together and openly share their ideas and struggles with one another. I think that is one major thing that would have helped our family out a lot if we were able to communicate with other families like ours. For the good of everyone in the situation, I think that approach would be much more helpful.

Given that your immediate family is fragmented right now, can you foresee a time in the future when your family will become reunited?

I don't know. That used to be my pipe dream. Now I'm starting to realize that people can only change in the direction that they want to change, not according to my design. We could always be a closer family on the surface, but would we be closer because we had developed relationships that made us want to be closer? It is a question of who do you call when you are having a struggle or when you want to share something? I don't think of my family in those times. I have people here in Charlottesville that I consider my family. I still struggle with that whole blood thing, maybe because I have an adopted brother and he is just as much a brother to me as the other brother. In some ways, even though I do not talk much with Peter, I feel closer to him than any of my other siblings because he talks about real things at the drop of a hat, whereas it is not that easy to communicate with the rest of my family. My parents are getting older and there is only so much energy that I am willing to pour into that. I'd rather put my energy into places where it will get reflected back to me … as cruel as that sounds. Yet, at the same time, I love my parents and struggle with feelings of guilt about not being a "better" daughter. Obviously I want to do the right thing.

Is there anything else that you want to add?

I often think about how my brother, Peter, has taken what he was given and has made a really good job of it. Of all of us, I think that he had the most challenges, partly because he was adopted. I just think it is a testament to his fortitude. I don't know how one would create fortitude, or in his case if he was just born with it. But I have seen that same characteristic in other people I have known who were adopted, and they just keep going. They eventually put the pieces together and then become this really key part of their community, despite all the odds.

BRITTON'S SIBLINGS

WE LEARNED from *In Their Own Voices* that **Britton Perry** had a brilliant career as an actor and teacher. He was born in Boston, Massachusetts, and was raised in Rochester, New York. He attended the State University of New York at Brockport and Emerson College in Boston. Brit enjoyed learning the acting trade. It was through this medium that he could express his feelings and when he was the happiest.

Britton grew up in an upper-middle-class family. His parents adopted him in 1970, shortly after he was born. Uncertain whether they could have children of their own, they were eager to adopt. Race was not an issue for them. According to Britton, they simply wanted a child.

He was taught that there was value in learning about different cultural histories. In spite of that, Britton's cultural orientation, outside his schooling, was in a predominantly white environment. Brit found that in order for him to make sense of his physical differences within a white setting and understand the African American experience, he would have to pursue those issues on his own. As a child he identified with his Native American roots; his exploration of his African American side began in middle school.

His life so far has been one of great cultural privilege and opportunity. He has accepted the challenge of exploring more about his ethnicity and contributing his time and his talents to communities. Through this struggle he is refining who he is.

In 2004, as reported in *In Their Parents' Voices*, Brit received a master's degree in information technology from Pratt University in New York City and married shortly thereafter. Now living in Washington, D.C., Brit and his wife, Pamela, both have professional careers and have started a family with their twins, Brooke and Quinn.

The following interviews are with Britton's sister, Amanda Perry, and his brother, Seth Perry.

AMANDA PERRY

OLATHE, KANSAS

OCTOBER 2006

Amanda Perry is two years younger than her adopted brother, Britton. She has three brothers, two older and one younger, but only Brit is adopted, and he is the oldest. As children, Amanda says about her relationship with Brit, "We had a pretty good relationship—though I was never super close with any of my brothers. We had different interests." Today Amanda describes her relationship with Brit in the same way. She attributes her lack of closeness to Brit, in particular, to, as she puts it, "almost living at opposite ends of the country and never living in the same city as adults." Still she remembers as a child that Brit always tried to take care of, and protect, her and her brothers. She says, "He still does today."

Amanda is 34, married, and has one daughter who is 6 years old. In addition to raising a child with her husband, she works as a customer service trainer. She indicates that her family's economic status is upper middle class. Amanda reports no religious affiliation. In addition to earning her high school diploma, Amanda has also taken college courses.

Where did you grow up?

We lived outside Philadelphia until I was almost 6, and then moved to Rochester, New York.

... Was this in the 1970s?

Yes, early to mid-1970s. We moved to Rochester in 1978.

Tell me about the community of Rochester and the neighborhood where you were raised.

It was an upper-middle-class neighborhood. It was a very strong neighborhood community with lots of kids and a great neighborhood school.

What made the community great?

There were so many families and kids that had lived in that neighborhood for a long period of time; you really knew all your neighbors and all their names. We lived on a street where each side of the street was one-way, separated by malls in the middle. There were two malls, and that's where all the kids would meet and play. There were a lot of neighborhood parties and picnics that took place. Everybody knew everybody, almost everybody, anyway. It was a very close-knit community. The rule was, you had to be home when the streetlights came on.

How many siblings do you have?

I have three brothers—two older and one younger.

How many are adopted?

One is adopted, my oldest brother Brit.

Did your parents talk to you about adoption and why they chose to expand their family transracially?

I was thinking about this yesterday. I was asking myself, when did I really know that my brother, Brit, was adopted. I really couldn't come up with a time or a conversation that I had with my parents about "Why is Brit different?" "Why is Brit's skin a different color?" "Why does he look different than me and my other brothers?" And I don't even remember having a conversation about adoption in general. I talked to my mom yesterday. And I asked her, "Mom, why did I never ask you, or why did we never have a conversation about this?" And she said, and now it all kind of makes sense, "Well, it was because you were raised knowing that your brother Brit was different and that your brother was adopted and just from a very early, early age you knew that and it was just accepted." So we never struggled with that awkward question": "Why is Brit different than the rest of us?"

In your neighborhood, were there other people who looked different, like Brit?

Yes. There were African American families in the neighborhood, and some other families that had adopted children also. My parents became close friends with another couple who had several adopted children, and they are still friends today. You knew which kids were adopted because you knew who their parents were. Another good thing was that the elementary school that we went to was very ethnically diverse. There were kids that were bussed in from different parts of the city.

What was your relationship like with your brothers?

My relationship with my older brothers ... when we were little, I think we had a pretty good relationship. They kind of watched over me. And they're not that much older than I am. Brit and I are just over two years apart, and then Seth is in the middle of us in age. At that time I was the baby, and my older brothers took care of me. As we got older, we also had a good relationship, although I was never really super close with any of my brothers, including my younger brother, who is four years younger than I am.

Did you have different interests than your siblings?

We all had different interests, yes. Brit especially had different interests; when he was in elementary school and into high school he was always kind of the joker, the actor. My brother Seth was heavily into sports and into academics. My youngest brother, Nathan was interested in music and matchbox cars. And I was the only girl.

What was it like around the dinner table at your house?

If I remember right, we almost always had family dinner. Dinner time was a time to talk about the day. We had a lot of very amusing and entertaining family dinners with lots of stories. Sometimes there were some arguments or disagreements. But I think just having that family time together, every night at 6 o'clock, was important.

During dinner, did you ever talk about race issues, adoption issues, or conflicts that happened at school because of race that any of your brothers dealt with or that you may have dealt with?

I don't remember a particular conversation. I am sure there were some, but nothing that I recall. I don't think we ever really talked about how somebody had said something to Brit about why he's an African American child in a white family. Maybe that kind of conversation came up, but I think because my parents had handled the issues so well early on, it was not so much of a problem. I don't ever remember a serious, heated conversation, or a time when a member of my family was really upset because somebody said something derogatory to one of us about our family.

When you were in school, were you ever confronted with the fact that you had a brother who was of a different race?

I don't recall that I was. We all went to the same elementary school, and I think it helped that all of our friends knew from early on that we had a blended family.

Was there a particular thing your parents said or did that helped you have such a good understanding and confidence about your family makeup?

I don't think it was anything in particular. It was just the fact that from an early age we had an understanding of it. I was never embarrassed that I had an adopted brother; actually, I remember feeling proud that he was my brother.

Tell me about your relationship with your extended family. Did any of your aunts, uncles, and cousins think that it was unusual that your family was racially blended?

I don't think so. From the beginning Brit was so accepted into our family and I never had a conversation with any of my cousins or any of my aunts or uncles about the fact that Brit was adopted or about the fact that we were a blended family. Again, I think from the beginning it was so understood and accepted, and that was just the way it was. Brit was part of our family, it didn't matter if he wasn't white like the rest of us, it didn't matter that he was African American.

Do you think being part of a blended family has helped you as an adult when it comes to understanding and interacting with people from different racial and ethnic backgrounds?

Absolutely. Even as a child, the fact that Brit was in our family really helped me understand and be more accepting of other people. When I was in kindergarten, I had maybe three or four friends and one of them was African American. After we moved to Rochester and I was in second grade I had two best friends; one of them was white and the other was African American, and she and I are friends to this day. I think the fact that I had a brother who was African American helped me become more accepting of people of other races.

Dating is huge in the lives of adolescents and young adults. Was it ever an issue for you as to whether you would date someone of another race?

No, I don't think it was. I never seriously dated anybody who wasn't Caucasian. But there were times when I had little crushes on boys that were of different races. It wasn't a mental choice ... things just happened that way. I never said to myself, "I'm never going to date anybody who isn't white." One of my best friends, who happened to be the only African American girl in our circle of friends growing up, had more of a hard time dating in that environment. She ended up marrying a white man. The fact that Brit was in my family helped me accept her and understand what she was going through. She did high school track and many of the girls on the track team were African American and they would give her a lot of grief, saying things like, "Why are you trying to be white? Why don't you accept who you are?" I would tell my friend, well, you've chosen *who* you are, and it doesn't matter what color your skin is. I think it was just a coincidence that most of her friends were white. I think I was able to help her understand that and give her some reasoning behind what she was going through.

Did you leave home to attend college?

Yes, I did.

When topics about race were discussed in your classes at college, what was that like for you, given your family background?

When I went away to college, I had a pretty good understanding of the different races in the world and people's beliefs and understandings, and that sort of thing. Not only because of Brit being in our family but also because of where I went to elementary school and where I went to high school. Seth and I went to an inner-city high school, and so we were faced with that from the first day of seventh grade all the way up through twelfth grade. The white students were the minority. Race was something that we had to deal with on a day-to-day basis. Seth and I had friends who were African American, we had friends who were Latino, and we had friends from other ethnic backgrounds, so we didn't have this big shock when we went off to college that there were other people of different races and viewpoints because we had basically grown up knowing that.

Did you have any role models that were persons of color?

No, but it wasn't intentional.

What is your relationship with Brit today?

I think Brit and I have a pretty good relationship now. We're not super close, almost living at opposite ends of the country and never living in the same city as adults. We try to talk on the phone and we try to get together as much as we can, but we know life just takes over and it is difficult. At this time in my life, I don't really have a close relationship with any of my brothers, only because we don't get the opportunity to see each other very much. As an adult I've never really had a particular sibling that I was closest to. I don't know if there's any real reason behind that. We all live in different cities and don't get to see each other very often, so that makes it tough.

What about your youngest brother, what was your relationship with him?

Nathan and I did not get along very well when we were growing up. I think that was just the age difference and that I was always trying to egg him on and he was always trying to get on my nerves.

Brit got married a few years back. Did you have the opportunity to go to his wedding?

Yes we did.

Tell me about the wedding.

His wedding was amazing and I was really happy to be able to go, and our daughter was a flower girl. I met a lot of his friends that I had never met before, because he had lived in New York City for so long, and I was in Rochester. It was a beautiful wedding, and we love his wife and truly feel she is a part of our family. The wedding was definitely a great celebration of their love for each other.

Brit, Pam, and their twin children are African American. How does the fact that your family is even more racially blended now affect you?

I've never really thought about it. I've never said, "Oh, now I have a niece and a nephew who are African American." It's just the way it is. Pam and my niece and nephew are now part of my family, and honestly I've never thought about it until you just brought it up. I was looking at a cute picture yesterday of the cousins. It was taken over the 4th of July and it was the first time we saw the babies. Seth's wife made matching shirts for all the cousins. They were really cute.

How old were the four cousins at the time?

My daughter was 5, Ronan was 3, and the twins were 6 months. My husband is a photographer, and he took the picture and he totally captured all their personalities.

How did you end up in Kansas from Rochester?

My husband had a job opportunity that we couldn't pass up, so we packed up and moved.

How did you meet your husband?

We met through his sister. I was working with his sister when I was 19. He was in the military at the time, and he came home on leave; we met and the rest is history.

Tell me about the community in Kansas. Is it as multicultural as Rochester was when you were growing up?

Not even close. We live in Johnson County, Kansas, which is a suburb of Kansas City. The area is not diverse at all, but other parts of the city are. Our daughter's first grade class only has 3 students that are not white.

As parents, if you and your husband were thinking about having another child, would you consider adopting transracially, given your background?

I think we would. I don't know if adoption is something in our future, but I don't think we would ever be totally against it. I don't think that conversation has ever come up. I personally wouldn't have any issues with it. I know transracial adoption is not easy for the parents. I know there are a lot of struggles the parents can sometimes have and siblings can sometimes have, and that the adopted children themselves can have. But I think if it is handled like my situation was, where it is just understood and accepted from the very beginning then I think it makes a smoother transition for everybody.

What were some things that both your parents did that you thought were helpful in that transition process?

Again, I would say the acceptance of everything and the conversations they had with us. I talked with my mom about this yesterday. Because Brit was already in the family when I was born, it's not like I'm six years old and then all of a sudden they bring home this little African American boy; the situation is a little different. My parents encouraged an acceptance early on and so understanding that Brit is part of our family was very positive. My mom said that she would tell us kids when we were little about when I was in her tummy and when Seth was in her tummy, and, if we had any questions about Brit, she would say something like, Brit was never in mommy's tummy, we had to go to a special place to find him, or something along those lines.

Is there anything else that you want to say about your childhood experiences?

The fact that Brit was in our family when I was growing up helped me to become more accepting of others, children of other races and ethnic backgrounds, just because of my brother. I think if I was in a family that was all white without any transracially adopted children, I might not have had the understanding that I had about racial and cultural differences and the acceptance that I had while I was growing up. I really think my experiences in my family has helped me through my high school years and I think into my adult years as well, to be accepting of people no matter what their skin color.

How has that mind-set carried through to your daughter?

She is also pretty understanding of different races and has several friends that are of different races. We've had some conversations about Uncle Brit and why his skin color is different than ours. Just in the past year or so. But I don't think she has ever brought it up. It was a conversation that my husband and I initiated, because we want her to understand at a young age.

Do you think transracial adoption is a good thing?

Absolutely, as long as there is acceptance by the entire family from the beginning. It has to be known and understood that no matter what race the child is, he or she will be loved unconditionally, just as any other child.

What would you say to other siblings in a similar family situation regarding the challenges that a brother or sister of another race may confront?

There may be some challenges, especially as children, where other children outside the family don't understand adoption. It might be hard to explain to those other children that the adopted child is part of the family, accepted and loved just like any other child.

In your family, it seemed like a lot of things were in place that made growing up with a multiracial sibling a wonderful experience. But knowing the challenges that did arise, how would you advise other non-adopted siblings in your circumstance about making sense of the complexities of this situation?

I don't think that I ever really had any conversations with people who had siblings that had been adopted. When I was growing up, my friends may have had questions, and I just explained it the way my parents explained it to us; the general understanding that we had from the very beginning that Brit was who he was and he's accepted in our family and we love him just like we love everybody else and that's the way it is.

One of the things I feel about Britton, even when we were younger and in high school, is that he was always trying to take care of us, protect us. I don't know if it was because he was the oldest. An example that comes to mind is the incident that happened to Nathan on the subway. For no reason, someone beat up his little brother. Brit was furious and hurt, understandably. I don't know if Nathan was assaulted by another white kid on the subway if Brit would have felt the same way. I just know that my brother Brit tried to protect his siblings. He still does today.

SETH PERRY

ROCHESTER, NEW YORK

2006

Seth Perry, aged 35, is Britton's younger brother but the second oldest child of four in the Perry family. Seth is married to Elizabeth, and they have a son, Ronan, who is 4. Seth has a Ph.D. in neuroscience and is a faculty member at the University of Rochester in New York. His religious affiliations are Quaker, Presbyterian, and Unitarian. Regarding Seth's relationship with his brother, Brit, he says, "Brit and I were very close growing up—especially prior to our teenage years." They shared the same group of friends up to the seventh grade and then went to different schools. Their interests diverged in about seventh grade. According to Seth, Brit was heavily involved in theater, and Seth was involved in athletics and was heavily focused on academics. As children, Seth conveys that his relationship with Brit was no different than with his birth brother and sister. Seth and Brit went to college the same year and stayed in contact somewhat regularly. Today he says he is still close with Brit. "We still see each other several times a year and speak or e-mail periodically. We also like each other's spouses."

What was your relationship with Brit when you were younger?

Brit and I were very close growing up, especially prior to our teenage years, when siblings are more apt to be spending time together. We did just about everything together when we were not in school, on vacations, etcetera. We rarely fought; probably less than most brothers do.

Do you remember when you first realized that Brit was black?

He's black? Somebody really should have told me ... no, I don't remember exactly when I first "realized" this.

Did you share the same group of friends?

Mostly so up until about seventh grade, at which point we went to different schools and developed somewhat different peer groups. But we still had the same group of "neighborhood" kids we hung around with, at least through late high school.

What about your interests? Were they similar to Brit's?

Starting in about seventh grade, our interests diverged somewhat in high school ... Brit was heavily involved in theater and some sports; I was heavily involved in athletics and had a high academic load as well, so our time together was more limited, except on vacations etcetera. But there was never any loss of respect for each other, nor development of animosity. We were still close; we just did not get to spend as much time together because of competing academic and extracurricular demands.

Do you think having a brother of a different race affected how you perceived yourself?

Not to any large degree, although I was cognizant of some of the burdens that came with being a biracial adopted child that Brit had to deal with. Being someone who stutters, I was familiar with being "different" myself, so perhaps I could understand it better than some ... although I hadn't really considered that perspective, at least not so explicitly, until now.

How did you perceive your racially blended family?

I was aware that our family was a little different, and I appreciated this and still do.

Did Brit have the same quality of relationship with grandparents, aunts, and uncles as the biological siblings had?

In almost all regards and instances I can think of, I would say yes, but I was certainly aware of the *possibility* that such relationships between Brit and relatives could differ because he was adopted. I was always glad that Brit was treated, and adored, the same by relatives, which is what one would always hope for and expect, but I can see that it may not always be the case.

Reflecting on your childhood and your adulthood years thus far, is your relationship with Brit different than it is with your biological sister and brother?

Not in the least.

Did you stay in contact with Brit when you went to college?

We went to college the same year, stayed in contact semi-regularly, and were always happy to see each other on breaks.

Did each of you date people of different races?

I don't think race was an issue for either of us in our relationships—neither as a reason "to" date someone or a reason "not to" date someone. The race of a partner—for both of us, I think—was more a matter of happenstance and circumstance than decision.

Do you think your parents did things they would not have done had they not adopted Brit?

Frankly, not really ... which I think is positive ... I think they would have done things pretty much the same irrespective of the race/sex/creed etcetera of their kids ... which is not to say they were not *aware* of the issues to be considered. It is just to say that they probably would have done it *anyway* and that it was going to be the right thing for any kid of any color.

Were there times, especially during your childhood, when you were jealous of Brit?

Not to my recollection, except maybe occasionally in the way siblings can be jealous of each other for being better at something than they are, though there was really very little of that between us.

Are you glad that your parents adopted Brit?

Of course ... he's my brother ... I was going to say he ate too much, he snored, and was a real pain in the ass, but I'm not sure everybody would know I was kidding—Brit would though!

Did you and Brit ever discuss issues surrounding the fact that he was African American or, more accurately, biracial, adopted into a family that was white?

Brit and I never spoke of these things or matters of race to a significant degree, at least not that I recall, though I think we probably had occasional brief conversations about race- or adoption-related matters. But I think there was some unspoken understanding between us, that we each were aware of some of the difficulties the other had to deal with. I was well aware of some of the name calling Brit had to contend with, both when he was younger—on rare occasions from our peer group—and in junior and senior high school—it was more of an issue then, was my sense. I knew that kids in Brit's situation are frequently not accepted well by any peer group. They're not black enough for the black kids or white enough for the white kids. Fortunately Brit had strong family support and developed many close friends, some of which had similar family situations, which served as a strong foundation of support when things were tough.

How did you react to the fact that Brit was seemingly treated unfairly at times because of his race or even because he was adopted?

I always felt somewhat protective of Brit, not because he needed it, and not in a physical way, because we were similar in age and he was quite capable of taking care of himself, but more in the way that I didn't want others—other kids especially, perhaps—thinking less or disparagingly of him because he was adopted or biracial. Most did not, of course—this was clear from his interactions and friends—and there was little I could do about such things anyway, but I *wanted* to prevent any unkindness that might arise, whether I could or not. I was also always very proud of his accomplishments, and remain so—for both the professional and personal success he has achieved despite enduring some tougher roads than many in reaching these accomplishments.

What are your thoughts about how Brit may have felt when he walked among the family in public, and how do you think members of society perceived him?

I was always aware of the *potential* for Brit to be treated differently because of his skin color, or his being of a different race than the rest of his family. I have vague memories of what I thought at the time were "disapproving looks" from others, when we would be doing things together as kids or in a store, etcetera. I worried about the potential for discrepant treatment from the various authority figures that one can encounter in their daily life, even in the most innocent or mundane situations. So I realized from early on that people probably didn't look at me with exactly the same "eyes" as they looked at him. Some did but not all. And this always bothered me. One example that brought this point home for me, I think, was when we traveled as a family to France, and Brit was subject to considerable more scrutiny from customs and immigration security at the Paris airport than the rest of us were—despite the fact that it was clear he was traveling with us (not that this *should* have mattered). I think—and my parents remarked something to this effect at the time—that this added scrutiny related to France's long and contentious history with the Arabic countries of North Africa and the Algerian riots that were happening at that time. Brit's skin color could easily pass for Arabic or Middle Eastern, which probably led the guards to conclude, erroneously, that he was a greater risk than others were. This is simply one episode that I recall clearly to this day where I remember being very bothered by the way Brit was treated just on the basis of his appearance.

It must be hard to have to battle the perceptions of others, especially when in your eyes their perceptions are not true.

I was also often bothered by the misperceptions that I felt others drew about how Brit fit into our family. Now that he is a father, Brit would be the first to tell you that he hopes—and, no doubt, prays—that his kids never do some of the things that he did when he was younger; in fact, I think the very thought of it scares the daylights out of him. I think we all feel this way as parents! Ah, the perspective of parenthood. Not that Brit was a bad kid or a troublemaker by any means; quite the contrary, he was a great, friendly, peaceful, compassionate, fun-loving guy, and still is. Just maybe a bit *too* fun-loving sometimes; nothing serious of course, but just enough "adventure" to keep his parents on their toes, and keep life interesting.

I suppose at least to some degree I admired Brit's ambition in this area, because I was just a tad more risk-adverse. We both still joke about the night—a school night no less—when, at about 1:00 AM, after I was finishing a long night of homework and washing up for bed (an early night for me … I told you Brit was more fun), I heard a suspicious noise outside the bathroom window, from the direction of Brit's room. It sounded like … nah, couldn't be. Well, better poke my head out and have a look. Sure enough, there's Brit on the side of the house, rappelling from his bedroom window using a water-ski rope! Knowing Brit as well as I did, I can't say I was particularly *surprised* to see him there, but given that my first concern was for his safety, my remark to him was "Why didn't you just use the door?!" Now, that would have taken all the fun out of it, wouldn't it?

Anyway, the long and short of it is, well, Brit probably got grounded more often than I did—a fact which I know he now actually appreciates, because it means his parents succeeded at doing what all parents instinctively wish to do: keep their kids happy, healthy, and safe. But this was hard for me for two reasons. First, it made it very easy for others, looking in from the outside, to think, "Well, Brit's the adopted child, and he's biracial, so he gets treated a little more harshly than the other kids." In fact, I know many of the other kids, and perhaps families, in the neighborhood had this perception, because I heard it many times. Even though we never really talked about it, I'm sure my parents were well aware of this dynamic, and probably bothered by it as well, but there was very little they could do about it. They needed to parent Brit and all their kids the way they felt best, and there was nothing they could do about the conclusions that others drew, right or wrong.

The second reason this was hard for me was because I sometimes felt guilty for not getting "in trouble" (with examples like the above) quite as often as Brit did, thus perpetuating this dynamic of misperception that I felt was unfair to both Brit and our family. It's not that there were double-standards in our family in regards to punishment (equal offenses merited equal treatment, in at least as much as practically possible), nor was our family overly strict; there were just some "rules" we were expected to abide by—just the kind of rules kids like to break (granted, I am *not sure* whether we had a "no rappelling out your bedroom window" rule, but perhaps my parents felt this one should be unspoken). Kids being kids, they will break the rules and push the boundaries sometimes, and some will do it more than others, adopted or not ... Sure, I had my fun and did my share of misbehaving, as did our other siblings, and we all got grounded, too; I broke curfew and back-talked or disobeyed, my sister was smoking out her bedroom window for a while—oops, did Mom and Dad know that? —and we "did the time" as a result. But Brit had a much keener sense of adventure than most mere mortals. Unfortunately, when the "usually slightly more mischievous" child happens to be the adopted child, this can create a "dynamic of negative or biased perspective," whereby it may be easier for outside observers to conclude—not necessarily fairly—that the adopted child is getting harsher or inequitable treatment just because they are adopted. And I don't think this dynamic does anybody a service—not the adopted child, the family, or the outside observers. In some ways, I probably wished that the roles were reversed and that I was the one who usually got "in a little bit more trouble," thus preventing the "easy conclusion" that Brit got worse treatment because he was adopted.

Not that any parents make 100 percent perfect decisions every time (I wish I did …), and I think all parents struggle with trying to keep things as equitable as possible among siblings, as much as possible. But at least as far as our family was concerned, I think any inequity, if ever any arose in the treatment of any of us siblings, was more by accident than concert—and/or tailored to what my parents felt the needs were of any particular child. In fact, there may sometimes even be a reverse dynamic, whereby sometimes one sibling might receive a harsher punishment than they might otherwise, precisely because parents may want to emphasis (to all their kids) that there is *not* a double standard in how one is treated versus another. I think this dynamic probably applies equally to all families, whether or not there is an adopted child.

Today, how would you characterize your relationship with Brit, and do you get along with each other's spouses?

Brit and I are still close. Relationships always change with the responsibilities of family and professional lives, but there is no affection lost. We still see each other several times a year, and speak or e-mail periodically. We also like each other's spouses.

In closing, is there anything you want to add?

I guess I want to close by saying that if there is one thing that I always felt very strongly, it was that even though I knew that I could never understand *exactly* what it was like to walk in Brit's shoes, I felt that I, as his brother with whom he shared a close relationship, wanted to try to be able to understand some iota of his experience. Because we both faced slightly different kinds of adversities, I think we both had some mutual unspoken understanding that we could understand some aspects of each other's experiences on this level. And that was, I think in retrospect, a powerful bonding force, and still is.

Ultimately, I believe—and we are still much too far from this point than I would like—the only way toward greater acceptance, tolerance, happiness, and peace in this world is to try to understand one another from a *human* perspective, rather than from a racial perspective. I hope we get there.

PART III

IMPLICATIONS OF SIBLINGS' VOICES ON
TRANSRACIAL ADOPTION

CLOSING COMMENTS

OF THE twenty siblings we interviewed, nine describe both positive and close relationships as adults with their adopted brother and sisters. Tom Baker, who was born after Shecara (pseudonym) was adopted and is the youngest of eleven children in the Baker family, describes his current relationship with Shecara in warm and joyous terms: "she is a hell of a lot of fun" and "we have a good strong relationship." Like almost all the white siblings, Tom emphasizes how having a black or biracial brother or sister affected his own perceptions of who he is and his feelings about African Americans. Dan Baker, second youngest of the eleven birth children, describes a close and positive relationship with Shecara as children. Shecara, who was five years older than Dan, was a "role model" for him. Now, as adults, they live far apart and, while Dan describes his relationship with Shecara as positive, they are not close.

Christopher Roorda, Rhonda's older brother also describes his ongoing close and positive relationship with Rhonda. He believes they are very similar emotionally and feels blessed to have her as a sister. She made his life "a whole lot more interesting."

Of Rachel Anker's three sisters, two describe very close current ties. The oldest sister was married and no longer living in her parents' home when Rachel was adopted. She also has a positive relationship with Rachel. Lynn claims that the biggest lesson she learned growing up with Rachel is that she doesn't see or define people by the color of their skin. All three sisters support transracial adoption.

Although they do not see each other as often as they would like because of geographical distance and busy work schedules, Mike and Chuck Adams, younger and older brother, respectively, to David Adams, describe their childhood and current relationships with David in warm and admiring tones. So, too, is Seth Perry's description of his past and current relationship with Brit.

They see each other several times a year, even though they do not live in the same city, and speak and e-mail each other regularly.

Of the remaining eleven siblings, none describes a hostile relationship or a lack of one. But there is a distance and coolness between several of the siblings. It is important to point out that the distance and the coolness may have nothing to do with the fact that the sibling in question is adopted or a person of a different race. Several of the eleven also characterize their relationship with their birth siblings as distant and cool. Scott Tremitiere, for example, chalks up his lack of closeness with all his siblings to geographical distance.

Catherine Tyler does not have a close relationship with any of her siblings, but she acknowledges that she feels closer to Peter, her only adopted sibling, because "he talks about real things unlike the rest of my family."

Hilary admires and respects her adopted brother, Keith, but, in her words, "logistics prevents them from having much of a relationship."

Amanda, a younger sister to Brit Perry, explains that she was never "super close" to any of her brothers because of different interests, but she feels she has a "pretty good" relationship with Brit today. Living at almost opposite ends of the country does not make it easier to have close ties with Brit, who she always felt tried to protect and take care of his younger siblings.

The three sisters to Daniel Mennega (Yvonne, Annette, and Michelle) all describe positive but not close ties to their brother. They usually see Dan once a year at Christmas time.

Adam Goff, one of two older brothers to Laurie, has mixed feelings about his sister. "She can be overwhelming and sometimes drives me crazy." As children they had a reasonably good relationship, although they did not share any of the same friends. Adam believes his relationship with Laurie is better than the one she has with her older brother Michael, with whom she has no contact.

Jean Roorda, Rhonda's younger sister by eight years, tells us that, growing up, their relationship was "awkward and sometimes conflicted as lots of sisterhoods are." The age difference was such that they did not share the same group of friends, and Rhonda took on more of a parental role toward Jean. Today they talk on the phone about once every two months and live almost a thousand miles apart.

Of the ten children in Tage Larsen's family, six were adopted and four were birth children. Anika Larsen, whom we interviewed for this volume, is the oldest of the birth children. Anika pursued her individual identity in order to stand out in her large family. She says, "Being one of ten kids I quickly realized how much I like individual attention and singing loud was a great way to get that attention." Although Anika did not specifically talk about her relationship with her adopted brother, Tage, she did indicate that "for the most part there's a core eight of us at this point who are really pretty tight and show up at every family event." Tage, who lives in Chicago, is part of the core eight.

Finally, an important point is worth repeating: the basis for the quality of the relationship that the birth siblings report often has little or nothing to do with the race and adoptive status of the siblings. In many cases, age is crucial. Some were old enough to be off at college or married before the adoption took place, and so there was little opportunity for a close relationship to develop. In some instances, geographical distance accounted for the difficulty in maintaining a close and positive relationship. And, in some cases, the personality of the siblings interviewed was such that closeness was not likely to develop with any sibling.

All the respondents believed that having a black or biracial brother or sister made them a "better, more interesting person," and also more accepting of racial differences.

AFTERWORD

MANY POWERFUL words resonate throughout this series on transracial adoption: *courage, preparedness, love, race, identity, responsibility, discipline, accountability, communication, honesty, continuation*. The hope is that now, in the twenty-first century, families, scholars, adoption agencies, and communities will seize their meaning in efforts to ensure that transracial adoption in America becomes ever more successful. Each of the three books in this series on transracial adoption is a unique forum for veteran adoptive families, including adoptees, parents, and siblings, to speak honestly about their experiences in a blended family; their struggles for identity; and their journeys in defining and redefining their relationships with members of their family and others over more than three decades. In those thirty plus years, these transracial adoptive families have had to try to make it work, paradoxically, within a society that still proves to be racially, culturally, and economically separated. The pioneers interviewed in these three books have forged a pathway for contemporary families embarking on similar experiences to move forward in their journeys with more direction, focus, and energy.

When Rita and I were collaborating on the first book, *In Their Own Voices* (2000), I was struggling as an African American adult transracial adoptee with how to love my adoptive family *and* simultaneously honor my own racial and cultural identity, personality, gifts, and talents. I also had to learn and relearn how to negotiate the societal terrain around me as an adult with dark skin. Perhaps by some I was considered successful. At 26 I had completed a master's degree, secured a good position with a respectable organization, and purchased my first home. Still, I felt severely off balance, and my boundaries were muddled. Sadly, in the process of trying to please and conform to those around me, I was losing my self-identity and self-esteem, my inner compass. As we were writing and interviewing participants for *In Their Own Voices*, I saw that many of the adoptees expressed, to varying degrees, similar realities.

Rachel, a 22-year-old African American transracial adoptee living in a mostly white community in South Holland, Illinois, was struggling with her identity. When asked about how the black community could help her, she said:

> [I would want the African American community] to accept me even though my upbringing is different from theirs. I'm an African American, *but I haven't been accepted into that community because of how I was raised.* For example, I don't talk like they do. But where have I been exposed to it? Nowhere. If I could be more accepted by someone … it doesn't even have to be an African American …
>
> I also struggle with my weight. A lot of white people want to be "stick thin." And I'm larger. I know I don't accept my body largely because my friends are white and thin.[1]

Rachel's advice for adoptive parents is that they should help their child to "know who they are so they don't lose touch with their identity."[2]

Ned, who is in his late twenties, is a biracial transracial adoptee who considers himself to be an African American man by society's standards. He is a schoolteacher and lives in Grand Rapids, Michigan, with his wife and child. Ned pointed out the challenges of finding and coming to terms with his multifaceted identity:

> Growing up as a transracial adoptee, I've always felt that I'm on a fence, half-white and half-black, somewhere in between everyone else. Or in school I'd feel like I was too black for the white kids and too white for the black kids. To this day I have similar feelings. Even in my workplace, I can fit in to a degree, it only goes so far. I still feel too black for my coworkers. At the same time I'm too white for some of my students. They say: "He talks too white, he's a sellout." I guess I have a lifelong challenge of trying to figure out where I fit in, who I am, and how I can find happiness in my particular life circumstances.[3]

Ned believes it is important for white parents to understand and relate to what their adopted black or biracial child is going through.

Jessica Pelton, 24, also a biracial transracial adoptee, grew up in West Rupert, Vermont. She has two other siblings who were adopted, one biracial (white and African American) and the other Korean. The only racial and ethnic diversity in the community of West Rupert was within her family. In response to whether her adoptive parents helped to nurture her racial identity, she said, "No. I have always felt, regarding my identity and ethnic origin, that my parents were not the source of information for me, especially when it came to the black experience. I don't know if that was fair of me. I just know I didn't turn to my parents for that. I felt like I was on my own."[4] In search of her identity, Jessica decided to attend a historically black college so that she could be around others who looked like her.

Today I negotiate every situation by trying to make myself as comfortable as possible. At this point in my life I'm sick of being concerned about always finding a balance for others around me. My feelings in a given situation are my priority now.

Actually, visiting this [historically black] college with my [adoptive] mom didn't look completely off. Here was this girl who looked mixed, walking with a white person who's her mother. You see that at this college. But my mind-set was that black people came from black people and that they regenerated into a group of black people. I see plenty of girls there who have white parents. A couple of girls I know were adopted into white families. Back then, my reality was that because I was with my mother I couldn't be considered black. I wasn't "black enough." When my parents come to visit me, I love walking on campus with *one* of them. Then the assumption is, "Oh, her father must be black" or "Oh, her mother must be black," depending on which one I'm with. But when I'm with both my parents, I feel that old familiar embarrassment.[5]

Jessica's biggest fear after college was the transition into black womanhood, especially given her childhood and adolescent upbringing. She asks: "Will I grab the next struggle and look it straight in the eyes or will I walk beside it?"[6]

The black and biracial adoptees featured in *In Their Own Voices* and the tens of thousands of other children of color who are adopted into white families in this country are put in a position (no matter how young or old the child is at the time of the adoption) where they must learn to recognize, adapt to, and ultimately transcend the race, culture, language, and rhythm of their white adoptive parents in order for them to genuinely grow to love their parents. This, by society's standards, is hard to do, yet many of these kids strive to adapt and conform to their parents' customs and environment well into adulthood because of their commitment and love for them. In talking with well over a hundred transracial adoptees throughout this country in a ten-year span, I found that many of these adoptees—African American, Korean, Chinese, Native American, Guatemalan—grew up or are living with their adoptive families in predominantly white, rural communities and small towns all over America. They sit in classrooms with mostly white peers, and when they worship they must sit in a church or synagogue where they are one of few persons with dark skin. Along the way these adoptees must walk on the sidewalks and, eventually, drive on the streets in these predominantly white communities in order to go to school, go to work, and even go out for entertainment. For the most part, their doctors, psychologists, teachers, priests, and ministers are white. Transracial adoptees must learn to cope successfully within their adoptive families and the communities where they live in order to participate satisfactorily as family members, friends, neighbors, patients, and coworkers.

It cannot be emphasized enough: transracial adoptees move beyond their comfort zones every day for the sake of their families, often at a significant cost. Collectively, as parents, social workers, scholars, and members of society, we need to ask ourselves if we are doing our best to equip this segment of the population with proper guidance and resources to help them in their difficult journeys.

Traditional adoption research, conducted in the early 1970s to the early 1990s, indicates that children and adolescents of color who were adopted transracially, whether domestically or internationally, tended to love their parents and siblings regardless of racial differences, and they were generally well adjusted and happy that they were given a permanent, stable home.[7] The children and adolescents reported normal to high self-regard and recognized that they were black, Korean, or Native American.[8] The parents interviewed in these same studies also expressed their contentment and love for their adopted children and were pleased that they had assimilated into their families.[9] The studies generally showed that, across the board, transracial adoptees living within similar types of families appeared to be developing as normally as were non-adopted children or children adopted into families of their own race. Based on this core empirical research, transracial adoptions were proved to be healthy for children and families, and they became the catalyst for federal laws that supported this kind of family planning. These laws, which apply today, are intended to encourage good adoptive placements regardless of the race, ethnicity, or nationality of the parent or the child.[10]

Of singular importance is that the adoptive parents in some traditional studies reported that they were "color-blind" in relating to their adopted children. In one such study, in 1977, Charles Zastrow compared forty-one white couples who adopted a black preschool child to forty-one white couples who adopted a white preschooler. All the couples lived in Wisconsin and came from similar socioeconomic backgrounds. Zastrow found that all the placements were successful, and he noted that "many of the TRA [Transracial Adoption] couples mentioned that they became 'color-blind' shortly after adoption; i.e., they stopped seeing the child as a black, and came to perceive the child as an individual who is a member of their family."[11]

The consensus that emerged from this traditional research was that love is enough when raising children of color in white homes. As a result, particularly for many transracial adoptive families moving forward, the race of the adopted child receded into the background, and the "color-blind" mind-set was embraced by white parents who adopted children of color. White parents were not held accountable by research, law, or the social workers who interpreted the law to include the child's racial and ethnic heritage and experience within the family plan. The unintended consequence for many transracial adoptees, especially those in their late teens and adulthood years, was that their identity and the knowledge of their racial and cultural heritage were compromised and sometimes lost.[12]

During the writing of *In Their Own Voices* (2000) and *In Their Parents' Voices* (2007), we had honest, in-depth conversations with the black and biracial adult adoptees, and then ten years later with their adoptive parents. These are amazing families that were blessed with the unique gift of transracial adoption. At the onset of forming their families through transracial adoption and birth, they received no book of instructions. So they traveled their path in the best way they knew, taking the bumps and the potholes as they came.

Many qualities made the participants we interviewed vital, such as their love and commitment to family, their faith-based beliefs, their work ethic, honesty, and the value they place on education. The qualities in these families instilled by the parents have unquestionably laid the groundwork for their children—both the adoptees and non-adopted siblings—to prosper. But what warrants addressing here, and is also relevant to contemporary families who are adopting cross-racially, is the downside of espousing a color-blind philosophy within the boundaries of interracial families.

Many of the interviews we conducted with the adoptees and their adoptive parents explicitly underscored the reality that the adoptees' race and cultural heritage were not integral to the identity of most of these families. In the initial stages of the adoption, only nominal conversations occurred among family members about the obvious racial and physical differences between them. In cases where an adoptee or sibling innocently raised the issue, the parents or another family member often would quickly change the subject to end any moment of surprise, discomfort, or embarrassment. On a social level, most of the black and biracial adoptees growing up within the borders of their families did not have meaningful relationships or contact with persons who shared their racial or cultural heritage, for example, black mentors, black godparents, and black family friends. It stood to reason that as these adoptees got older and were grappling with their racial identity, they did not feel comfortable or even have the language to talk with their white adoptive parents about their personal struggles relating to race issues or about the connection they felt to the African American community. Their adoptive parents, before adopting transracially or in the early stages of adopting, had not developed an adequate knowledge about African American history and the African American experience; nor, at the outset, had they created an atmosphere embracing the child's ethnic community and heritage. For the transracial adoptees in these families, the color-blind philosophy left them to haphazardly fill in the gaps of their racial identity by themselves as young adults.

Within the nucleus of many of the families we interviewed, the entire family appeared to be far more comfortable, particularly in the initial stages, to overlook racial differences. Every family arguably had vested interests in maintaining the illusion of a normal family as a way to avoid uncertain terrain or at least change the family dynamics. The problem is that the failure to integrate our children's racial and ethnic identity within the family prevents these children from becoming well-balanced adults, proud of *all* that they are.

It is difficult, of course, to redesign our families, especially in later stages. As an adoptee, I understand the desire to maintain balance within the family, as I myself experienced considerable imbalance; before I was formally adopted, I had already been relinquished twice, first by my biological parents (and community) and then by my foster family of two years. As a child I understood the feeling of abandonment, and it scared me. I wanted to do everything in my power not only to love my adoptive parents and siblings but also to shield them from my pain and loss, and from the questions I had about my racial identity and heritage, as well as society's blatant reaction to me because of my transracial status. As I entered my teenage years I kept my conflicted identity a secret from my family, as I thought my parents would love me less or grow tired of me because I was different.

What led me at last to change the pattern were the very attributes that caused me to avoid the problem in my earlier years. Unlike most of the adoptees featured in *In Their Own Voices*, I was raised in a multicultural community in the Washington, D.C., area, where I was exposed to people from many different races, nationalities, and ethnicities. I saw modeled before me black people (and others) who were schoolteachers, legislators, social workers, pastors, lawyers, entrepreneurs, and artists. In addition, I was blessed to have an African American godfamily and, later, an African American godfather. Expectations of what I could become were set high for me. Over the years I had also built a library of books that included African American history and literature, so as a child and adolescent I had a good foundation for accessing information about my African American heritage and experience. But I was immobilized by the fear of tapping into those resources, because I thought I would be stepping outside the "hidden" boundaries of my adoptive family's perceptions and their expectations for me.

In adulthood, I could no longer minimize my racial identity, personality, or the differences between me and my adoptive family. Who I was forced me out into the open socially. I did not anticipate fully, however, that my commitment to honor myself was weakening my ties to members of my adoptive family, whom I loved dearly.

The color-blind philosophy did not just impact my life negatively, but it may have undermined the integrity of transracial adoptive families throughout this country. This is a short-sighted plan that prevents adoptees from confidently feeling that they have permission to explore their racial identity (or adoption issues) within their adoptive families without the risk of losing or weakening their status in the family or their relationships with family members. That many of these children of color are trying to develop their racial identity within the vacuum of their white adoptive families, and mostly white communities, is not helpful to them.

In the late 1970s, the National Association of Black Social Workers expressed legitimate concerns about transracial adoption of black and biracial children by white families. The Association's spokesperson at that time, William T. Merritt, said, in part, "Black children in white homes are cut off from the healthy development of themselves as Black people. The socialization process for every child begins at birth. Included in the socialization process is that child's cultural heritage which is an important segment of the total process."[13] During that same period, in 1972, the respected researcher Leon Chestang, also concerned about these types of placements, posed critical questions for white parents who chose to adopt transracially in the article *The Dilemma of Bi-racial Adoption*. Among his questions were these: "Are they [adoptive parents] aware of what they are getting into? Do they view their act as purely humanitarian, divorced from its social consequences? Are they interested in building world brotherhood without recognizing the personal consequences for the child placed in such circumstances?"[14] He concluded the article on a more positive note compared to other critics, stating: "Who knows what problems will confront the black child reared by a white family and what the outcome will be? But these children, if they survive, have the potential for becoming catalysts for society in general."[15]

Transracial adoption is a beautiful and unique gift for children and families, and requires added responsibility on the part of the adoptive parents and, eventually, the adoptees and their non-adopted siblings. In the twenty-first century, it is even more pertinent that adoption agencies and ultimately families (including adoptees and their siblings) implement strategies—within the statutes of current law and the integrity of good adoptive families—to remove the ineffective, color-blind approach that has persisted for more than thirty years and replace it with a multidimensional approach that will help families build a long-term plan that includes the adopted child's racial and cultural heritage. The integrity of transracial adoption of black and biracial children calls upon both the white and black communities in America to open the lines of communication and work toward eliminating divisiveness and mis-understandings, and, for the children's sake, to build meaningful relation-ships with one another one step at a time. No longer should we argue about whether transracial adoption is a good or bad policy. It has proved to be a good policy for families, but it must include the positive and valuable investment of the black community and other ethnic communities.

THE VOICES OF THE WHITE NON-ADOPTED SIBLINGS

Most fascinating to me personally, as well as in my career as a student of tran-sracial adoption, are the siblings' interviews included in this final volume. In my own struggle for identity, especially during my childhood and adolescent years, I did not think about how the lives of my white siblings would be shaped growing up with a black sister. From my one-dimensional standpoint I saw my brother and sister as my siblings who I loved and who exemplified their own individuality and Dutch heritage, but because they were "privileged" in American society I thought they would move through life untouched by tran-sracial adoption.

By listening to the stories of my siblings and the stories of the other remark-able men and women in this book, I recognized for the first time that this group, too, has a voice that needs to be heard in the discussion of transracial adoption. Whether these individuals were raised in rural, small-town commu-nities or in multicultural neighborhoods, all of them continue to be changed by this experience. For far too long, white non-adopted siblings have had to navigate their course silently within their transracial adoptive nuclear families and in society, at times struggling to understand their own identities.

The siblings in this book are, by and large, successful in their professional roles and in their personal lives. Many have started families and established their own traditions, providing a nurturing foundation for a new generation of children. Others are contributing to society creatively by using their gifts and talents to break down the barriers of racism or by tapping into their experience of having been raised in families with adopted siblings of color. Unheard and unseen, however, is where the story of transracial adoption takes on another dimension through their eyes, and at its heart is the color-blind philosophy.

As readers, we are reminded again that this philosophy impedes the growth of everyone in the family, not just the adoptees but also the birth children and the adoptive parents. Catherine, who was raised in a rural area in upstate New York with two brothers, including her adopted brother Peter, and a sister, is estranged from her family as an adult because of the residue of pain and un-answered questions lingering from a color-blind childhood. In her own words: "a family who is open-minded enough to raise a child at home with Down's syndrome and adopt someone of a different race ... you'd think that the logic would follow that my parents would be politically aware, politically active, and openly discuss things at home, but that was not part of our family life. We just sort of lived as though nothing was different from anybody else." Living "as though nothing was different from anybody else" caused Catherine deep inner pain. She loved her biracial brother as well as her sister with Down's syndrome; yet she was silenced within her own family from being able to talk with her parents and learn about the obvious differences between her and her brother and sister.

The tone of silence in the household was set by Catherine's parents early on, and so Catherine, along with her brothers and sister, not wanting to break the code of silence, passively agreed not to talk about these important issues. Catherine may very well have struggled against feelings of shame she may have felt about discussing race and Down's syndrome, because her family was unable to talk about those differences in a natural, open, and honest way. Clearly things work better within a family when there is honest communica-tion about issues going on within the nucleus. If her parents had empowered Catherine and her siblings with information about Down's syndrome, race, adoption, and cultural issues, and freely allowed them to ask questions about these issues, then every member of the family would have been better able to support one another.

Catherine's way of surviving today is to stay away from her family. Almost poetically, she conveys in her interview that even though she and her adopted brother, Peter, don't talk often, she feels closer to him than the other mem-bers of her family. She has learned as an adult that because Peter dealt with his own tough issues in his life growing up and learned from those real experi-ences, he became an affectionate and honest person. She believes that, as a result of Peter's efforts to understand himself, he is the only person in the fam-ily who has gone on to nurture strong healthy ties with his wife and children. Catherine sees Peter as a role model of how she wants to live her life.

My own brother, Christopher Roorda, grew up in the Washington, D.C., area with me, his adopted sister, and Jean, his younger sister of nine years. Even though he was raised in a multicultural setting, the responsibility that his parents placed on him to protect his black, adopted sister was at times overwhelming, exacerbated by a community that, unlike his parents, saw his color (and the color of his adopted sister). He talks in his interview about caring for his sister, Rhonda:

> When we were younger I was kind of like the protective older brother. I very much disliked that role at times. But because our parents said I should do that, I did. I felt like I should protect her, if nothing else because I had an advantage—I was taller than her. She was kind of shy and she seemed to sense that she was very different from us, the rest of the family, in terms of appearance. Also, there were times when people in our community in Takoma Park and generally in the Washington, D.C., area directly questioned her about that. So I would feel like I would have to step in and defend her and explain why she was different. Sometimes I would tell people that she was my adopted sister, and not some vagabond off the street.

Christopher "Duffy" was about 9 or 10 when he took on the role that he refers to in his interview as the "protective older brother." In effect, he was buffering Rhonda from racism, a huge task that his parents may not have known about. Christopher was, perhaps, resentful of having to protect his sister in this adult capacity, because it was not his job to do so. He was a child. It was his parents' responsibility to protect all their kids and equip them with the tools and language they needed to develop as a unified family in a society that remains racist in varying degrees. Unfortunately this was not done satisfactorily. Within the Roorda household, the family was living a color-blind reality, and so family members were unable to discuss with one another the tough issues affecting each individual and to devise a plan on how to respond to public statements made by people who were curious, angry or uneducated about transracial adoption.

What happened, instead, in the scenario Christopher paints is that, because he loved his sister and saw her suffering, he stepped up to protect her even though he was unprepared and, as a child, probably scared. Christopher protected his sister in public settings where there were white and black people who were sometimes confrontational to both him and Rhonda. The consequence for Christopher was that he had an unfair burden to carry silently for many years, because he did not feel he had permission to talk with his parents or his sisters about his feelings.

Chuck Adams was raised, with his younger brothers David and Mike, in the rural, predominately white community of Sioux Center, Iowa. Through reading, Chuck learned about people from many different cultures and ethnicities. Even though he speaks about the support within his family, he cannot help but reflect on his concern about how his younger, biracial-adopted brother, David, behaved outside the home. He states:

> As far as David goes, as a kid, I sometimes thought that outside of our family the wrong kid seemed to always be the black kid, and that David didn't care about that perception. In my opinion, I thought my brother was too flippant about issues like that. I thought he was too willing to make himself into a stereotype. He would see certain stereotypes of black people on television and would act like them. I would tell him that he did not want to be a stereotype but to be himself, whatever that was. But he liked to get attention, and for him that was a good way to get attention.

As an older brother, it was very frustrating for Chuck to see David willingly play out stereotypical images of black people to gain acceptance in the white community of Sioux Center. Chuck hoped that his brother would strive to be an authentic individual at home and in society, especially given the negative images of black people portrayed in the media. It was very difficult for Chuck to watch helplessly and see someone he loved avoid the responsibility to grow as an individual with a healthy and informed racial identity, and instead choose to gain public admiration by being a comedian at the expense of himself and his race. Undoubtedly even more disheartening for Chuck was that within the community of Sioux Center there was no access to African American role models, mentors, or even family friends that could offer David and the rest of the family real-life examples of positive individuals striving for excellence in their own lives.

Recently a mother who heard me speak at a workshop asked, "Are my husband and I harming our birth children because we adopted a child transracially?" Based on the interviews in this volume, I replied: "No, as long as you and your husband are preparing all of your children to live in a world that is not color-blind."

An example that came to mind was Scott Tremitiere and his sister, Michelle, who were growing up in their family in Pennsylvania with thirteen other siblings, twelve of them adopted transracially. They experienced racial injustice as a family and found solutions together as a family. Whether it was the Ku Klux Klan who burned a cross in their front yard or siblings in the family who were harassed in school because of their skin color or a black brother who was dating a white girl whose family was racist and unaware that their daughter was dating a black man, the parents explained these very difficult situations to their children and gave them the vocabulary and encouragement to ask questions when they were confused about these bigoted, unfair acts. It was understood in the Tremitiere family that everyone was supported and individual interests were nurtured. Through their imperfections, race, adoption, and birth issues, the Tremitiere kids today have been courageous enough to build (and use) a reservoir of tools that allows them to navigate successfully all over this country and the world. When an adopted child's racial identity is overlooked within the family, all of the children are disadvantaged.

The amazing gift in transracial adoption is found in the process of discovering our interests, our racial and cultural identities, and our stories freely and together within our families. It is also found in the friendships we develop that are made in communities across racial, cultural, and social economic boundaries. The ground work covered in that journey gives each member of the family heightened discipline, confidence, and purpose. To make this happen requires extra tools, extra love, extra support, and extra communication, but in the process everyone benefits.

This volume contains additional illustrations of men and women who have tapped into their reservoir that grows as they continue their journeys with honesty and openness. The potentially positive aspects of transracial adoption extend beyond any one person and will impact future generations. Good things happen when we join together while acknowledging our differences, all the while delving deeper within ourselves in order to love one another fully. Perhaps Catherine said it best: "When adoptions happen, society as a whole matures. We move toward a greater understanding of one another and greater maturity through the process."

Rhonda M. Roorda

NOTES

1. Rita J. Simon and Rhonda M. Roorda, *In Their Own Voices: Transracial Adoptees Tell Their Stories* (New York: Columbia University Press, 2000), 166.
2 Ibid.
3 Ibid., 326–327.
4. Ibid., 61.
5. Ibid., 65–66.
6. Ibid., 70.
7. Rita J. Simon, Howard Altstein, and Marygold S. Melli, *The Case for Transracial Adoption* (Washington, D.C.: American University Press, 1994).

8. Ibid.; Joan F. Shireman and Penny R. Johnson, "A Longitudinal Study of Black Adoptions: Single Parent, Transracial, and Traditional," *Social Work* 31 (1986): 172–176; Ruth McRoy, Louis A. Zurcher, Michael L. Lauderdale, and Rosalie E. Anderson, "Self-esteem and Racial Identity in Transracial and Inracial Adoptees," *Social Work* 27 (1982): 522–526; and idem, "The Identity of Transracial Adoptees," *Social Case Work* 65 (1984): 34–39.

9. Charles H. Zastrow, *Outcome of Black Children–White Parents Transracial Adoptions* (San Francisco: R&E Research Associates, 1977).

10. Multiethnic Placement Act of 1994, P.L. 103–382 Sections 551–553; 108 Stat. 3518; and Interethnic Adoption Provision Act of 1996, P.L. 104–188, Title I. Section 1808(c), 110 Sat. 1904.

11. Zastrow, *Outcome of Black Children–White Parents Transracial Adoptions*, 81.

12. Amanda L. Baden and Robbie J. Steward, "A Framework for Use with Racially and Culturally Integrated Families: The Cultural-Racial Identity Model as Applied to Transracial Adoption," *Journal of Social Distress & The Homeless* 9, no. 4 (2000): 309–337.

13. William T. Merritt, chair of the Committee on Transracial Adoption, speech to the National Association of Black Social Workers National Conference, Washington, D.C., 1972, quoted in Rita J. Simon, Howard Altstein, and Mary Gold S. Melli, *The Case for Transracial Adoption* (Washington, D.C.: American University Press, 1994), 40.

14. Leon Chestang, "The Dilemma of Bi-racial Adoption," *Social Work* (May 1972): 100–105.

15. Ibid.

LaVergne, TN USA
18 May 2010
183148LV00001B/6/P

DATE DUE

FEB 1 0 2014 — ILL			

HIGHSMITH